The ~~~~~~~~ ~~
the Knights Templars

Best Wishes Bev—

Judith

http://www.norma.org/long

Best Wishes for

Luck

http://www.nnn.org/long

The Last Mass of the Knights Templars

Judith Long

VANTAGE PRESS
New York

This book is a work of fiction, and substituted persons of the author's choosing are included. Names of characters were chosen from the ranks of acquaintances or simply made up, and are not intended to represent any real person. Any similarity to real persons, living or dead, is purely coincidental.

FIRST EDITION

All rights reserved, including the right of
reproduction in whole or in part in any form.

Copyright © 1998 by Judith Long

Published by Vantage Press, Inc.
516 West 34th Street, New York, New York 10001

Manufactured in the United States of America
ISBN: 0-533-12656-8

Library of Congress Catalog Card No.: 97-91410

0 9 8 7 6 5 4 3 2 1

THANKS TO EVERYONE

who believed in my work and encouraged me to keep writing even during the most difficult days. First to Mary Hanson for doing the first editing process and for providing the critique that was necessary when the subject matter involved the Catholic Church. Then to my sister Nancy who has believed in me all my life and loves a good story. To Madeline Olund, a dear friend and admirer who questioned my positions and inspired me to achieve higher goals for myself. To other friends whom I have loved, admired, and listened to in my life. Thanks to all for allowing me to be myself and to open windows which permit me to explore the world.

Preface

In the year of our Lord 1119, an Order of Knights was established by Hugh des Payens and Godfrey de St. Omer under the direction of Bernard of Clairvaux who was also a priest and the founder of the Cistercian order. He was well respected in Europe and his advice was sought after frequently. These two men were the first Knights of the Order to be sworn in with the vows of poverty, chastity, and obedience to Rome.

There was deemed to be an urgent need for such an order to protect and assist pilgrims on their way to the Holy Land and to religious shrines throughout Europe. Not only had many pilgrims been robbed and beaten by gangs of thieves, but there were even some thieves who masqueraded as pilgrims in order to gain the confidence of the other pilgrims and then loot the camps at night while they were sleeping. These new Knights were to be the Soldiers for Christ and examples of outstanding men who were wholly trustworthy and always ready to do good deeds in the service of others.

In earlier times civil and royal knights were less than exemplary and fell into practices of drunkenness, gambling, and debauchery with loose women. The Knights of the New Order were to possess the dedication and chastity of monks and have the fighting strength of giants.

The Order's reputation grew as the two Knights toured France, Spain, England and Italy. They were soliciting funds, looking for men of noble reputation and dedication, and reconnoitering for land that would be used in the work of assisting the people of the Church. Large amounts of wealth began to pour in and their mission to help the Church was beginning to be realized. The Knights of the Temple were extraordinary in their discipline and obedience before, during, and after battle. These attributes made them extremely valuable to the pope and greatly desired by kings. They served in the Crusades and in the protection of lands from invaders.

The lives of the Templars were modest and routine. They lived in community as did many of the monks in those days. Their residence was constructed of masonry and was designed to include specific structures. Most central in the estate was a chapel constructed with a round roof designed after the Church and Holy Sepulcher in Jerusalem. The temple contained two large halls that were used for gatherings and meetings of state. Around these rooms were several smaller chapels that were used in religious services and private devotions. The officers and commanders had their own private houses.

The church was connected to a long building called the cloister, or dormitory, that held corridors opening to cells or small sleeping rooms. Each cell contained a cot with bedding materials, chest, and chair. There was a large common room at the end of this building where the servants slept.

The only possessions that a Knight could have were a lance, sword, armor, which included a coat of chain mail, helmet and white over-garment with a red cross on both sides. Each man was also supplied with several excellent horses. The Knight's previous personal identity was suppressed after he joined the community in order to promote common life and the unity of purpose. The names of Knights that are found in history records are those associated with heroic acts of gallantry.

In the Hall of the Knights the walls were covered with trophies of wars including various kinds of helmets, swords, shields of many designs and colors, and shining coats of mail. This hall served as a meeting room where reports were given about current activities and orders issued for the following day. The Knights also used this hall as a dining area. The floor would be covered with beautiful rugs, and great long tables were set with linen coverings. The diet of the Knights was more than ample because they had hard work ahead and were not to appear frail.

The Templars built and equipped castles in many parts of Europe. They also had an ever-growing trail of supplies that went to the Middle East. There were frequent attacks by Muslims which the Knights had to continually suppress. On the western front the Knights fought the Moors for the people of Spain. Always, the Knights were called upon to save the day and each time they were successful. When there was a victory in a foreign land, the Knights would be left behind to maintain that territory. Castles would be built and a route for transportation of goods and people established. This excellent system saw the movement of gold, silver, armor, horses and men going to and returning from their missions.

The Templar Knights won many concessions from both the state and Rome. They were made independent of the state, reporting only to the pope. They were even exempt from paying taxes or from having any official obligation to the state. Money and gifts of every description came into the Templars' quarters. Their wealth and influence grew immeasurably over a very short period of time. In 1187 the Knights left Jerusalem after many battles with the Muslims. They chose to make their headquarters in Paris and built the largest of their communities just north of the Seine River on the Right Bank.

The Paris headquarters was very large and able to house over three thousand individuals including servants, stone masons, priests, sergeants, Knights and other protected persons. It was known that this Temple would defend any individual who was hunted and even kings were known to have found shelter here at times.

The Benedictine Order also maintained a monastery within three to four miles of the Knights' Temple in Paris. Their monks were known to have played a key role in the establishment of the Order of Hospitalers and eventually created a dual role that permitted some of the monks to fight. The Knights of the Templars, Hospitalers, and Teutonics became great defenders of the Catholic Church and its properties.

The Last Mass of
the Knights Templars

1

I first must tell you a story that occurred in the year of our Lord, thirteen hundred and ten. A story that will chill your soul and make your blood run cold. The story of a fight between good and evil that once transpired in this world.

The air of the fall was cool and the evidence of autumn's touch on nature was beautiful. Maple trees were showing rich colors of reds and yellows. The oaks and ash were changing to shades of brown. Most of the summer flowers had disappeared, with the exception of the hardier red roses and late autumn daisies. The grass was still fresh and green due to recent rains, and farm animals were content in their grazing without a thought of the approaching winter.

The people of France worried over the state of an unsteady economy. The sales of retailers were in a slump and there was no sign of relief. The commoners became skeptical about any unnecessary spending and used their commodities carefully. Organizations that had always tried to assist the poor were straining within their budget limits and had to approach again and again the purse strings of the more fortunate. King Philip the Fair was continually increasing taxes to gain finances in order to proceed with his ventures. The methods used were frequently unfair and wrong. Peasants, afraid that soon they would be penniless and might find themselves begging on the streets, created an air of uneasiness which permeated the city and the land of France.

Shops opened as usual on October the fifteenth, the owners hoping for a good day without any more disheartening demands from King Philip. Their stores were overstocked due to the reduced purchasing habits of the people. Maybe today there would be a change in the mood and practices would return to a more normal pattern. The Temple Square bustled with business as usual. The stables were very active with farriers trimming the hoofs of the Knights' horses and servants currying them with loving hands. Stone masons and other craftsmen were repairing part of the southern chapel wall and several spots around the perimeter wall that protected the community. Chickens and geese could be heard as their keepers fed them their day's rations. Nearby, farmers milked their cows in the field instead of the large barn. It was a sunny day and everyone was taking advantage of the opportunity to be outside. Cattle grazed contentedly in the lush pastures that lay between the Templar community and the Benedictine monastery. The farm was important for the Templars to provide provisions for its entire populace.

Inside the Temple, Sir Guigo Adhemar was continuing his instructional sessions with two young monks who had applied for membership with the Templars. He usually liked to instruct his recruits in the North Chapel because of the closeness to God that he felt in the area. Guigo was a man of much learning for his time. He had attended the schools of Florence and had taught in them for a few years before his father suggested that maybe his best opportunity could be found with the Knights Templars. He found the brotherhood very compatible and was soon giving his best to the organization. Guigo was a man of strong bearing; six feet tall, and his weight a lean one hundred and ninety pounds. The full head of shiny, sun-blond hair and beard gave him the appearance of a Viking who had recently arrived from Norway. His skin was toughened by the weather's beating sun; the time spent in wind-swept terrains; and battering battles. These elements had removed any trace of softness from his skin. He did love to be in command even if it was just overseeing the instruction of young recruits. The manner with which he taught instilled pride and loyalty into the hearts and souls of students. One did not have to guess that Guigo was indeed a man of dedication, a man whom God would be proud of always.

"The most important aspect of knighthood with the Templars is loyalty to God, respect and protection for our brothers and our fellow members in God," said Sir Guigo. "Life on this earth does not matter if you will truly be a warrior for God Almighty. There will be a place waiting and prepared for you in heaven with all the honors and glory imaginable."

"Does it not matter to God that we might put to death another fellow human?" inquired Richard, one of the young monks. Richard was twenty-two years of age and had spent the past ten years with a Cistercian group near Avignon in northern France. He was young appearing for his age, and the elders of the elders of the community had debated long about the likelihood of such a youngster joining a warrior group. His fair skin and innocent speech made him appear as one who might have been better off locating himself in a cloistered monastery. Yet the young lad's attitude and brave determination convinced even the toughest members to permit his knighthood.

"You are permitted to take the life of anyone who does harm to one of God's children; this is the honor that will be bestowed upon you with other privileges of knighthood," replied Sir Guigo. He knew from experience that the power given to them was not to be handled lightly and that serious thought would always precede the using of the sword or lance when in conflict with the enemies of the Church. Their code was to fight and even to kill an unjust aggressor.

The North Chapel in which Sir Guigo was conducting instruction that day was one that was frequently used for the continued lessons of the Knights and for morning and evening prayer. Its high arches which came to a pinnacle were constructed from stone that had been quarried in northern Italy near the Alpine mountains. The stone was chosen for this particular temple because of its quality and color, a dark gray marble. Scroll designs were etched into the columns that rose from a cobbled black granite floor. There was an assortment of grotesque gargoyles placed over the entranceway that were intended to frighten away evil spirits and men. A long hallway lined with pillars and doorways led from the North Chapel to the administration chamber. Lord Chancy was there today discussing the need for greater precautions to be taken when Master Jacques de Molay was traveling about France. Lord Chancy was a well respected aristocrat of the Paris society and did under all circumstances maintain a disciplined life. He was the owner of a shipping company that he had inherited from his wealthy and adventuresome grandfather. The company's exports dealt mainly with fine furs from northern countries and precious jewels that were mined throughout the world. He was a man whom Master Molay trusted and he had been a priceless friend of the Templars.

"It's time, I tell you, that you should begin taking one of the Knights on your journeys when you travel through France. There have been too many unusual occurrences lately. Why, just the other day my butler saw Guillaume de Nogaret leaving St. Martins. You're aware that he's one of King Philip's assistants? Now what do you suppose he was doing there?" asked Lord Chancy. "And there also have been rumors of the local clerics having meetings in King Philip's palace."

"You worry too much, my dear friend," replied Master

Molay. "Stories during these troubling times are many and fanciful. It's true that King Philip has for some time tried a variety of methods to wring more money out of us and the church, but Pope Clement indicates that we must hold fast to the law and our beliefs. We've come too far to recant rights that have been bestowed upon us by God and the Church."

Master Molay was himself once a knight and now headed the Templars. He was directly responsible to Rome for the Order's activities. His stature appeared so stately that it impressed most everyone with whom he came in contact. The Knights admired his unwavering sureness and his ability to make decisions quickly.

Jacques de Molay was a man of vision and inspiration to the Order. He, most of all, reverenced God and the Catholic Church and could be found frequently praying in the chapel. Now at sixty years old and beginning to show the gray hairs of age, he would often write his pope and ask him whether a younger man might not be found to resume the administration of the Templars. He knew that the political scene was not the brightest for the church, but he had the faith to believe that someday the air of evil would lift and the church would prevail.

There was a knock at the door which led into the adjacent chamber. Master Molay turned toward the entrance and called, "Come in quickly."

The large oak door swung inward and Squire Lawrence approached Master Molay. Stopping just four steps away he bowed and handed the Master a letter.

"Thank you, Squire, I will study this momentarily."

He walked over to the window of the chamber and parted the draperies slightly. A troubled look came across his face and he stared out beyond the protective walls to the beautiful landscape. No one was ever able to read Master

Molay's mind and at this moment he was even more inscrutable. Lord Chancy hesitated to disturb his deep silence or troubled thoughts.

"Well sir, if you don't mind, I will be returning to the Chancy estate. You will let me know if there is ever anything with which I can assist you?"

Lord Chancy moved slowly toward Master Molay with hand outstretched. The two gentlemen shook hands and then Lord Chancy gave Master Molay a brief embrace. A slight trace of moisture appeared in the eyes of Lord Chancy as he turned to leave.

"Thank you for coming to visit me, Lord Chancy, and please give my regards to your family. Mind you that if anything unusual occurs you will be the first to know," Master Molay told his friend as he followed him to the door.

"Very well," Chancy replied as he put on his black woolen cloak and left the room.

* * *

The serenity of the calm French countryside was suddenly shattered that afternoon by the shouts and clamor of armor in the Templars' courtyard. Master Molay ran quickly to his office window and looked out toward the court walls. The men of the community were running everywhere. Soldiers on horses and on foot were coming into the yard in great force and shouting at the scattering men.

"Everyone here is to remain calm and stay within these grounds," yelled one of the sergeants from the French guard. "We are here to take into custody only those who have been suspected of wrongful acts. They will be under investigation by the inquisition upon the order of King Philip."

The soldiers moved aggressively about the estate shoving, knifing and knocking down men of the Templar group. Many of the Templar Knights and sergeants were trying to make a valiant stand to defend the Temple grounds and its members. About forty near the main entrance to the Temple building executed a magnificent stand with their swords and shields flashing in the light. There was no sign of surrender within the brotherhood as they fought fearlessly against unbelievable odds. Another group of Knights and sergeants, with the help of servants, held a defensive position near the rear of the Temple building. They were determined not to allow the French to capture Master Molay or the other leaders within.

The numbers of French troops now within the courtyard were seven hundred. Bodies of slain men lay strewn about the once beautiful and peaceful grounds. The cries of the dying mixed with the moans of the wounded as they fell to their knees. The odor of blood and sweat began to permeate the air. The sound of clashing blades and knives sinking into flesh made the evening seem like the end of humanity. Why in this particular country with its great desire for the improvement of civilization and progress in society, was such a dreadful occurrence taking place? Not even the pope himself could stop the inevitable calamity that was about to happen; nor have the most learned scholars been able to properly explain why such a ghastly incident transpired.

When the fighting seemed at its peak, Master Molay and six of his assistants appeared at the Temple entrance. He held up his arms and called loudly to the struggling soldiers. "Stop, I tell you, and put an end to this abomination! If it is I that King Philip wants, then I will go with his escorts, but please stop this bloodshed and leave alone those who are not wanted by the King."

Master Molay slowly approached the commander of the French who was still on horseback and said, "Take me to your King, but I order you to immediately release those not in question."

"All right," replied Lord Albright, "You and your immediate court along with the Knights in this Temple Square will come with us now." Lord Albright was the head of the King's Paris garrison and a formidable opponent in battle. He demanded strict obedience from his men and they had learned to respect him and fear him in many ways. The successful discipline and strategy of war that had been the trademark of the Knights had been passed to the military leaders of many countries. Kings of many lands recognized the superior intelligence and training of these soldiers and instructed their commanders to adopt similar strategies. Lord Albright was one of these commanders who knew that he was dealing with a superior group and was not about to take chances.

* * *

All across France, on that day, the Knights Templars were being arrested and taken to the prison in Paris. This prison was located north of the river Seine just across from the palace and other administrative offices of the French government. Its four towers were six stories high and constructed of granite. The walls around the perimeter were three stories high with an occasional located window near the upper half. The diameter of this prison was approximately two city blocks and had the capacity to hold eleven hundred prisoners. The commander of the prison garrison was General Leonard who held the reputation of being one of the toughest prison commanders known by the military personnel of that day. It was said that he was specifically chosen by King Philip and that no one was to underestimate the seriousness of their crimes, especially those committed against Philip's kingdom.

Then suddenly there arose out of the west a terrible wind, which was followed by a lashing thunderstorm. Gales whipped at the men huddled in the doorways of buildings around the palace grounds. Large raindrops and hail pelted the city and surrounding farmlands. As the thunder rolled and the lightning flashed the guards and French captains began to worry about the seriousness of their deed. The cells into which the Templars were thrown were dismally dark and damp. Mice and rats could be seen running across the floor and into crevices about the structure. The large wooden doors banged loudly behind them as the last glimpse of daylight faded. Sore and angry, the men called to each other through the heavy doors.

"Master Molay, where are you?" called Sir Guigo, as he tried to peek through a crack in the entrance frame. He had suffered a sword wound to his right leg and several blows to his head and upper torso.

"God, please help us," whispered Guigo. "How can a thing like this happen? What is going on?" The other prisoners in his cell moved about trying to make themselves comfortable on the straw that was strewn about the floor. Their wounds were being attended to only by one another. The darkness that soon followed left a dreadful and ominous feeling throughout the prison. All became quiet except for the occasional moan from a man or the sounds of swearing as someone felt an animal crawl across his leg.

The following day, the Templars were brought before the local magistrate in the Great Hall of Justice near the palace on Cité island. The crowd was unusually excited, maybe because the very idea of the Knights being under arrest was unbelievable. These criminals were men of a religious order who had an outstanding and celebrated reputation all over Europe. What could have happened that made the king angry? The officials presiding over the event sat expectantly behind a large wooden table at the far end of the hall. The clothing they wore indicated their position in society, and their aloof attitude seemed coolly calculated to intimidate all present. Along with the captured Knights were also arrested servants, farmers, sergeants and priests of the Order. Their interrogation was to be conducted by the best inquisition masters in Europe. The head of this fanatical group was Guillaume de Norgart, a Paris judge and certainly an enemy of the Church.

"You Templars here today are under arrest to answer charges which have been filed at the clerk's office. There will be an inquiry into the attitude, behavior, beliefs and activities of the Knights Templars. This information will be of great importance to the King, the Pope and the people of France," said Guillaume as he stood before the group. His comrades seated beside him had given him the right to speak for them. Guillaume's attitude toward the church was known to be extremely hostile and he challenged any subject that might potentially affect the church's domain.

"You, the members of the Knights Templars, will be undergoing questions that have arisen during the past several years. You will cooperate and answer appropriately to those examining your case," Guillaume paused and stroked his clean-trimmed, black beard. "It is important for you to realize that your souls are in peril and that King Philip is very anxious for this unfortunate situation to be resolved with the utmost expediency. He has given me full authority to find the evil in this sector and to eradicate the sources from the country."

"Why weren't questions brought to the attention of myself or Master Molay first, according to proper protocol?"

asked Sir Hugues de Pairaud as he stepped forward from the group of Templars. "Queries have not been uncommon to the men of our Order during these past few years and we have dealt before with them appropriately. Why has this sudden arrest and imprisonment occurred at this time?"

Sir Hugues was a knight of great nobility whose reputation was known all over Europe. His curly brown hair and blue eyes made him attractive to women and gave him an air of courtly stature. Always dressed in his coat of mail and covered with the white cloak of the Templars' dress, he was a man of distinction and a formidable foe when cornered. This was just such a time, and Sir Hugues was outraged by the actions of this tribunal.

"It is imperative that Pope Clement be notified of this event and that we be given the right to travel to his court in Avignon. He is the one to whom we report, and we will answer only his questions. I otherwise find this act of hostility towards the Templars malicious and unworthy of men in your position, and insist that you immediately set us free." Sir Hugues' voice was deep and the tone that he used sounded strong. His bearing of six feet, two inches and two hundred and twenty pounds usually brought aggressive individuals to an immediate halt. The loyalty and lasting faithfulness of this knight for his community and to the entire Order was an attribute that Master Molay had long admired. The knighting of this man had been a gift of great significance to the Templars; Sir Hugues' leadership throughout France was not only inspirational but respected.

"You will not leave Paris, and you will not leave the prison," replied Guillaume, with a sneer on his lips. "You and your friends are to be questioned regarding accusations made against you. The only kindness that you will receive will be the reluctance we exert by not executing the lot of you at this very moment."

A horrified, hushed silence filled the Hall for a moment, then General Leonard stepped forward and addressed Guillaume. "If it is the court's desire, I will now take the prisoners back to prison. Will there be anything . . . "

General Leonard stopped abruptly as Sir Hugues suddenly approached him from behind.

"Lord Guillaume, why not allow a duel with lances and swords to be held in the palace courtyard? We could settle this argument that you have brought against us in the proper manner. I will be the knight to challenge the knight of your choice on the day of your choice."

Lord Mason rose from his chair behind the table and walked over to Guillaume. He was a magistrate of the court and had been occasionally questioned about his loyalty to the King. There had been other similar circumstances regarding inquisition matters which had arisen during the past several years, and the method for dealing with questioned subjects was satisfactorily established. He leaned toward Guillaume and with hand raised to his ear whispered something that could not be heard in the court. Guillaume thought for a few moments, then took several steps toward Sir Hugues.

"You will have no right or authority to ask or demand methods by which to resolve the complaints that have been lodged against you. You and your men will be taken immediately back to prison to await the questioning that has been arranged. Now, General Leonard, please take them away." He waved his hand at the Templars as he turned his back on them. The men remaining behind the table stood as Guillaume approached them, then followed him from the hall.

General Leonard motioned to his soldiers that the time had arrived to return the Templars to the prison. They moved forward in a line with spears held horizontal so that the prisoners would move out before them. The walk back to the Tower prison occurred much too quickly for Sir Hugues. He was trying desperately to reach Master Molay and Sir Guigo, who were ahead of him by twenty feet. Quickly he moved forward through his men, excusing himself if he seemed to push roughly.

"Master Molay!" Sir Hugues called, as he struggled to make headway. He reached out and grabbed the garment of his master.

"What are we to do now?" asked Sir Hugues with the sound of urgency in his voice.

"We will have the right to our attorneys and will commence to prepare our defense. They have nothing against us that will endanger our Order," replied Master Molay with an anxious but tired look on his face. "I must get word to Pope Clement at once and inform him of this terrible situation. Also, this evening I think we should all make special prayers to God and asked that we be blessed with guidance from the Holy Spirit."

That evening, and many evenings thereafter, the Templars frequently were found praying in their cells. The events that were beginning to unfold made even the bravest knight sweat cold drops of perspiration and pray that God might present them a merciful end. Day after day the Knights or some of their associates were taken from the cells to an adjoining building. It was here, deep within the French prison compound that the Templars were examined by the inquisitors. Torture beyond human endurance was used to try and break these men, acts that would make even the Devil squirm. Still no word of confession crossed their lips.

Many of the Templars were hung naked for days with ropes tied about their ankles. The blood that rushed to their heads and was unable to be pumped back up their bodies, soon caused them to be rendered unconscious. There were some who had their feet held over flames until the flesh was roasted. These were seen later with nothing but bones protruding from the lower leg. Others were given nothing to eat and slowly began to die of starvation. Wood and steel slivers were also driven beneath the fingernails of a prisoner until pain swept the consciousness from the man. So the torture continued for several months, and then one evening....

"Master Molay," said Sir Hugues, as he finished the last morsel of bread, "do you think that God will ever permit us to leave this dreadful place and return to our temple lands?"

Molay sat quietly with his legs crossed on the cold, damp stone floor. His shoulders were slumped with fatigue that comes after days and weeks of torture not only to the physical body but to the mental faculties.

"I don't know what will become of us. Even Pope Clement seems to have turned his back on our problems. Why hasn't he and the Cardinals done something to rescue us from these awful circumstances?" pondered Molay sadly. He slowly drew his cloak around his body in an effort to shield himself from the penetrating cold and darkness.

Later that night as Sir Hugues lay on his straw pallet, he silently wished that there was a priest in his cell so that he could make his confession and obtain absolution. Instead, he prayed that God would forgive him for the weaknesses of his flesh; for the sins of pride that he had committed; for the lack of faith in time of despair, and for not having been able to anticipate this tragedy and prevent it. He asked God for His continued love and mercy; for hope of a better life to come; for God's people across the land during this, their darkest hour; and for Master Molay as the awareness of their hopeless situation slowly settled upon him. His arms and back ached as he tried to find a comfortable position. His stomach was empty and painful as it had been for many days. He thought of the past years that he had spent with the Templars and the wonderful times that the brothers had together. He wondered how things might have turned out if he had married Lady Ann of Sorbonne instead of joining the Knights. He loved her very much and could still remember her long brown hair and dark brown eyes. Her small frame was pretty in the lovely dresses she wore and her spirited humor was the charm that gave her family its joy. He would never know again the softness of her touch against his cheek, or the tender caresses he once received when they were courting. They had almost married. Yes, he almost had children and a home to return to at the end of a fatiguing day's labor. But, alas, this was not meant to be. He was introduced to Master Molay during a hunt that brought the party near the Templars' property. After meeting the other knights and spending several days with the Templars, he decided to investigate the Order further. There was a special aura of nobility in the Order, a feeling of pride and a sense of accomplishment which filled the lives of the group. And, most of all, it was serving God with all of one's abilities. As he now remembered the past he was suddenly filled with a deep sadness. If only he could have seen this problem coming and could have done something to prevent it! Master Molay had depended on him for advice and guidance during the past several years. Hugues' heart became heavier as he began to realize the possible outcome of this inquisition. As he dropped off into a fitful sleep, hostile forces were even at that time planning the Templars' destruction.

* * *

The clatter of armor and shouts from guards brought the Templars to their feet early one spring morning the following year. Soldiers opened the prison doors of several cells and began to usher the men out at sword point. There was confusion about the prison even among the guards because of the unusual order that had been given. A total of fifty-eight Templars were marched from the dungeon to a field across the river from the palace. They were tied together in groups of four or five with a large, rough, wooden post in the center. Straw piles were hurriedly arranged beneath them and cloth pieces were tied tightly over their mouths. Tears could be seen in the eyes of the brothers as they realized what was about to happen. The soldiers began to throw fiery torches at the feet of the prisoners. Soon the morning air was filled with the pungent aroma of burning flesh and the cries of the bound men.

Sir Hugues could feel the warmth turn to heat beneath his feet. Those feet that had once carried young children to safety; that once helped the elderly find their way home; those feet which once carried the banner of the Christian cross through the toughest battles, and had brought Sir Hugues to the altar of God so that he could receive communion. These were the feet, this was the man who had served God and his order, the Knights Templars all his life. Now, fires like those of hell would open for him the gates of heaven.

The French troops began to slowly step backward as the heat intensified and the smell worsened. Sir Hugues de Pairaud, Visitor of France, Preceptor of Normandy, Oliver the Templar, Guigo Adhemar, Raymond Robert, and many more silently and in great pain gave their souls to God. The smoke of that blazing fire blended with their gentle but pure spirits as westerly winds lifted the essence heavenward. Then a great darkness fell upon the land and upon the hearts of the French people.

2

The year was 1995 and the place was Duluth, Minnesota. Springtime had finally arrived in the northland after an extremely hard winter. Of course, most winters in Duluth are an endurance test, but this year had the greatest snowfall in history and it took record time to clear the drifts from the streets because of continuous winds.

The coming of spring always heralds glorious feelings of ecstasy that are sometimes hard to explain. Warm breezes stir the yearning heart and delicate senses. Emotions surge with the appearance of green in the lawn and buds protruding on deciduous trees. The fragrance of old leaves from the previous autumn permeates the air and mixes with the smoke from fireplaces in the neighborhood. The sky is a brilliant blue with wisps of snowlike clouds drifting across the horizon. Finally, the sun is spreading its warmth over the land and people are responding with their usual spring rituals. Short-sleeve shirts are seen, as well as short pants on adventuresome young people jogging along residential streets. There are even those who are brave enough to be sunbathing on porch tops or on driveways near house and garage. Yes, springtime is a wondrous occurrence each year and brings people of all ages out of their homes and into the fresh spring air.

Classes at the College of St. Scholastica were continuing as usual, even though the students felt that it was useless with the weather being so nice. Still, there were studies to completed before the end of the semester, and exams to take before final grades could be expected. The college was known widely for its scholastic excellence and broad curriculum. Students loved the friendly and supportive environment that is promoted by the Benedictine Sisters.

The Benedictine property is located near the top of a hill that overlooks Lake Superior, on the most western prominence. On their grounds are located the Health Center for the elderly, the college and dormitories, and many acres of land for leisure. In the center of the complex is the original structure which resembles European Romanesque architecture, the Monastery. The building's shape is like the form of a Latin cross, and located directly beneath the center of the cross is their main chapel. To the north of the Monastery is the College administration building and student dormitories. The grounds have a variety of beautiful trees and bushes of every species that can be grown in the northern climate. It is a college campus that stimulates the eager mind to search for knowledge and personal growth.

Professor Lyle Longsworth busily gathererd his lecture materials together after a full day of classes. There was a knock at the classroom door. He was a little tired after five lectures, but happy with the job. His tweed jacket was rumpled around the lapels and his sandy brown hair appeared wind-swept. As he opened the door he brushed the lint off his trousers and ran his fingers through the hair that had fallen into his eyes

"Hi, are you Professor Lyle Longsworth?" asked the uniformed gentleman standing in the open doorway. By the style and dark color of his uniform he was obviously a UPS employee.

"Yes, I am Lyle Longsworth. What can I do for you?" replied Lyle as he smiled pleasantly at the courier. His smile at this time of the day was manufactured and automatic. He would never let anyone know how he was truly feeling or how glad he was that classes were over for the day.

"I've a special delivery for you, if you will just sign your name to this receipt," said the UPS fellow, handing Lyle a clipboard with pencil.

Lyle reached for it and then signed his name on the appropriate line while wondering what sort of package might be coming to him.

"Thank you, Professor, and here is your package," said the delivery man as he handed the brown wrapped parcel to Lyle. The wrapping appeared to be used grocery bag material with hay bale twine tying it very tightly closed.

As he handled the parcel carefully and walked back toward his desk, he heard the door close behind him and wondered why it had taken the delivery man so long to take his leave.

Lyle sat down at his sturdy oak desk and leaned back in the chair while examining the parcel more closely. *What do you think this is?* He slowly righted his chair and began to carefully open the package. The air had become stifling in the room and he wondered when administration would turn on the air conditioning. It was hard to control the temperature of buildings properly in the spring and autumn because of the variability in outside weather. Still, he wished that something more reasonable could be arranged for the comfort of the instructors and students.

The twine had to be cut off the package because the knots were extremely tight. Lyle pulled his five-inch, pearl-handled knife from his pocket and removed the twine skillfully. The paper wrapping came off easily and soon he was staring at a black box about the size of one which contained shoes. He opened it and pulled back the tissue paper that was surrounding the object. There, inside the center of many tissue layers was a journal that appeared to be very old. The paper had yellowed with age and the pages looked to be extremely delicate. He gently picked up the journal with shaking hands and noticed a small piece of paper protruding from under the first page. Removing the piece of paper carefully, he examined it and found a message addressed to himself. The language was French and written by his friend Ben Sully from Paris.

Dear Professor Longsworth, my friend,

I have come across the most extraordinary discovery recently. I found this manuscript while going through an old chest in the cellars of St. Martins Conservatory. As I am aware of your interest in the Crusades and related historical events, I thought you might find this information invaluable. I will talk with you more about this soon. Please keep this material confidential for the present time.

Sincerely, your friend,
Professor Ben Sully

Lyle wrinkled his brow and wondered what this material could contain and why his friend had decided to send it to him. Something of historical value usually was not permitted to leave the country of its origin unless permission was granted by the government or its owner. Ben must have been onto something of great interest. Lyle gently lifted the first page of the aged manuscript and folded it back. It was obvious that Ben had sprayed the fragile paper with a preservative because all brittleness was gone and the paper had the touch of fine leather.

Chronicles of Pierre Dubois.... the Knights Templars and King Philip.
Dated: 1314, following the execution of Master Jacques de Molay and the suppression of the Order of the Knights Templars.

Lyle took a slow deep breath and wiped the perspiration that was beginning to form on his forehead. His heart pounded in his chest and he wondered if this was really going to be as exciting as his imagination was telling his body. He decided that it might be safer to read this material in the security of his home, just in case someone unexpected might drop into the classroom. The journal was carefully wrapped again in the tissue and returned to the black box. Lyle gathered his books and papers into his briefcase, picked up the black box and his laptop computer before turning out the lights of the classroom.

It was 6:30 P.M. and he remembered to stop at the Benedictine Chapel for the evening Mass of Holy Thursday. Earlier in the day the Bishop would have celebrated a Mass with the priests of the diocese in attendance, and would have consecrated fresh chrism oils used in anointings at baptisms, confirmations, and the prayers for the sick and dying. By now the clergy had all taken a portion of the holy oils and placed them in safekeeping for use in their individual ministry.

Lyle thought about the many rich and ancient rituals of the Church that made his connection to the study and teaching of history seem almost sacred. He was a deeply reverent and thoughtful man who viewed every facet of daily life in a spiritual context.

As he approached the chapel, Lyle remembered that just ten years ago he had embraced Catholicism and was formally inducted into the Church on Holy Saturday at the Easter Vigil Mass. It was hard to believe that in two more days he would celebrate his tenth anniversary at another Easter Vigil Mass. Where had the ten years gone?

Mass had already begun when he entered the chapel and the sweet, clear voices of the nuns was rising as they sang the ancient chant, *"Kyrie Eleison.... Christe Eleison.... Kyrie Eleison."* Once again mankind was pleading with the Creator and Lord of the universe for mercy and forgiveness. The melody wove its way into the inmost depths of his soul, and his heart was filled with indescribable feelings of adoration. Then the festive ringing of the bells began as the entire assembly broke into song with *"Gloria in Excelsis Deo....* Glory to God in the Highest and Peace to His people on earth." As Lyle added his own voice to the singing, he felt himself to be one with all creation and with the Creator Himself. He was so deep in thought and feeling of gratitude that he barely heard the readings and responses, until it was time to stand for the reading of the Passion of Christ. Now he was fully aware, and was listening intently as the story of the Passion unfolded and he could hear the crowd call, "Crucify Him! Crucify Him!" His own heart ached, and he yearned to assuage the thirst and ease the pain of Christ as the crucifixion took place. Now the last words of Christ were solemnly recited by the priest. "It is finished." The assembly knelt silently and Lyle also sank to his knees. When the group arose for completion of the story, Lyle remained on his knees, unaware of the people around him. Then he arose and sat during the brief homily but was still deep in his own thoughts. It was not until the celebrant announced the washing of feet of several representatives from the assembly that Lyle again became present to the congregation.

The cantor was singing, *"Mandatum novum do vobis....* I give you a new commandment to love one another...." and again Lyle was immersed in his own thoughts and feelings of gratitude and adoration.

The celebrant was beginning to incense the altar and the assembly, when Lyle noticed how lovely the essence from the incense blended with the smoke from the candles.

The wisp gently floated upward and Lyle sent his prayers along with it. The bread and wine were now being transformed into the body and blood of Christ, and as he went slowly forward to receive this gift the choir sang *"Christus factus est pro nobis...."*

The priest then stripped the altar, and the sanctuary was darkened with the exception of a lone candle in the rear of the chapel. Lyle felt his heart swell with the love that he felt for Christ, and was unsure if he would be able to stand following such a moving mass. He stopped by the entrance and picked up his belongings as he left the chapel. On the way down the front stairs Father Marcos called to him from the doorway.

"Professor Longsworth, do you have a minute?"

"Sure," replied Lyle as he turned and set his things on the steps. The evening was bringing on an ever-darkening sky and stars were beginning to show themselves.

"Wasn't that a beautiful mass?" asked Father as he approached Lyle. "I was wondering if you would be interested in coming to our house for Easter dinner along with a few of our friends? Father Gramlly will be there, along with Professors O'Mally and Fritze."

"Why, yes, I think that would be great," Lyle answered with a warm voice. He had always admired Father Marcos and his great understanding of the role of religion in society. Lyle thought the priest was about sixty, and silently marveled at the man's athletic abilities. He was known to be quite a tennis professional and avid biker. Lyle had himself bicycled the north shore of Lake Superior on many occasions and always wondered at the strength this priest demonstrated. Father Marcos had been the resident priest for the Benedictine Monastery for seven years and enjoyed it greatly. His original order was located in France and his presence in Duluth was often wondered about, but never questioned. Why so far away from home and why Minnesota? Still everyone loved him and had adopted him into their lives.

"Come about 4:00 P.M. and we'll have a wonderful time," Father Marcos said as he turned to ascend the stairs on his way back to the Monastery.

"Okay," called Lyle after him. He picked up his belongings again and headed toward home. His place was approximately two miles away, down toward the lake. The evening air was cool now that the sun had set and Lyle walked quickly to keep himself warm. The streets were well illuminated by the city's street lights and the traffic headlights prevented the night from becoming too dark for safety.

Lyle's home appeared small compared to many of his neighbors', but he didn't mind because it was the perfect place for a bachelor like himself. The house was once the home of a gardener who worked for a very wealthy man in Duluth. The main home or mansion was located further back from the main road. A winding lane entered the property at the northwest corner of the estate and passed his house, then continued on about fifty yards to the mansion. The structures were made from sandstone that had been quarried sixty-five miles south of Lake Superior. They were stately buildings and frequently reminded Lyle of castles he had once seen in Spain. He could now begin to see the lights shining from his study window as he approached his residence from Hawthorne Road. He always left a few lamps on when he knew that he would be coming home after dark. He also varied the location of the lights left on so that nobody could predict whether he was at home or out.

It's good to be at my residence again, Lyle thought as he opened the front door with a key from his pocket. He turned on the hallway light switch and set his briefcase and computer on the woolen rug. He then walked down the hall a few feet and entered his library on the left. Going over to the fireplace, he arranged four oak logs so that there would be enough ventilation and struck a match to the kindling beneath. Punching on his answering machine, Lyle went over to his desk and placed the black box down. He wanted to read more of this manuscript but wanted to get everything arranged first. He was such a perfectionist, almost to the point of being ridiculous at times; at least, that was what he kept telling himself. After making sure the doors were locked and he had put his school materials in the office, Lyle went upstairs to his bedroom and changed into his evening robe and slippers. He was remembering Ben Sully from a conference that they attended together in Paris two years ago. The seminar's subjects were about international historical discoveries from around the world. Ben was about forty-five and very handsome. There was the slight graying of hair at his temples and in his mustache that made his black hair quite noticeable. His love for life was very apparent and had Lyle extremely fascinated. The women of Paris were always calling on him and, surprisingly, he usually found time to see most of them. Ben was gregarious, adventuresome; Lyle was much more serious in nature, always surprised that Ben enjoyed his company.

Stopping by the kitchen on his way back to the office, he made a toasted cheese sandwich with lettuce and tomato for himself, then poured a brandy. Entering the library again he chose to sit in his favorite leather armchair that was between his desk and the fireplace. He again unwrapped the journal from the box that Ben had sent him and turned on the lamp as he sat down to read. The hand printing was somewhat difficult to read, but Lyle, being an expert in the old French lettering tried to make out the message.

It was the year 1297 that the Knights of the Temple began to be scrutinized throughout the French court. Their riches in properties, gold, jewels, and other valuable materials became common knowledge amongst the leaders of the empire. Their expertise was also common knowledge and great respect was to be accorded them. Their presence in the kingdom and their increasing functions as ambassadors was an embarrassment to Royalty and legislators.

I found a use for the talents that were given me in the form of writing and began to devise a method of making myself useful to King Philip. I began to document the complaints and discussions I heard in the courts, universities and communities. I then began to prepare documents about the Knights Templars and their behavior. Of course, the intent of this information was to give strength to King Philip and his officials. It was soon obvious to me that King Philip appreciated my literary achievements and he invited me to the palace. After having dinner with the royal family and being entertained by the court's jesters, he asked me to accompany him into the drawing room where we would taste cognac that had recently arrived from Italy. He then told me that he deeply appreciated the writings that I was doing and that they would be of great benefit to France someday. He then asked if I would like to be appointed to his economic council, and that this service would pay extremely well.

Of course, I accepted the position and began immediately to make plans for future publications.

Lyle rubbed his eyes and took a sip of brandy. This was unbelievable! Such a document would be priceless to the French government, or for that matter, anyone who was interested in artifacts. He had studied about the Middle Ages and the Knights of the Crusades many years ago. He was always led to believe that they had committed an unforgivable offense to God and their nation. But, now, maybe there was another story, perhaps a political front, and maybe—

Lyle wondered if he should try to contact Ben in Paris. He glanced at his watch. It was 9:00 P.M. Duluth time, so it must be 4:00 A.M. in Paris. Lyle reached for the telephone and began to dial the operator, then he returned it to its place. It was too early in the morning to awaken anybody, even Ben.

He leaned over and picked the computer up off the floor, then placed it on the desk. *I'll send Ben an E-mail note and he'll see it when he awakens,* Lyle thought as he turned on the computer's power. *Now, let's go online and then pull up mail.* Lyle was busily clicking the keyboard and didn't notice the wind beginning to rise outside. Suddenly there was a strong breeze that blew through a partially opened window and the draperies flapped vigorously. *There had been no forecast given regarding a storm or bad weather approaching,* thought Lyle as he crossed the room to the window and peered out. The sky was clear and only the stars could be seen shining brightly through the trees. The beginning of the waning moon appeared in the easterly sky and there wasn't a stir anywhere in the bushes. Lyle returned to the desk and completed the following message to Ben:

Professor Sully, my friend,

> *Your package and message arrived here today. I'm most interested and curious about the contents. Please advise me regarding your intentions.*

> *As always, your friend,*

> *Professor Longsworth*

Lyle sent the message off and returned to the reading of the manuscript. He selected his favorite smoking pipe from a tray on his desk and filled the bowl with cherry Borkum Riff tobacco. The brandy was still available and he took a sip while reclining back in the chair; then struck a flame to his pipe. He remembered the stories of the Crusades and the knights in shining armor that defended the honor and glory of their kings. Lyle closed his eyes and could picture rolling green hills with valleys lined in trees. On one rather large hill was a castle with walls higher than the cliffs of Dover. A winding trail found its way upward toward the castle, until it disappeared within those silent walls. There were banners of white, red and blue waving high above the towers, and feather-like clouds floating in the distance. Suddenly, over the hill opposite the castle came the charge of many soldiers. Out in front of the brigade were beautifully clothed knights on large white horses. As they held their lances forward and tightly clutched their swords, they surged forward toward the castle's walls. Then out through the gates charged another army. Yells of victory could be heard above the clashing metal, and cries of pain apparent after the fall. On they fought bravely until not a sound could be heard. Then silence came and all was still. From another hill came a silent procession, walking slowly, two by two, down toward that lonely battlefield. Melodic voices could now be heard gaining strength. *"Ave mundi spes Maria.... Ave mundi spes Maria...."* Where had he heard that sound before? A single melodic line that was sung in unison and free of rhythm. The closer they came the greater was the distinction in their voices.

"*Lyle ... Lyle ... Lyle ...*" They were calling his name from a distance.

"*Lyle ... Lyle ... Lyle ...*" A cold breeze chilled his bones and he tried to cover himself but couldn't seem to find his garments. Suddenly he awoke with the curtains again moving by the window and the fireplace giving its last flicker. *Good Lord,* thought Lyle as he pushed himself to his feet and hurried over to close the window. He seemed to detect the fragrance of incense in the room and vaguely wondered who else might have been there. Then, from somewhere out through the window of his office he heard the music he had just experienced in his dream. It was a Gregorian chant, like the melodies sung by the monks of Santo Domingo De Silos. Lyle shook his head and pinched his leg until tears moistened his eyes. Still the melody floated through the window and held him captive. Then, all was silent again. Lyle slowly closed the shutters and went over to stir the fireplace. He needed to get warm. Finishing his brandy, he remembered the trip he had taken to Spain four years ago. The group he was with wanted to stop by the old Benedictine Monastery near Burgos and spend a portion of the day with the monks. A memorable occasion, one that would stay with him forever and provide him with many spiritual memories.

So much for day-dreaming, thought Lyle. *I must retire for the evening and return to the manuscript tomorrow.* He walked over to the desk and lay the journal again inside the box. There was a special feeling about this evening that he couldn't quite identify as he turned off the lights of the library and headed for his bedroom.

* * *

The next day, Good Friday, Lyle attended the Lenten services at Holy Rosary. This was the Cathedral for the diocese and very lovely. It again was typical of Romanesque architecture that was used by the Catholics for many large churches. The cathedral overlooked the city of Duluth and the shores of Lake Superior. The people of the city were friendly and proud of their community. Years ago the population was mainly composed of Scandinavian descendants; now most every culture is represented in the area and the business climate reflects the progress. There was great diversity in occupations, prosperity, education, and interest. All lived together harmoniously most of the time. The main business of the region stemmed around tourism and there shows a steady growth in the number of visitors during all seasons of the year.

Lyle was glad he lived here and that his grandmother, Madeline, had decided to stay after the death of his grandfather. Lyle, her only living grandson, made it his responsibility to see that her every need was met. He was a striking man of forty-two and had a very distinctive appearance. His stature, just shy of six feet, supported a slim but strong frame. The clothing he wore consisted mainly of jeans and tweed jackets, although he did possess three fine dress suits for the more auspicious occasions. As a graduate of the University of Notre Dame University, in Indiana, he had stayed on to be an assistant for Professor Laden before accepting this teaching position at St. Scholastica just ten years before. He had always dreamed of being an archaeologist, assigned to unexplored areas of the world and uncover lost artifacts. One never knew though, maybe someday his chance would come. In the meantime he read a variety of books with an enormous appetite.

That evening Lyle returned home after having dinner at Rock's on the North Shore. He checked about the house to see that all was in order and stopped to read a message that his housekeeper, Gladys, had left for him on the kitchen counter. Slipping on his smoking jacket he went into the library and turned the computer on. First "Menu" then to "America Online." After entering his identification number he waited until hook-up was completed.

"You've got mail," came AOL's voice. Lyle's pointer immediately clicked onto "New Mail" and he brought up a message from his friend, Ben Sully.

Professor Longsworth,

Received your message today. This discovery could lead to an ex-

citing search if you are interested. Have you as yet studied page ten? If you are so inclined, please join me soon and we will embark upon a most interesting adventure.

Respectfully your friend

Ben

Lyle unlocked and opened the top drawer on the right side of his desk. He carefully reached in and withdrew the manuscript. Sitting down in his leather and oak office chair, he began to thumb through the pages. On page ten he stopped and began to read from the top.

The capture of these significant members of the Knights Templars was indeed a terrible blow to the Order. It is doubtful that they will ever again regain their previous standing of importance in the country.

Most of their properties were confiscated, with riches going to the King and his favorites. I also heard of an escape by twelve Knights, that occurred on the day of the arrest. It was reported that much gold and jewels were taken by these men. I was asked to assist in the locating and bringing to trial of these Knights. Guillaume de Nogaret was to be the one to whom I would report. We were good friends and calculated that King Philip would have use of our services in the future.

Lyle scratched his head and stretched his legs. Could it be that Ben was onto the whereabouts of the Templar Gold? With about six hundred and eighty years gone, could this valuable deposit still be traced? What a wild notion! It would be like hunting for a needle in a haystack. *But wouldn't it be a great adventure!* Lyle was on his feet now and pacing the room. He would have to obtain as much information about the Order and their place in society of that time. Maybe he could talk with Father Marcos and find out whether he knew anything about the Templars' fate. Ben would probably not mind if he talked to a friend in confidence.

He could envision himself crawling in through a dark tunnel that emptied into yet another underground room. Only a fiery torch that he was carrying lighted the darkness ahead. The air was filled with a foulness from years of decay and isolation. The threads in the knees of his jeans were beginning to break away from the roughness of the ground, and the palms of his hands were starting to burn after pressing them on the ground for so long. As he squeezed through an extremely narrow crevasse, Lyle noticed a thin stream of light coming from a small hole about twelve feet away. He inched his way onward until he was at the opening. Reaching up he tore with his sore fingers at the rock that surrounded the area until the opening was large enough to squeeze himself through. On the other side, Lyle stood up and stretched his fatigued body. Rubbing his hands together, he noticed blood coming from several scratches. The pain didn't seem to bother him, especially when he observed a large table at the end of the room he had entered. He walked closer, moving through dust and cobwebs. His respiratory rate had increased as well as his pulse. There, on the table were five chests and one of them was open—revealing a large amount of coinage. He picked up a piece and rubbed it on his clothes, then held it up to the light that was coming from above. *Gold!*

Slowly, Lyle was beginning to return back to reality. The sequence of events that were occurring seemed to him to be leading somewhere. First, the manuscript came; then Friday evening and the Gregorian music he had heard at Mass and then again at home. The idea of being led into an adventure excited Lyle. He was being enticed into this expedition! He decided to send a reply back to Ben.

Dear Professor Sully,

You might have guessed; yes, I am extremely interested in embarking on this adventure with you. I hope you have more details. When do we start?

Sincerely,

Lyle

He clicked on "Send" and the mail was gone. What a masterpiece of ingenuity, the invention of the computer. Lyle rubbed his eyes and again settled back to read more of the manuscript.

Most of the information included were dates and excerpts from propaganda that spoke of suppressing the Order of the Temple. One article, *De recuperatione,* was directed at the need for another Holy War and the King's lack of finances. Pierre Dubois went on to state that the King would be able to bring about peace in the Holy Land, if only they could obtain the large cash supplies of the Templars and Hospitalers. He spoke of reform and the need to consolidate the military knights under one head, the King.

Just then the computer said, "You've got mail." Lyle moved the mouse so that he could click on "Read."

Dear Professor Longsworth,

So you're home! Yes, I do have more details and am continuing to work on them. Please let me know when you can come to Paris. We will commence as soon as you arrive. Bring the manuscript with you and a friend if you'd like.

As always, your friend,

Ben

Lyle clicked onto the Web and began to search for Knights Templars. The information there was generic and only skimmed the surface. He decided to go to the library the following Monday and research information on the Order. There would have to be a lot of information regarding such an important organization in the Middle Ages.

The telephone rang about 10:00 that evening and Lyle roused himself out of his easy chair.

"Hello," he said as he yawned and adjusted his clothes. The room had become cool and dark.

"Hi, Lyle," came a familiar voice. "How are you? Do you know who this is?"

"Why, of course, my dear grandmother," replied Lyle as he eased himself onto the phone chair. "I've been great, and what about you? I've been planning on coming to visit you soon; would Monday evening be too soon?"

"No, that would be just fine. I'm planning on a trip to see your folks in Georgia next month. Do you want to plan on traveling with me?" asked Madeline, with great enthusiasm.

She was such a joy, thought Lyle, always upbeat and going somewhere. How fortunate for him to share her genetic makeup. Still, a woman of ninety flying about the country, participating in bridge groups, always out for dinner in the evening with friends might be pushing her luck. But, if she had the desire and her health, she should do whatever she wanted. Lyle admired her stamina and her ability to always make the most of her natural beauty. White hair and sparkling blue eyes set off by an ever-winning smile, did indeed describe Madeline. *A woman about town*, thought Lyle. *Yes, she would live a long time.*

"Well, Grandmother, I was beginning to make plans for another trip abroad. Something recently came up and I'm investigating it with a friend," said Lyle. He didn't like to say no to his grandmother. "Maybe next time you're traveling that way, I can go."

"Oh, of course, don't let a thing like this bother you. Monday, I'll take you to the Country Club for dinner and you can fill me in on what's happening in your life. Okay?" asked Madeline.

"Yes, that would be great. Shall I pick you up about 6:00 P.M.?"

"Exactly the time I had in mind. Meet you then and take care, love." Madeline hung up the receiver and Lyle heard the click. It would be nice seeing Grandmother again. She was a real source of inspiration and he could always count on her to challenge and then support his endeavors. Then she would be there at the end applauding his success.

* * *

The Sunday Easter Mass was beautiful as usual at Holy Rosary. Lovely spring flowers adorned the altar and sanctuary. The church was crowded with ladies in new spring dresses and men in freshly pressed suits. Children were exceptionally clean and tidy, as well as on their best behavior. The mass celebrated the risen Lord and His continued dwelling with His people. Lyle enjoyed the homily that Father Adrian gave, especially the sincerity with which he spoke. It was almost as if he personally knew Christ and knew what He was feeling.

After mass, Lyle went for a drive along the scenic north shore of Lake Superior. He enjoyed seeing the growth that was occurring in nature with each passing day. His 1965 dark green Jaguar XJS glided gracefully along the blacktop road as if it were on a cloud suspension. The air was fresh and the sky a bright blue. He felt at peace with himself and with God. This evening he would have dinner with Fathers Marcos and Gramlly. Also, his friends Professors O'Mally and Fritze would be there to liven up the occasion.

As Lyle pulled his car onto a turnout that overlooked Lake Superior, he noticed a black car pulling out. Not an inexpensive car either, probably close to sixty thousand big ones. He was sure the car was a series 7 BMW. *Who could be driving one of those in this part of the country,* he wondered. Also, the gentleman in the driver's seat appeared unusual, with a dark hat and a rather large bushy mustache. The sunglasses obstructed the driver's face from Lyle's keen eye, and soon the car was out of sight. But not until he noted the license plates were from California.

Lyle got out of the car and strode along the shoreline sand and rocky coast. The sea gulls were making their daily rounds to locate food from passing boats or friendly tourists. Their loud cries broke the tranquility of nature's sublime surroundings but did not distract from the reality of nature. The wing span of these birds must have been three feet across, and their bills three inches long. When feeding these creatures, one had to be very careful; they had been known to remove fingers from the unwary.

In the distance, a large ore boat was traveling from Thunder Bay to the harbor in Duluth. The ports for international trade in the lake cities made them an ongoing point of interest to residents as well as tourists. The lighthouses and foghorns helped to create a climate and culture of the sea. Many individuals had moved to this area of the country just to be a part of the activity that surrounded the lake, which Lyle loved. He knew that he'd never again move inland. As he began to make his way back to the Jag, he wished that he owned a boat so that he could tour the islands and search out those hidden inlets. He wanted to explore the unknown and find the treasure lost. *Find the treasure lost!* He suddenly awakened from his dreamlike walk and realized he was soon going on a treasure hunt. Now he needed to return home and dress for dinner.

* * *

"Good evening Lyle, come in and make yourself comfortable," said Father Marcos as he led Lyle into the living room. "Let me take your coat, and please make yourself a drink from the liquor cabinet." The room was warm from the fire and very attractive. Hardwood floors were partially covered by two separate Persian rugs of extraordinary colors. One wall was totally shelved with books, exact number unknown. Two large French Provincial sofas faced each other about eight feet apart. The coverings were imported tapestries of inestimable value. Extra armchairs were about the room, each with an end table, vase or statue nearby. Lamps were conveniently located so as to provide ample light for the reader or invited guest. Notable artwork was displayed on one wall and large, spacious windows overlooked the lake. Indeed, a room of taste for a priest from France. Lyle smiled his approval to Father Marcos as he walked over to the mahogany bar and selected a drink.

"Hey, Lyle, how are you?" asked a voice from a chair near the fireplace. "How are classes progressing this spring? Or has the fever of spring overcome your ability to comprehend present conditions?"

"Frank O'Mally!" exclaimed Lyle as he poured a J&B scotch over ice. "I'm great and yes, classes are going well and no, spring has not as yet made me take leave of my senses."

"When are you going to have Marge and me over to your place for dinner? You promised a year ago and still nothing has happened. Oh, I know, you probably have something sinister going on there after dark. But that's okay with me, we'll join in." Frank was smiling as he rose and took Lyle's hand in a friendly shake.

"Don't get impatient Frank, the right time will come," replied Lyle as he seated himself in a chair near Frank. He was always impressed with his colleague who was the most popular professor on campus. His humorous anecdotes, created especially for the students, made boring subjects quite fascinating. His tenure was in mathematics and geoscience. One of a kind and a blessing for St. Scholastica. Lyle vowed silently to himself that he would try to have them over for dinner soon.

While they were deep in conversation, Father Marcos was welcoming the other guests and attempting to make them comfortable. There arose a delicious aroma of food coming from the kitchen and Lyle could detect his stomach beginning to growl from hunger. As he cautiously rubbed his middle he noticed John Fritze entering the room.

"Hi, John," called Lyle as he stood and approached Professor Fritze. "Let me make you a drink and then you can join Frank and me by the fireplace."

"Thanks Lyle; make mine a brandy Manhattan," replied John as he brushed his suit and then ran his fingers through his black hair. "I'm dying to tell you all about the recent decision of the college board."

"Well I bet we've already heard it," said Frank as he stood and approached the bar. "Think I'll refresh this drink while you professors watch."

"Don't keep us waiting, John; give us an unabridged version of the news," Lyle said as he returned to his chair.

"I'll tell you all as soon as we're seated in this comfortable room" replied John, placing a couple of ice cubes in his glass as he headed for the softness of Father Marcos' favorite armchair.

"The board has decided to combine a few classes for the remainder of the term."

"Why would they possibly want to do that?" asked Lyle. He leaned forward and looked at Frank questioningly.

"They think it would be a unique experience for the students to combine certain subject materials and see what they can develop," John exclaimed, excitedly. He stood and crossed the room to the window. "It's an experiment to test the ingenuity of the students."

"This will indeed be quite an achievement, if these young college people work together and meet the challenge," added Father Gramlly as he entered the room with Father Marcos. They stopped by the liquor cabinet and made drinks for themselves. Father Gramlly had a twinkle in his eye and a slight smile beginning to curl his lips. Always an optimist, Father Gramlly had always been deeply involved with the college students. Now, almost seventy years old and slightly lame in his right leg, he was becoming even more interested in the curriculum development of the college. Ever since he returned from a pilgrimage to Yugoslavia, Father appeared to be driven toward a greater sense of commitment in the youth. He believed that the future of the church lay in these young people, as frivolous as they were, and that a greater commitment needed to be honestly felt by their elders. It was as if he had experienced a renewal of life and a deeper relationship with God.

"What will the instructors do?" inquired Frank as he stood to shake hands with the priest.

"That is something that is still to be resolved. It has been suggested that a sabbatical could be taken if there is something pressing in that person's life, or it may be that the two professors will desire to work together to develop new teaching methods," replied Father Gramlly to the wide-eyed professors. They couldn't quite believe that St. Scholastica was being so bold in its effort to be the most progressive in education.

"Well, it certainly will provide some with a convenient opportunity to delve into new arenas of research and adventure," said Father Marcos as he glanced at Lyle. There was a moment of silence as everyone in the room looked at Lyle. He felt his face turn several shades of red and wondered remotely whether they might know about the manuscript he had received. *Did Father Marcos know what he had been secretly planning?*

"I for one would like to take this opportunity to undertake a class or two at Notre Dame," indicated Frank with a smile "This is a chance in a lifetime and I'm certainly not one to pass a good thing by."

The atmosphere of the room was laced with an air of expectancy as the men began to figure ways of spending their newly found time, or ways of combining lecture material so as to make it meaningful. The warmth of the room was not only coming from the fireplace but, Lyle noted, it seemed to be generated by all persons present. Comfortably, they smoked their pipes and sipped on aged liquor while smells of food being prepared were drifting about the house. The music of Mozart's *Don Giovanni* was blending with conversation as did the occasional noise of the housekeeper in the kitchen. *What a life,* thought Lyle as he walked over to the bar and helped himself to another J&B. *It can't get much better than this....*

"Father Marcos," called the housekeeper, Rosa, from the doorway. Father stood and strode across the room. She spoke quietly to him and he nodded.

"Dinner is served, my friends," he said as he raised an arm and motioned them to come.

That evening's dinner was a delight. Beef Bearnaise, baked potato, mixed vegetables, hot rolls, fresh green salad, and a bottle of French 1997 Beaujolais to drink with dinner.

The delicious meal was capped with apple pie à la mode which inspired everyone to release a notch on his belt.

After great applause was given to Rosa for such a magnificent repast, Father Marcos suggested they retire to the living room and have a smoke. Lyle, who had been quiet for several minutes now, was wondering if he should talk with Father Marcos about his recent acquisition. He must know whether or not this entire episode was beginning to get out of hand. Was he imagining too much? Father would be able to evaluate the situation from a different perspective and reflect sound judgment when it was time to give his opinion. *Yes. I'll do it. Now for the right moment to get him alone.*

Father Gramlly was getting into deep conversation with Frank and John as they cooled themselves by an open window. Lyle crossed over to Father Marcos, who was inserting another log into the fire.

"Father, could I speak privately with you?" asked Lyle, brushing a few crumbs from his shirt.

"Certainly you may. Please, let's go outside and select more Pinewood."

Father Marcos led the way to the rear door of the house and motioned for Lyle to follow. Outside, they headed toward the woodpile that was stacked to the right of the door.

"Now, what is it that you would like to discuss?" Father Marcos began to pick out a few good-looking split logs. The air, slightly chilly and breezy, had started to blow from the west. Lyle folded his arms and wondered if he was making a mistake.

"I've received a document from a friend of mine in Paris," he began. Then he related the sequence of events and his thoughts about the opportunity that lay ahead. The words rushed from his mouth as he relayed Ben's ideas and tentative plans for the search.

"My, but you've certainly been busy," observed Father

Marcos as he stood staring at Lyle. "This sounds like quite an adventure; I almost wish I could go with you."

"Then you don't think I'm crazy and imagining too much?" asked Lyle in disbelief. He had been certain that Father would laugh at him or think that he really needed a sabbatical for a prolonged rest.

"No, I think that you might be onto something very interesting not only from a monetary standpoint, but from a historical fact-finding position. This information you received may have been sent to you for a purpose."

"I'd like for you to read it, if you've got time," Lyle said as he rubbed his arms.

"That would be great, Lyle. Should I drop by your place tomorrow evening?"

"Tomorrow I'm going out to dinner with my grandmother, but Tuesday evening would be good," replied Lyle, hoping that Father would consent.

"Great, shall I come about 6:00 P.M.?"

"Yes, and I'll have Gladys fix us some dinner," said Lyle with a tinge of anticipation in his voice. He began to wish that it was Tuesday evening. How ridiculously anxious he was becoming about all of this!

The two men gathered up the necessary logs and proceeded back into the house. The remainder of the evening went quickly as the guests conversed about everything from weather to the current state of the economy. Only the chiming of a grandfather clock in the hallway alerted Lyle as to the lateness of the hour. Giving his farewell and thanking Father Marcos for a wonderful evening, Lyle gathered his coat and departed for home. The night was getting cooler but was not distracting Lyle from his elation. As he studied the brilliance of the star patterns and breathed deeply of the fresh air, he wondered what would happen next.

3

Northwest Airlines Flight 356 taxied down the runway of the Duluth International Airport early on the morning of April 16th. There was a trace of fog in the lowlands that was spreading its light-gray hood over most of Lake Superior. The weather had stayed quite springlike over the last few weeks, despite forecasters repeatedly saying that winter wasn't over yet. Spring flowers were popping up all over the city and the surrounding countryside. The usual multicolored tulips and crocuses mingled with white spring beauties in the neighborhoods and in the woods. Lyle was going to miss the next few weeks of spring here, but was not saddened because of the challenging trip lying ahead of him.

As the Boeing 747 lifted into the air, the surge of excitement grew within him. This was sure to be an exciting escapade. All the necessary arrangements had been made, but still he hoped that he hadn't forgotten anything. Grandmother was a little sad and yet elated that this opportunity had been presented to Lyle. The college president seemed pleased that Lyle was taking advantage of such an unusual and historic opportunity. If the trip portended half of what Lyle anticipated, it would be a positive image for the college, especially for the history department. Lyle realized that the strong endorsement of his close colleagues and the college administration gave him additional pressure to succeed. *To succeed!* Not just simply to have an adventure and to learn for his own purposes and self-satisfaction, but to succeed meant to discover, to reveal, to publish, to bring a new relevance to his classroom at St. Scholastica. *Oh God,* thought Lyle, *help me to make a difference and to do credit to history. This mission must be a success, or I will seem a naive fool.*

Father Marcos had read the manuscript that had been sent from Paris and had agreed that it was authentic and historically significant. He said that Lyle should feel free to contact him if anything arose for which be might be of help.

Upon the advice of Ben, Lyle had decided to invite a friend to accompany him on this trip. The first name that jumped into his mind was Doctor Bill Burley of New York University. Bill, well known as a maverick, sort of a misfit in medicine, but an extremely brilliant man. He was a little older than Lyle, but one would never have guessed that by his lifestyle. His wife, Laura, always threatened to leave him if he didn't settle down and become a responsible husband, yet she never accused him of infidelity and always remained a devoted wife. He had supported her in opening one of the most fashionable women's shops in New York and among her clientele were notables such as the mayor's wife and the spouse of the World Bank CEO. It had been good for Laura to maximize her limitless potential and she was partially satisfied knowing that her contribution to their marriage was worthwhile. She reconciled herself with the many absences of her husband and sublimated her loneliness with her established business.

Bill had traveled extensively and some of his escapades were known to have been quite hazardous. He seemed to have an unquenchable appetite for excitement. He wanted to experience everything from safaris in the African jungle to mountain-climbing in the Andes, to crossing of the Atlantic in a small sailboat with two of his boat-maker friends. One could even say that medicine was Bill's hobby and adventure his vocation. Lyle thought he might be game for this journey even though it would be on short notice. Sure enough, when he answered his phone that Tuesday evening, he only heard half of the report that Lyle gave before answering affirmatively.

Lyle had packed only two bags and a briefcase which contained his lap-top computer and a few books that related to the Templars. Then of course, he brought the manuscript that Pierre Dubois had written. The money he carried was mainly in the form of travelers checks and a couple of credit cards for emergency use.

The plane was leveling and the seat belt sign had been turned off. Captain Bolyes was speaking over the intercom relating the usual flight messages and notice of the smooth flight anticipated. Lyle reached for his briefcase and removed one of the books. Reading on an airplane had always been difficult. He had previously experienced sickness and had always stopped focusing on the material just before it was too late. This time he was so engrossed with his subject matter that he didn't notice his stomach starting to churn. Suddenly, he gasped and clapped his hand over his mouth. Standing quickly, he turned and ran down the aisle toward the rear restroom. He barely made it inside the door, when all hell broke loose and he slumped over the commode letting the devil out. *God,* thought Lyle, *why did I have to start reading?*

The remainder of the flight into New York's Kennedy Airport was uneventful. There were a few low clouds in the sky with a trace of sun beginning to shine through. The runway appeared wet as the airplane settled into a smooth landing and taxied across the field to the assigned gate.

Lyle disembarked along with the other travelers and proceeded to the baggage area. The nausea in his stomach had greatly diminished since he had placed his feet on solid ground. *Hopefully, the remainder of the expedition will go without a hitch,* he thought as he located his luggage and turned toward the entrance of the terminal. A redcap came quickly out of nowhere and asked to assist Lyle to a taxi. The ride into New York City proceeded without incident and soon they were in the midst of honking cars and bustling people. Nowhere did life seem more real or chaotic than in this city, and yet they were all able to function relatively well together. From the surface it appeared that everyone rushed to nowhere, but after getting to know people and the system, you realized there was purpose in this design. It was about 1:00 P.M. and the peak of the business hour was in full swing. Just then it started to rain heavily. Some made a mad dash for cover; others just opened their umbrellas without blinking an eye. Thunder clapped above and the rain came down with great force. It was beginning to be difficult to see out the front window of the cab, even with the wipers going. Of course, rain or any other kind of weather never slowed down a New York taxi.

The yellow cab pulled up in front of the Plaza Hotel on Fifth Avenue and 59th Street, and Lyle stepped out onto the sidewalk. The cabby retrieved the luggage from the trunk. People were scurrying about, probably making arrangements for their evening lodging or for an elegant dinner in one of New York's most famous restaurants. A hotel porter took charge of the luggage; Lyle paid the cab driver, entered the hotel lobby and proceeded to register.

Lyle had prearranged to meet Bill for dinner that evening in the Edwardian Room adjacent to the hotel lobby. They would go over the information Lyle had acquired and discuss pertinent details that could lead to a successful exploration. Lyle wanted to shower and then relax in his room that afternoon before the evening's activities.

At 6:00 P.M., Lyle roused himself from a peaceful nap

and glanced at his watch. The suite was pleasantly decorated in several shades of blue and white. He always enjoyed the art work in these older and more elegant hotels. So much so that he didn't even mind being on the eighth floor, although he would have preferred a lower level.

It was time to get ready for dinner. After slipping on his dark blue suit with a white shirt and an attractive blue striped tie, Lyle quickly ran a comb through his hair and placed one of the white carnations (from a china vase on the table) into the buttonhole of his lapel. He made sure everything was in place before he left the room. Checking the doorknob to see if it was securely locked, he was then certain that it was safe to leave his valuables. He headed toward the elevator. He noticed a hotel bellhop waiting for him at the elevator and smiled in gratitude while finding his place within.

"Floor, please?" asked the bellhop. *He seems to be preoccupied with something,* thought Lyle. There was the appearance of worry on the man's face and a distant look in his eyes. *He must be about sixty years old with that graying hair,* thought Lyle, but the bellhop had a very strong physique, and there was also a noble quality about him too. This was probably the type of man that would enter a Military Order today if there were such an organization in existence. Or, if he were outside of these circumstances, he would pass for a successful business man of means and education. And here he was, a bellhop. Lyle tried to look him in the eye, but the man kept averting his glance.

"Lobby, please," replied Lyle and proceeded to the back of the elevator with the expectation that other passengers would enter and exit before they arrived at the entrance level.

The lobby was still busy. Lyle looked about the area carefully and located the Edwardian Room to the far right.

He walked over to the entrance and introduced himself to the maître d'.

"Good evening; my name is Professor Lyle Longsworth. Do you have my table ready?" asked Lyle as he moved his eyes over the dining area. It was very attractive, with long purple velvet draperies and sparking crystal chandeliers. Large round and oval vases with a variety of colorful flowers were placed about the room, complementing the expensive oil paintings on the walls. Somewhere off to the left a piano was being elegantly played, and a few couples danced gracefully nearby.

"Yes, Professor Longsworth." The maître d' straightened his cuff and lapels. "Please follow me."

He turned and proceeded through the line of tables until he came to a section near the upper edge of the room. After pulling out a chair for Lyle, he placed a wine list on the table.

There were some very interesting people in New York! It was a place where you could be anything you wanted and almost nobody would bother you, a place where colorful characters and ambitious entrepreneurs had free rein to develop and grow as much as they wished. Lyle hoped to attend an opera here at Lincoln Center and have dinner at Windows on the World someday.

"Hi, Lyle," came a voice from behind him. "Is it really you?" Lyle turned around quickly and a big smile appeared on the questioner's face.

"Dr. Bill Burley! I'm sure glad to see you," said Lyle, as he stood and put his hand out.

"How was your trip? I heard that there was some bad weather approaching from the west," quizzed Bill, as he shook the outstretched hand vigorously. They both sat down and Lyle motioned for the waiter.

"What would you like after your strenuous day at the

office?" asked Lyle as he leaned back in his chair and glanced at the menu. Bill was looking great, just as he had imagined.

"Well, I think I'll have a gin martini, and I know you're going to have a J&B, right?"

"Yes! You've got a wonderful memory, Bill. How is Laura?" Lyle, glad that Bill had consented to embark on this enterprise with him, knew that his wife was probably swallowing her anger. She was proud of Bill in his position as a successful professor of medicine at New York University, but could not help resenting his enthusiasm for exciting travel and dangerous adventures.

"She's great and, as always, looking beautiful. However, I'm worried about her total lack of interest in my work," laughed Bill as he landed a resounding slap on Lyle's back. "I'm sure she does not approve of this escapade but she also will not refuse to let me go with you," he added as he began to sip the drink that was placed before him.

"This should be quite an education," stated Lyle as he also took a taste of his beverage. "Have you ever read much about the Crusades of the 11th to the 13th century? Or about the Knights Templars who were sponsored by the Catholic Church?"

"What I know about this era you could put in a thimble," Bill answered. "But I've got a desire to follow the smell of gold. You did say there was the possibility of locating treasure, didn't you?"

"Yes, there is a good possibility of finding some of their lost treasure," responded Lyle with enthusiasm. "I've got the most unusual sense of positive expectancy about this; it's really quite uncanny!"

Lyle then told Bill of the experience he'd had at Easter time, of Father Marcos' thoughts regarding the manuscript, and of his conviction that there was some special reason for him to travel to Paris and assist Professor Sully.

"I believe you for some reason. I'm not at all concerned that this expedition might be a wild goose chase."

"Let's order dinner and afterward I'll show you some of the material I have in the room," said Lyle as he began to study the menu. He was anxious to have his friend evaluate the manuscript from Paris and to review the plans for their trip.

After a delicious dinner of Maine lobster and a great bottle of 1986 sauterne, *Chateau Massereau*, Lyle summoned the waiter and asked for the check. Leaving a generous tip, they stood and headed back toward the lobby and the elevator. They were unaware of dark eyes that watched them from the far left. Unaware that even as they enjoyed the evening's entertainment, there was foul play at hand.

The elevator came and the bellhop that Lyle had previously come into contact with was in attendance again.

"Eighth floor, please," said Lyle politely.

The movement of the car was quite soft as it glided upward. Then the elevator stopped; the bellhop opened the door, leaned out and looked down the hallway in the direction of Lyle's room. He suddenly moved out of the elevator and ran down the corridor. A succession of loud noises and grunts came from the direction of his own room. Lyle and Bill stepped out of the elevator and looked toward the source of the racket. The bellhop was wrestling with a large, muscular man who had a knife in his hand. His face was frightening. Puffy red cheeks held two small dark eyes that peered out with a hateful stare. His stocky neck had folds of fat, and his hands were also large and crude with dirty nails. A large, snarling, red mouth dripped saliva on the bellhop as the struggle continued. The intruder was fighting to regain his footing when the bellhop landed a blow to his chin that knocked some of his teeth out. The body rocked heavily off the wall and landed in a large heap on the carpeted hall.

Lyle and Bill were running toward the scene when the bellhop lifted his hand for them to stop. He reached in the pocket of his uniform and retrieved a set of keys. Placing one of the keys into the keyhole, he unlocked the door and entered the room cautiously. Lyle was behind him then and together with Bill, they searched the room for other signs of intrusion. After about six minutes of examining the suite and uncovering no mark of damage or noticeable tampering, the bellhop started to leave.

"Thank you, sir! Could I ask your name?" inquired Lyle as he walked with him to the door.

"Raymond Robert, sir, and I will have the intruder taken to the hotel security office. Please don't let this incident distract you and your friend from the business at hand," replied the bellhop as he turned and left the room. He picked the man up off the floor and swung him easily over his shoulder. Then he made his way down the corridor without another word to the speechless professors.

"My God," exclaimed Bill as he closed the door. He looked shakened and was breathing heavily. "Let's have a small drink." He crossed the room to the bar and poured himself a glass of brandy.

"That was rather miraculous, don't you think?" asked Lyle as he joined Bill. "Do you believe that man was about to take something from my room?"

"Oh, he was probably just a thug looking for a simple place to break into in hopes of finding money or other valuables. The bellhop appeared to have handled things like that before."

Together they sipped their drinks as they went over and sat down near the window. The evening had been shattered with this unusual incident, but the men were still silently anticipating events yet to come. Bill removed his pin-striped jacket and tie as he finished his drink in one swallow. Lyle instinctively began to wonder if someone was after the manuscript. There was a good probability that this journal might be in demand if it could ultimately lead to wealth. People did commit some awful crimes to gain money, but who could possibly have known about this precious journal? Lyle vowed silently to himself to be extremely careful in the future and quietly asked God and the Saints to protect them on their journey.

"Why don't we open the window for a little fresh air, Lyle?"

"Sure, make yourself comfortable and then you can look over the manuscript," responded Lyle as he also removed his jacket and parted the curtains to open the window. The night was slightly cool and soon a refreshing westerly breeze was filling the room. The sounds of engines running, horns honking, and sirens screaming filled the night air and filled Lyle with nostalgia. It was a grand city.

"Here's the document I was telling you about earlier," said Lyle as he removed the manuscript from his briefcase which had been hidden behind the draperies. Bill took the aged parchments and gently began to turn the pages. Several minutes went by as Lyle stood looking out over the city.

"This is great stuff, by God," exclaimed Bill as he stood and walked over to where Lyle was standing. "Who were the Templars and why were they so important?"

"From the reading I've done, I'll tell you what I know," replied Lyle as he again selected a comfortable chair. "They were an Order of religious men developed by the Catholic Church, who were to be a fighting Order. They were given the authority to defend the rights of the Church with lance and sword. Their popularity grew dramatically over a very short period of time. They were so effective in battle techniques because of their discipline that they became favorites of rulers and kings of many lands. They gave positive influence and assistance to Spain fighting the Moors during the 11th century which resulted in the growth of the Templar Order in that country. They were also rewarded by King Alfonso I with gold and many properties. Upon his death, they were even bequeathed one third of his kingdom."

"They must have become very influential with their contacts, to include both rulers of kingdoms and leaders of the Church," said Bill as he placed his feet upon the hassock. "Did much money pass through their hands?"

"The Knights Templars did become great handlers of money and properties, not only for themselves but for those who chose to transact business dealings through them. Since they had the strength to defend and protect, which they did very well, they were the most likely candidates to hold wealth. They became great bankers throughout Europe and the Middle East. They also became the first organization to develop a sophisticated system of credit. Their castles were their strongholds for immense deposits and they defended these treasures to the death."

"How did the Church relate to this Order, you know, their activities and influence?" queried Bill.

They stood and walked back over to the window. The night breeze was beginning to increase and was refreshing as they breathed in deeply.

"The people loved the Knights," responded Lyle. "They were being protected from bandits and from those in power who frequently took advantage of the working class. Their hostels were havens of rest and refreshment for the people when they were journeying or taking pilgrimages to Santiago, Rome or the Holy Land. The poor were also the recipients of charity from these men and the knights helped create organizations whose only work was to assist the needy either with food or with helping them find gainful employment."

"The attributes of these heroes seem too wonderful to be true," stated Bill.

"It was uncommon and very unique for these men of the Church to undertake such a mission. There were also many friends of these Knights who enjoyed being with them on special occasions. They became known as `oblates' or the `third Order' and gained personal strength in their association with the Templars. Their missions and philosophies became entwined together and civilization during that time became elevated. A revival of respect toward Christianity swept across the continent which ultimately increased the authority of the Church."

"Well," said Bill stretching his arms and giving a tired yawn. "This certainly has my attention and I'm eager to be taking off. I shall pack my bags tonight and give Laura something special to remember me by," He gave his friend a sly wink as he said this.

"Yes, do all of the above and with great care," replied Lyle as he went over to the desk. "Let me check our flight time." He leafed through the papers in his briefcase and retrieved the airline tickets. He handed an envelope with Bill's name on it to him, and opened his own.

"We leave Kennedy Airport at 9:00 in the morning on Air France, flight 863," Lyle said excitedly as he thought about the trip. "And don't forget to bring your passport."

"I'll meet you in the International Terminal at the Air France desk at 8:00."

Bill found his jacket and started to move toward the door. Lyle was trying to think of anything else they should do before the next day, but couldn't come up with any more last minute instructions.

"Okay then, until tomorrow. You have a good evening

and give my regards to your wife," Lyle said as he opened the door and gave Bill's hand a hearty shake.

That evening, as Lyle went through his belongings again to see if everything was there and in order, he decided to call Ben Sully. He sat on the edge of his bed and picked up the receiver.

"Operator, please connect me with Paris, France. The number there is 33-1-42-66-97-38."

Lyle waited as the operator began making the connection. He thought of his recent experience in Duluth and wished that his friend Father Marcos had been able to come with him.

"*Bonjour*," came a familiar voice over the wire.

"Hi, Ben, how are you? This is your old friend Lyle on the verge of becoming delirious about the trip. By the way, I did tell a few friends about it—hope you don't mind. How is everything there?"

"Lyle, I'm sure you were careful whom you told about this expedition. You won't believe what has happened here recently. Yesterday, on my way home from my office at the University, a car ran me off the road."

"Were you hurt? What in the hell!" blurted Lyle in disbelief.

"No, I wasn't injured, just badly shaken. Two men in dark overcoats got out of this sedan and approached me. I, of course, also exited my car and started toward them. I was really upset. One guy was big and fat with a hideous mustache," related Ben in a voice that was beginning to reflect anger. "He told me that I had something that belonged to his boss and I must at once deliver it to him or something awful would occur."

"Do you suppose he was talking about your recent discovery?" Lyle asked, not wanting to say too much over the phone in case it was being bugged.

"I have a feeling that may be it. Anyway, I told them that they had made a mistake in identification and that they should reexamine their sources. I was not the one they were looking for. I'm not sure I convinced them, but I was very indignant and assertive. I then asked this big fat guy who his employer was, thinking that I might begin to worry them a little. He said something about my needing to pay more respect to the great Monsieur Jacques Gerard."

"Did they rough you up or try to force you to go with them? Do you think it concerns our trip? Did you notify the police? What will you do now?" The questions were pouring out of Lyle as he began to show a little more anxiety.

"No, I'm not going to do anything. I don't know what they are talking about and if I did, I wouldn't tell them. Nothing is going to spoil our research, okay? That's something I want you to promise me."

"I promise, Ben," Lyle replied. He was pledging to Ben that he would continue this project despite all odds and he knew that Bill would too. Then he told Ben about that evening's unnerving experience outside his room and the manner in which the bellhop defended him.

"Wow, I think you should be careful also, Lyle. This discovery may be more widely known than I thought."

"The friend I'm bringing with me is great and I know you will enjoy his company. He's got an aggressive nature and a strong determination that will surely assist us."

"When do you arrive in Paris?"

"We're leaving on the 9:00 morning flight from Kennedy on Air France, flight 836 and should arrive there about 8:00 tomorrow evening. Will you meet us at the airport or shall we come to your residence the following day?" Lyle inquired as he began to settle down again. He knew he must be calm and have nerves of steel now.

"I'll meet you at the airport and then we'll stop by my place for a nightcap."

"Great Ben, meet you then and please be careful."

"Will do and *bon soir*," came Ben's smooth French farewell.

The telephone suddenly awoke Lyle from a deep sleep. He jumped up and grabbed at the receiver on the table near the bed.

"Good morning, sir, this is your wake up call. Please have a wonderful day," came the recorded female voice. He couldn't believe that he had slept so soundly. Quickly he took a shower and shaved before collecting his things together. He then placed a call to the front desk and ask that a taxi be ordered and that a bellhop come for his luggage.

After checking out he followed Raymond, the bellhop, to the front doors and waited until a taxi arrived.

"Thank you very much," said Lyle as he slipped a fifty-dollar bill into the hand of the man who had saved the previous evening from ending in disaster.

"Have a good trip, sir, and please come again," replied Raymond as he loaded the luggage.

The ride to the airport was uneventful—if you can describe a drive in one of New York's cabs uneventful! Lyle arrived at Kennedy Airport and had the cabby take his luggage to the nearest redcap to have it checked through. He then explored the area for the Air France ticket desk, hoping Bill had already found his way there. Alas, Bill was not to be found anywhere. It was only 7:30 and Lyle found a seat affording him a view of the area. The terminal was very busy; people beginning their business travels for the day, heading to numerous destinations. He hoped for good flying weather and safe journeys for all the passengers, particularly himself.

"Lyle," came the voice of Bill as he strode up to Lyle's seat, "I'm here and on time, how about that for punctuality?" Bill had a broad smile across his face that showed his sparkling teeth. Always an optimist, he projected himself favorably to people around him and they liked him for this characteristic.

"You're a source of continual admiration and respect," Lyle said as he stood and shook the hand of his friend. "Is everything okay with Laura?"

"Yes and I'm happy to report that even she is pleased with this trip. I told her about what we discussed last evening and she is solidly behind me."

"That's great," continued Lyle as he picked up his briefcase and motioned Bill to follow him. "It's probably time we made our way to the departure desk. I'm anxious to get aboard."

The walk through the long concourse to the location of the Air France boarding station seemed like miles. They smiled pleasantly at a group of airline stewardesses on their way to an assignment.

After checking in at the desk and obtaining their seat assignments, the friends went over to the airport window and gazed out across the concrete field. There seemed to be hundreds of shiny silver planes moving about, getting ready to ascend once again into the blue beyond. Then Lyle noted a jetliner approaching their terminal entrance. It was smaller than what he had expected. In fact it looked almost like a Lear jet.

"Do you suppose that's our plane?" asked Bill. He started toward the check-in counter with the intention of inquiring about the small plane. Words were exchanged between Bill and the ticketing officer, then he returned smiling at Lyle.

"Yes, it is our plane. There weren't enough passengers to use a larger one, so the airlines decided to use this Lear. It is supposed to be their best in accommodations and comfort. They're now in the process of submitting a new flight plan to Control," said Bill with a voice that sounded very upbeat.

"Very well," replied Lyle as he adjusted the coat over his arm and gazed again out at the plane. It was a beautiful white model with red and blue stripes around the nose and back to the tail section. Lyle wondered how fast it could go and whether he would be allowed to visit the cockpit.

An announcement came over the loudspeaker system just then. "All those departing on flight 836 for Paris should have their boarding passes ready when entering the gate. Those holding tickets for this flight may now proceed with the boarding process."

Bill and Lyle gathered their belongings and, giving one last look about the area, started toward the ramp. As Lyle showed his pass to the flight attendant, he noticed a familiar looking man near the opposite window. He was wearing a dark cashmere coat and matching hat with a purple band about the crown. He also wore a pair of large sunglasses that hid most of his face. The black mustache was the part that made Lyle study him carefully. A slight chill passed down his spine. Could this be the same man that Lyle had seen in the BMW on the North Shore of Lake Superior? Could there be a possibility that someone was following them? Lyle glanced once more at the figure before he passed from view through the entryway that led to the plane. The man hadn't moved and didn't appear to be watching them, but it was hard to know for certain with those glasses hiding his eyes.

The inside of the plane was great. *It must seat about thir-*

ty, thought Lyle as he found his assigned location and placed his coat in the locker above his head. Bill was busy seating himself near the window and appeared to be making himself comfortable. *This aircraft has an exceptional safety record*, Lyle remembered. It was modeled after the military T-33 jet fighter that had an almost perfect flight record; statistical data touted its superior design over and over again. Pilots had indicated that the aerodynamic design of the plane made it very responsive and maneuverable which is why it had such high safety ratings. The power thrusters were perfectly balanced for speed and reliability. The engines and fuel system had the latest anti-power failure features that had never faltered after thousands of tests. The cockpit was equipped with the most current technology which made the handling of the Lear jet a shear pleasure. All safety measures were included in the overall construction of this model and it had turned out to be one of the most popular planes among big business magnates.

After the pilot and stewardess made the passengers aware of the rules of flight and checked out all necessary safety devices, the plane began to move away from the gate. Lyle glanced out the window and again noticed the gentleman in the dark overcoat standing by the window near the jetway. Lyle settled back in his seat and fastened his seatbelt while hoping that he wasn't becoming paranoid.

The Lear jet lifted off the ground at the end of the runway in an effortless pass into the sky through the wind. It seemed exceptionally agile in the air and extremely responsive to each command of the pilot, almost like a perfect lady who loves her man. *It must be wonderful to be able to fly a plane like this*, Lyle mused.

The two friends settled back and began to discuss more of the history of the Crusades. Lyle related to Bill all that he had picked up from his recent reading and they talked about different approaches to locating information and ultimately the Templar gold.

Time passed quickly as the jet skimmed through the atmosphere and raced toward a new world for Lyle. He was leaving yesterday and approaching tomorrow where new horizons would be opened. If only he and Bill could discover more about this manuscript and help Ben in his quest!

Suddenly, there was a violent jerk in the plane's structure and then a sound that was very similar to an explosion which startled everyone. The lights dimmed and a crackling sound could be heard coming from the exterior. The stewardess' voice came over the speaker, "Please fasten your seatbelts and return your seats to an upright position." Lyle quickly locked his clasp and checked to see if Bill was okay.

"What is going on?" asked Lyle as the stewardess passed him on the way to a small area in the rear of the plane. She seemed to be relatively calm and taking this incident in stride. Of course, he knew that emergency drills were practiced frequently so that the employees could prevent panic among the passengers.

"I don't know yet. Just be calm and I'm sure we'll find out soon," she replied as she continued on her way. The plane was beginning to shake much more violently now. They felt themselves surge upward suddenly and then the bottom of the sky seemed to drop out. They gasped for air and were thrown back into their seats as the plane again swooped upward. Thin cries for help could be heard in the dimness but no one seemed to be panicking yet. The stewardess grabbed at the backs of the seats as she tried to make her way forward again on the unsteady floor. Suddenly her legs wouldn't hold her up and she crashed to her knees.

"Let me help you," called Lyle as he leaned out into the aisle, and held out his arm, trying to reach her.

"Don't get out of your seat, sir," she replied as she struggled to regain her footing on the bucking floor. Her cheek had received a cut across the jawbone and was bleeding onto her white shirt. She staggered and grabbed for Lyle's hand.

"Thank you sir," she choked as he pulled her forward. The dim light in the cabin was even fainter and the voice of the captain could barely be detected over the noise.

"I think he's trying to inform us of rough weather," said the stewardess, giving a forced laugh.

"Where do you think we are?" asked Bill as he leaned across to see if he could help.

"By my calculations," answered the girl, trying her best to be well-poised, "we should be near the coast of France."

"Then the captain should be contacting the nearest airport for assistance, right?"

"Yes, I'm sure he is," she said as she again began to move toward the cockpit. "I'll try to find out something from the pilot."

The other passengers were trying to be cooperative. No one had left their seats and no one was screaming. Someone several rows in front of them had vomited and the odor was beginning to permeate the air. Lyle was himself starting to feel sick and he hoped that this new condition wasn't contagious. *Bill is sure taking this whole thing very well*, thought Lyle as he tried to lean back in his seat again. He reached for his briefcase that was beneath the seat and placed it in his lap. Just then, there was another explosion that seemed to send the airplane into a spinning dive. Everyone gasped for air and clung onto their seats as the night became black around them.

"Hang on, Lyle," called Bill through the dread that was now becoming a reality.

"Do you suppose it was a good idea to have selected the seats near the rear?" asked Lyle as he clutched his case and leaned forward.

"It must have been the right thing, because you requested them," replied Bill. The darkness magnified the terror within their bodies. The sound of rushing wind and screeching metal chilled even the heart of the bravest. They could no longer hear the sound of the captain trying to inform them of rough weather and they had forgotten the pleasure of the previous flight's hours. Hunched over, the men each silently whispered a pleading prayer to God and began to experience a cascade of thoughts that revealed both hope and fear. Lyle hoped that he could live through this ordeal, but he knew that he was okay with God if he didn't make it. He had loved his life at the college and all the wonderful friends he had made there. He worried about his grandmother and wondered what she would do when he wasn't around Duluth anymore. If only he could have done more.

Bill was reminiscing about Laura and hoping that he had provided sufficiently for her. He wondered if he had really been fair with her in placing himself in so many dangerous situations. He hoped that she knew of his immense love for her. She had been a wonderful, caring and understanding wife and he would not have traded her for anyone else in the world. His eyes began to tear as he remembered the farewell she had given him. "Don't let anything happen to you, you old goat," she had said with a smile that brightened her face. He tried to swallow a knot that was forming in his throat when he felt Lyle grab his arm.

"I think I hear the ocean," Lyle said as he leaned over Bill and peered out the window.

There was a sudden sound of steel splitting and a jolt that knocked the breath out of Lyle. The pitch-black darkness and whistling wind were rushing around them like a rasp upon their flesh. They felt themselves falling, falling though the blackest void that ever existed. Clutching the arms of their seats they prayed as they spun off into a space that no man dared to enter this way before. *The plane must have been ripped apart,* concluded Lyle as the scene in front of him changed from the inside of an airplane to the darkness of the night sky. His briefcase was tightly clasped with one arm and with his other hand he clung fiercely to the seat. Wind whipped past their faces as they tumbled through space in their broken portion of the plane.

Then, after what seemed like an eternity, there was a resounding splash that knocked the breath out of them for a few moments and they realized they had hit the ocean. Dark, cold wetness soon enveloped them. They held their breaths as they felt themselves being sucked down into the unknown depths below. *We must have crashed just off the coast of France,* thought Lyle as he opened his eyes and tried to accustom them to the water. All was blackness and they still hadn't reached the bottom. God, I hope this settles down soon, thought Lyle as he continued holding onto his briefcase and the chair. *I won't be able to hold my breath forever.* He could feel Bill starting to move beside him.

A soft thud could be detected as the wreckage came to rest on the ocean floor. Bill struggled with his seatbelt as the tail section of the plane settled upright. Lyle tried to unbuckle his belt with one hand but couldn't get it open. The water was becoming bitterly cold and the air that he had started down with began giving out. He slowly began to release his breath in a tiny stream of bubbles that floated upward. *I must get loose of this seat,* he thought as he weighed the possibility of being found on the ocean floor years from now with one hand gripped to the armrest and the other to his briefcase.

Abruptly, Lyle could feel a strong hand on his arm and another hand starting to unfasten the belt that was holding him captive. He felt the strap give way and the hand, still on his arm, start pulling him from the wreckage. Slowly they were rising in the water as Lyle wondered if his lungs would burst within his chest. Had Bill gotten loose to assist him? Could they make it to the surface in time?

The water parted over their heads as they broke the moonlit surface of the Atlantic Ocean. Gasping for fresh air and sputtering vigorously, Lyle splashed about as the hands pulled him toward the shore. It wasn't Bill, but someone much larger and stronger, someone who didn't say a word as he helped Lyle onto the rocks. He painfully crawled onto one of the larger stones and fell in exhaustion as the night wind blew over him. The racing of his heart had begun to quiet when his rescuer broke the silence in a low voice.

"Shall we proceed up the embankment now?"

Lyle slowly got to his feet and looked ahead at the large rocks that they had to climb through. *It will be impossible*, he thought. He couldn't remember the last time he had tried to scale rocks.

"Follow me, sir," came the voice of his rescuer as he started on a narrow path that wove its way upward. Lyle slowly stumbled after him, still clutching his briefcase. Their steps led them past what seemed like great boulders and narrow passageways which had probably not been seen by man in many years. Finally, breathless and feeling desolate, Lyle arrived at a plateau. It was large enough to sustain the growth of trees and some shrubs, even though it still seemed isolated and barren in the darkness.

"Lyle."

He looked toward the sound of the familiar voice. There was a fire burning about twelve feet away and he thought he could make out the figure of Bill silhouetted in the flickering light.

4

The evening was relatively comfortable, if one enjoys camping out in nature under the stars Their new friend, Oliver Temple, so he called himself, had fortunately been spending the weekend on the coast and had constructed a campsite for himself by the seashore.

"Bill!" Lyle exclaimed as he rushed over to his almost lost friend. "How did you get out of that plane without a scratch?"

"It was unbelievable," replied Bill giving Lyle a big hug. "I can't understand why we aren't both dead. Such a perfect flight on a beautiful aircraft and then *boom*, it's over."

"I know, I can't believe we're really standing here talking about it."

"Pardon," said Oliver as he arrived from the darkness with an armload of dried branches. "It was an awful sight, that's for sure. There, right above me, about fifteen degrees to the west," he was pointing at the sky. "I heard an explosion, *fort bruit*, and then a flash of light. I watched as the tail section of the plane was ripped off and took a plunging course toward the earth. I had hoped that it would land in the water and fortunately for you both, it did. I heard the splash, just a short way out and decided to go in and search for survivors." Oliver added a few more pieces of wood to the fire.

"It's a miracle that you were here tonight, you know. How can we ever thank you?" asked Bill as he found a comfortable spot on the ground, close to the fire. His clothes were still about fifty percent wet. "Exactly where are we?"

"This is the northwest coast of France," replied Oliver. "Out there is the English Channel." He had a heavy French accent that rolled off his tongue like music coming from a French horn. It was beautiful to listen to. He had obtained some cooking utensils from his tent and was proceeding to prepare some food for the men.

"The closest town is Treguier. It's located about four miles down the coast and three miles inland. It's a delightful little town with all the activities and local color of a coastal village. That's where I left my motor vehicle."

"Are you going there soon?" inquired Lyle as he joined Oliver by the fire. He had slipped out of his jacket and had placed it on a nearby rock to dry, then wrapped himself in a woolen blanket that Oliver had laid out for him.

"Yes, I'll be leaving here in the morning and heading back to town. I will be pleased to take you with me. Now, I wish that you would have some coffee and a bowl of soup."

Oliver gave each a bowl of garnished black bean soup and a piece of rye bread. He poured them a cup of strong French coffee and then joined them around the fire. The night was cool but not chilly enough to be uncomfortable. The stars were bright in the dark sky and the only sound interrupting the silence was the ocean breaking her waves upon the rocky coastline. It was a peaceful sound and one that made Lyle mindful of his recent experience. He would have had one more experience trapped at the bottom of that lovely sea, if it had not been for the heroic efforts of Oliver! Trapped, with those peaceful waves rolling over his head. *Thank you, God*, thought Lyle remembering home and friends.

"Darn, I bet my briefcase and its contents are ruined," blurted Lyle as he jumped to his feet and ran over to where he had dropped it. "It's supposed to be watertight, but I doubt if anything could have survived getting wet under those conditions." He sat down on the grass and placed the case in front of him. Carefully, he inserted a key that he had taken from his pocket and slipped it into the lock. After turning it until he heard a click, he popped open the lid and raised it to look inside. He felt around the computer and then picked up the manuscript.

"Well, what's the verdict?" called Bill from the fireside.

"It's all dry," exclaimed Lyle in disbelief. "Not a single drop of moisture anywhere." He got up and strolled back to the others with his treasure in his arms.

"At least we can go on with our investigation now, if we don't run into any other mishaps."

"What do you make of an accident like this, Bill?" Lyle was starting to wonder about the possibilities of sabotage.

"It is strange. The Lear jet is one of the safest aircrafts built today. And there was an explosion, no, there were two," answered Bill as he finished his food and placed the empty bowl near the fire.

"I noticed a strange gentleman at the airport," began Lyle hesitantly. "I swear that he looked like the man I saw in Duluth shortly after I received the manuscript from Paris."

"That may be a coincidence, Lyle, but not when you tie in the intruder who was intercepted outside your hotel room in New York."

"And, Ben told me when I called him later that same night, he was run off the road on his way home! Two men had tried to scare him. He thought they might be after the document."

"You might have something, Lyle," Bill was beginning to feel uneasy. "There might be a organized group after the same things we are. And they don't sound like the kind of men I'd relish running into either."

Oliver had returned from cleaning the cooking utensils and was pulling out extra blankets from his belongings. They wondered why he was remaining quiet and if they could trust him. But, of course, he was probably shy and didn't want to interfere too much into their business.

"Oliver, come, we would like to tell you about an interesting theory that we've been discussing," ventured Bill as he moved over and created a sitting area on the ground. "We're on a mission, here in France. We have important information that may be worth a great deal and there may be problems starting to develop because of it."

Bill began telling Oliver about the sequence of events that were beginning to add up to a suspicion of conspiracy. Oliver listened attentively without interrupting. His eyes gazed into the fire and his arms encircled his knees in a relaxed position. He seemed calm, thought Lyle as he studied the man across the fire. The face was strong with a firm, wide jawline and deep-set eyes, but with a kind crease around his lips and across the brow. His arms were brawny and muscular with large hands that knew the position of a peaceful clasp. *He must be a laborer to have such an athletic physique,* figured Lyle. *Maybe even a bodyguard for an important financier. Then maybe, a Knight of the Templars might have looked something like this gentleman too.*

"Your story does sound like there may be some conspiracy going on," said Oliver after listening to the report. "I think I'd be extra careful from now on." He rose and stretched his body lazily. "Tomorrow, we will go to Treguier. Tonight, you will sleep here and regain your strength." Walking over to his tent, Oliver brought out two sleeping bags.

"Here, place them by the fire and you will be relatively comfortable for the evening. I'll see you at daybreak."

Bill took the sleeping bags from Oliver and began to spread them out on the ground. *It must be about 10:00 P.M. and still April the seventeenth,* figured Lyle as he removed his shoes and crawled into the bag.

"Bill," whispered Lyle as he leaned over toward his friend, "You know, we don't as yet know very much about this guy. Don't you think it was unusual for him to be here at this time, to save us from the wreck? Maybe he is a part of this conspiracy?"

"Yes, but I think his presence is more providential then coincidental," replied Bill as he yawned and folded his arms behind his head. "There are in this world both good and evil forces. It is fortunate when we can identify both. I have a good feeling about Oliver and I'd like to trust him, at least within reason until we get to know him better, okay?"

So much had happened in the past forty-eight hours that it seemed like a month had elapsed. Lyle settled back into the sleeping bag and gazed at the brilliance of the stars. He respected Bill's judgment and would follow his advice. It was wonderful to be alive and to be out in nature, immersed in the greatness of God's universe. Only a speck in the vastness of creation, yet significant to God. Lyle took a deep breath of the fresh night air and closed his eyes peacefully.

* * *

"*Bon matin*," called Oliver in a cheerful voice. Lyle opened his eyes and looked about. The sun was just coming up over the nearby hills, casting a pleasant brilliance on the surrounding landscape. The sky was almost luminous with a blue glow and the breezes were a sweet freshness that roused the human spirit for another day. Waves continued to lap gently on the rocky shoreline and gulls were proclaiming, with shrill cries, their ownership of the land.

"Good morning to you," replied Lyle as he crawled out of the bag and shook his arms. The tightness of sleeping bags was notorious for giving unrelenting cramps to the human body. *Why do people continue to use them,* Lyle thought, *and why hasn't somebody designed a more practical bag that permits full range of motion to the body while it sleeps?*

"I've made us a little breakfast to enjoy before we leave," said Oliver as he signaled them to come over and eat. Bill was beginning to stir and the sounds that came from his bag were fortunately unintelligible. He crawled out, dressed quickly and ran down the trail toward the ocean. Lyle guessed that he was going to wash his face and take care of other morning activities.

"I hope you enjoyed the night. It is going to be a beautiful day." Oliver smiled broadly and motioned with his arm toward the morning sky.

"Yes, I think it will be," replied Lyle as he walked over to the fire, where the morning coffee was brewing. "Thank you again for all the help that you've given to my friend and me. And don't say it was nothing."

"It was what was expected of me, *mon ami,*" answered Oliver as he handed Lyle a cup of hot coffee and a biscuit.

Bill returned in a few minutes and joined them for breakfast. His face appeared fresh and pink from the ocean water and his hair was neatly combed. Despite the previous evening's dreadful event, he was beginning to show exuberance about beginning another day. A big smile played upon his lips as he laughed about the gulls that were starting to bother them for food.

"Hungry old buzzards, aren't they Oliver?" he remarked, throwing them some crumbs.

"*Oui*, they are indeed. It must be wonderful to be a beautiful bird and free to fly high above the earth," he answered with a faraway look in his eye. There was something special, surely not objectionable about this fellow. Something that made you take second thoughts.

After they finished eating, Oliver packed up his belongings with the assistance of his new friends. They helped him load up, each carrying some so as to divide the weight. It seemed strange to Lyle not to have his own belongings in hand as they began walking east on a trail that had been used hundreds if not thousands of times in the past.

The coastline was unusual. Rock formations were of a violet-pink tone, a beautiful color that Lyle had never seen before. The strange rock arrangements appeared like weird animals from some mythical legend and the more you were among them the more you began to imagine movement. Large overhangs protected numerous caves beneath that housed a variety of fowl and other creatures that lived by the sea. The winding pathway wove its way between large granite boulders and evergreen bushes that reached out to scratch the trespasser. Lyle skillfully maneuvered himself and his pack while keeping up with the others.

The sandy edge of the water was beginning to grow larger as they continued along the rocky path, giving way to a lovely beach filled with beautiful white sand. The ocean air was redolent with many fragrances from the surrounding country that made you instantly aware of the customs of the people. In the distance, Lyle could see tiny fishing boats tossing gently upon the ocean waters, and cottages lining the shore above the rocks. The harbor in the distance contained beautiful yachts for the romantically challenged and many established resorts for the tourist with time to enjoy the country.

"This way," said Oliver as he turned to the right at a branch in the trail. "This leads to the town." He led the way up the path, moving effortlessly among the rock and brush.

Lyle was beginning to feel a little breathless, but swore silently to himself that he wouldn't let anyone know.

They reached the outskirts of Treguier and Lyle immediately fell in love with the place. On either side of the town were two rivers, Guindy and Jaudy, which flowed into the ocean. Just four blocks away stood the Cathedral Saint-Treguier and as Oliver explained, it was the best loved of Brittany's nine cathedrals. It was built in the 1330s, a masterpiece of ingenuity and artist delicacy. Grand granite arcades stretched upward and supported the cloister nearby. Three towers rose above the gigantic edifice that was composed of many different colored stones. Richly decorated arches and walls enclosed the adoration chapel which held the Eucharist, the body of Christ. Lyle, awestruck, stood enchanted before this awesome spectacle of man's love and dedication for God.

They moved on into the village square where people were beginning to stir about in their daily activities. The fishermen were gathering their bags and lines in their arms and laughing about the day's prospects as they headed off toward the boats. The market was bustling about with wine and cheese makers clamoring for business. Sidewalk cafés had signs welcomed visitors and countrymen alike to sample their fresh oysters and mussels. Women clothed in a variety of bright colors were busy sweeping and cleaning the entrances of shops. Their cheerful faces seemed to show all that they were happy with another bright day. Children played together on the cobblestone streets and their cheerful voices filled the atmosphere with a relish for life.

"Come, we will have refreshments before we proceed on," said Oliver as he led the two to a table under a large red and white striped umbrella. The flowers in nearby containers were releasing the most enticing fragrance and the air was filled with the sounds of friendly chatter from townsfolk.

"This is a wonderful village," said Bill with the sound of satisfaction in his voice. He was impressed by the old fashioned ways that were still being practiced in a slower pace and the joy that was obviously felt by the people. "This would be a magnificent location to retire to someday."

"It is refreshing, isn't it?" queried Oliver with a twinkle in his eye. "So nice to know that happiness isn't always found where all the money is."

"*Bienvenue*, what will you have, *monsieur?*" asked the café waiter, He was dressed in black trousers, white shirt, red suspenders and a black cap. His eyes sparkled with humor and he radiated pleasantness.

"Three coffees," replied Oliver in French. "And some of your sweet cakes."

The three men ate with great relish and gladly accepted seconds when the café waiter returned. They talked of France and the kind of people who had settled here many years ago. Lyle was surprised to learn from Oliver that Paris had existed before the time of Christ and that France had at one time been the crossroads for many an invading power.

"The original people of France were known as Gauls and were considered barbarians who fought desperately against becoming civilized by the Romans. Nevertheless, they were converted to Christianity and became fearless defenders of the Church. Then, Spanish Arab rulers began to exploit the region and weakened the strength of the empire. Charlemagne became one of France's fiercest leaders in fighting the incursions of neighboring countries. He fought the Lombards of Italy, the Saxons of Germany, and the Arabs of Spain. He was so favored that Pope Leo III made him Emperor of the Romans to show his gratitude and that of his people for defending their land and the Church." Oliver seemed to be very knowledgeable about not only the history of France but also informed about the underlying reasons why events occurred as they did.

"Time marched on as soldiers from the Scandinavian lands invaded Paris and destroyed much of the city. North Africans challenged the Provençal coast and plundered most of Burgundy. France had one king after another who had steadily given most of the land to nobility. The realm was breaking up and giving way to provinces such as Burgundy, Normandy, Provence, and Brittany. As the Roman Empire was falling, the Christian church provided the needed unity that brought people together and this helped in maintaining the principles of God's law. Hughes was then appointed king by divine right of the French." Oliver paused and glanced at his friends.

"You're probably not interested in all of this..." he began as he ran his fingers through his dark, glistening hair.

"We are," exclaimed Lyle. He was just surprised that this man was relating to them material that was so pertinent to their mission.

"Well, the Church continued to grow spiritually and numbers expanded throughout Europe. The people were happy and contented with the protection that the Church gave them and in turn they supported the Church's authority. There was one man who was a Christian King and who defended the honor of the Church along with handing down justice to the people. Louis IX undertook the first Crusade to the Holy Land and drove the Muslims from the Holy City, Jerusalem. After some time, the Kings who followed began to be more concerned with the growth of their own military strength and in conquering lands for their own monetary gain than for strengthening the Church's position. Although they continued to support the Crusades, they were focused more on the building of great houses and gaining vast quantities of wealth for the throne. Taxes were imposed upon the people to help with the funding of the King's adventures and soon the population was reeling under the heavy load. By the year 1300, France was the strongest military power in Europe. Philip IV was known as *le Bel* for his handsome looks and stately dress. The goals of the king were great. He wanted to bring together all classes, noblemen and serfs, clergy and military orders under one control. He wanted supreme command over all and to change the economic base of the country from agriculture to industry."

"I remember from history," interrupted Lyle as he leaned back in his chair and folded his arms behind his head, "that Philip is remembered for his progressive ideas and is heralded for bringing France together."

"Yes," replied Oliver, sipping his coffee. "He did do a lot to forward civilization during his reign, but he did these things at the cost of making his countrymen suffer from his overtaxation and by creating enemies of major organizations around him. He ordered the Church and clergy to pay taxes and was denounced by Pope Boniface VIII, who was outraged at the states' interference into their affairs. The French cardinals, bishops, and priests refused to comply, so Phillip sent William de Nogaret with a garrison of soldiers to Rome and tried to overthrow the Vatican. The Pope's soldiers fought bravely and withstood the assault from the French. William and thirteen of his accomplices were subsequently excommunicated by the Pope.

"Phillip was also widely known for his particular choice of assistants. They were usually lawyers with an outstanding knowledge of Roman law and considered to be brilliant but with little regard for morality and respect to precedents or history. They disliked the power that the Church had over the people and the wealth that belonged to them. Soon, these lawyers began to devise methods of making the Church seem at odds with the government, so as to justify their aggression."

"Weren't there enough forces to defend the Church?" asked Bill, who was thoroughly enjoying this journey back through time.

"The Vatican did have its soldiers and special forces, but they weren't organized to fight against large armies from neighboring countries. They were supposed to be God's servicemen and used in the defense of the Pope. There also were Military Orders, like the Knights Templars and Hospitalers, who were extremely strong, but they were either not prepared for what was happening or were instructed not to interfere."

"Shortly after the assault, the Pope died and the French government moved the papal throne to a northern French town called Avignon. Phillip IV had a French monk, Clement V, elected Pope in 1305, one who had studied law and had been archbishop of Bordeaux. He was to serve in this position until 1314 and then he became involved in a most hideous trial and execution of a Military Order. I will never forgive him for refusing to assist in freeing the men of the Knights Templars," Oliver said with a noticeable strain coming to his voice. He turned his head away so as to conceal a tear and to avoid looking into the eyes of his friends. His jaw was clenched tight so that one could see the muscles contracting on his jaw.

"Oliver," interjected Lyle as he reached over and placed a hand on his companion's arm, "That is part of what we were telling you this morning. The manuscript that I received is a portion of the evidence that we're collecting. Your relating to us this information about what occurred in history is also very helpful. Hopefully, at the end of this journey we will understand more fully what happened and perhaps find some of their hidden gold."

"Hey, let's lighten up a little," said Bill. He stood and took a few steps about the table. "We're analyzing events that occurred over six hundred years ago! Everyone makes mistakes, even popes, kings and every ruler that has tried to make improvements in this world. It's just kind of interesting now," he said with a smile on his face that gave mischief to his eyes, "to delve into moments from the past; find treasure that was hidden away for unknown reasons; search to understand ideas that thrived years ago; and to understand ourselves better now in order to make a superior world for mankind to live in."

"Right, that is what it's all about," replied Lyle. He also stood and brushed a few cake crumbs from his trousers, then turned to Oliver. "You know so much and have lived in this country where we are only visitors. We appreciate your sharing your knowledge with us about this land and its past. Maybe now we should see if we can find a way to Paris." He gazed over the village square looking for a car rental agency.

Glancing at his watch, he noticed it was almost 12:00 noon. Time was moving rapidly and they had a lot to accomplish before they would go to bed that night.

"Sirs," offered Oliver with a look of respect on his face, "may I offer you the use of my services? He stood and reached in his pocket for the payment of their breakfast. "Please follow me." Turning toward the square, he started walking across the cobblestones, heading toward the opposite side of the courtyard. The noise of activity had subsided temporarily during the noon hour. Warmth from the sun was penetrating every corner of the neighborhood and a pleasantness radiated everywhere. A variety of birds were making themselves at home in the village. Lyle noticed them drinking and bathing in the center fountain without disturbing anyone. A few townspeople were feeding them bread crumbs and loving the attention that these little feathery creatures were giving them.

They approached a shiny black Rolls-Royce sedan and Oliver placed a key into the lock on the driver's side. The long lines of the car were classic, and accentuated by silvery chrome that highlighted the corners of the body. The windows were moderately tinted so as to reduce the brightness of the sun, but not to interfere with the occupants' visual acuity. Opening the door, Oliver reached in and flicked a switch that unlocked the remaining doors. He then went around to the trunk and opened it. Lyle noticed him reaching in and returning with a black chauffeur's cap and jacket. Oliver quickly removed his hiking slicker and folded it carefully into the trunk, then ran a brush through his dark brown hair. He placed the camping gear in beside the clothes and closed the lid firmly. Putting on the cap and then the chauffeur's jacket, he stepped to the passenger door and opened it.

"Please, if you will honor me and accept the use of my car," stated Oliver, quietly but firmly. He motioned toward the open doorway and bowed respectfully. *Wow*, thought Lyle, *how do you think we came upon this luck?*

"You mean to tell us that you are a chauffeur, and this is your vehicle?" asked Bill in surprise.

"Yes, I do operate a business and would like to offer you my service."

"This couldn't be more advantageous," replied Lyle as he turned toward Bill. "What do you think, Bill? It seems to me that this service would, so far, fit into our plans perfectly."

"Yes, I agree. What a stroke of luck! Let's do it," Bill answered enthusiastically. He turned to Oliver and extended his hand to secure the arrangement. With a broad smile that showed his beautiful white teeth, Oliver took Bill's hand. Lyle slipped into the rear passenger seat and marveled at the lovely interior. Light beige leather seats seemed to still be new, and the aroma indicated as much. Darker brown trim highlighted the edges of the seats and armrests. The tightly woven floor carpeting was also in dark brown, and immaculately clean. There was a cabinet in front of him that probably contained refreshments, Lyle guessed.

Bill climbed into the car on the opposite side and gave a sigh of comfort. Oliver turned around from his position in the driver's seat after adjusting the mirrors.

"Well, how do you like it?"

"This is wonderful! We'll have to talk prices soon," replied Lyle as he adjusted his position to maximize his comfort.

"The only thing I need to know now is your destination."

"We need to go to Paris," said Lyle as he reached into his briefcase. He pulled out a paper that contained some of the travel information and looked at it for a few seconds.

"The hotel that I made reservations for is the Crillon. They said it was located on the Des Champs Elysées."

"Yes, I know the place. That is one of the finest hotels in Paris and world famous. It is an old mansion that is near the Rue Royale and is very impressive. It and the mansion beside it are an example of the early Louis XVI style. In 1778, the Treaty of Friendship and Trade was signed there between the King, Louis XVI and the independent States of America. I've also heard that Benjamin Franklin was among those who were present that day. I'm sure you will find your stay there most pleasant," said Oliver, as he started the vehicle and checked over the gauges on his dashboard.

"It does sound superb. I was wondering if we shouldn't let our folks know what happened to us. They must have heard by now about the crash," noted Bill.

"I was just thinking the same thing," responded Lyle. "Maybe when we get to Paris we can give them a call. It would be terrible of us to let everyone think we are dead! They will have us eulogized and buried by this time next week."

"But it might be better for the bad guys to think that we were dead, though. They would stay off our tail then," said Bill with a ominous tone to his voice.

"Yes, it might help with that aspect, but I couldn't stand the thought of anyone grieving on our account."

"You're probably right, besides," said Bill, "it might also be better for our research if the people we come into contact with know who we really are and do not think we're some impostors."

"Okay, we'll contact them when we reach Paris. At least that will give us a few hours of reprieve."

The Rolls moved smoothly over the road's blacktop surface as they headed along the shoreline highway D786 toward St. Brieuc. There was not a cloud in the azure blue sky, nor any obstacle now to hinder them in their progress. The countryside was dotted with quaint little farms that bred some of the finest stallions in the country, whose owners trained them to be champions in racing, cross-country, dressage, and to be carriage horses. This area also maintained a stock of splendid Percherons that were at one time almost nonexistent throughout the world.

Lyle noticed that some of the attractive old houses were wonderfully preserved from the 16th century. Many were still being occupied as homes, although some of them had been converted into sites of historic interest. Dinard was an unusually well preserved and lovely town along the northern coast. Figs, palms, tamarisk, and camellias grew there in great numbers. The posh hotels, gardens, wealthy villas, and picturesque parks made this town a lovely place to pass through on their way east. From the high cliffs, Lyle could look out across the azure sea and see the disorder of reddish sandstone and slabs of black schist along the coast. Enormous waves crashed noisily across the boulders of the Grande, disturbing colonies of cormorants and guillemots that were nesting in the Petite Fauconniere bird sanctuaries. Oliver informed them that on a very clear day one could see all the way to England.

"Oliver," said Lyle quietly, so as to not interrupt the beauty of the moment, "it would be great if we could stop at a clothing shop so we could purchase a few things. I feel naked without any belongings. Would you know of a place on our way?"

"Yes, I do know of a shop here in Dinard," he replied, nodding affirmatively.

"Great," added Bill as he leaned forward in his seat. "We would be most grateful if you would take us there. I was beginning to wonder if I'd be washing these things out by hand tonight," he said pointing to Lyle's smudged shirt.

After Oliver maneuvered the Rolls through the cobblestone streets, he pulled up in front of Masuer's, a men's clothing shop, and waited in the car while the two Americans proceeded to purchase a few articles of clothing and a couple of new suitcases.

On their way again, Lyle and Bill felt much more comfortable, now that they had a small wardrobe with them. Nothing like being hundreds of miles from home without a change of underwear.

As they passed near Mont-Saint-Michel, Oliver pointed to the left, and toward the ancient monastery that stood towering above the lowlands.

"That is indeed a landmark that was been well preserved. Its erection began in the 8th century by a bishop who was supposed to have received a vision from the Archangel Michael. In 1017, the Benedictine monks started to make additions to the oratory and constructed a harbor for boats to bring in supplies. After a few centuries, the abbey began to be encompassed by shops and homes for the peasants. Hotels were established to house pilgrims on their way to Santiago, Rome, and the Holy Land. During the Hundred Years' War those inside its formidable walls felt safe."

Oliver had pulled off the road to allow the men to take a good look before leaving this site.

"It was partially destroyed during the Revolution; it was used for a while as a prison; then rebuilt to its former glory. Inside there is a Knights' Hall and a Guests' Hall that are located beneath the Church and cloister. The large structures you see now were constructed from granite and firmly implanted into the protruding granite hill that rises from the coastal waters. The decorations that presently adorn the interior are beautiful and are excelled only by the wonder of St. Peter's in Rome."

They were moving along again and Lyle laid his head against the plush neck rest of the Rolls. The Knights had a place within the abbey walls. It seemed to him that this evidence of a link between the Knights and religious orders was appropriate. If the Benedictines created the Hospitalers and related to them, then the Cistercians might have continued relations with the Templars.

Lyle's eyes closed as he thought about the Knights Templars and their plight. He hoped he and Bill could unravel some of the mystery and if they were lucky, become a little more wealthy.

The miles moved smoothly beneath the wheels of the Rolls-Royce as it glided on toward Caen. Oliver pointed out to them that the D-Day beaches were just off to the left and asked if they wanted to stop and take a closer look at them. Lyle said no and that they would have to visit them another day.

The rolling hills and pastures of this Normandy area were very picturesque. Farm fences made of a combination of stone, timber and mortar matched the houses and outbuildings. Apple orchards on the hills were just beginning to blossom and fill the air with their sweet fragrance. Roadside stands remained from the previous year's sale of apples and dulcet cider. Dairies also speckled the landscape with large herds of cows that produced milk for drinking, butter, and the sharp creamy Camembert, Livarot, and Pont-Eveque cheeses.

"North of here is an interesting spot to visit sometime," Oliver said, interrupting their thoughts. "There was a grand abbey of Jumieges near Fécamp, one that was greatly admired by William the Conqueror. It is located on the rocky coast in a setting of pine and spruce trees. The Romanesque structure was modeled after Notre-Dame and constructed of white granite. Its two stately churches with two towers that are still standing despite their seemingly forsakedness. The abbey was owned and operated by the Benedictines until the 1700s, when it was disbanded because of the Revolution. This monastery had educated many monks who researched and documented history. No one now knows where their written materials disappeared to after they departed the district. These monks also operated a small seaport harbor nearby and were known to inner circles as having significant connections with exporters."

"It sounds like the Benedictines had many monasteries throughout France. It's too bad that so many of them were destroyed by the Revolution," said Lyle with sadness in his voice. "I think the Order helped to provide stability that the people needed in their lives. They also helped to create a civilized way of living with the promotion of the Benedictine Rule."

"Yes, the Church has done more for civilizing the world by promoting God's law than any other form of government in history. All of the laws that now exist have their bases in God's ordinance. We are now on the last leg of our journey to Paris. We'll be there in about thirty minutes," Oliver said as he glanced at the dashboard clock. It was about 6:00 in the evening and the traffic was increasing as they neared the city. Both Bill and Lyle had their eyes on the scenery, as they both loved traveling to foreign lands. The culture of other people was something to respect and admire, especially ancient civilizations. The French had an antiquity filled with a wealth of information, of lessons to be learned for all societies now and yet to be born.

As the Rolls drove along the Avenue de la Grande Armée, they arrived at the Arc de Triomphe and preceded on Des Champs Elysées until they reached the Place de la Concorde Obélisque. Oliver turned the vehicle to the left and headed for a large mansion near the Hotel de la Marine.

"This is your hotel, the Crillon. The building to the left houses the Offices of the Admiralty. I'm sure you will have a pleasant stay here," Oliver said as he pulled under the entry canopy and came to a stop. A hotel doorman came to the car and opened the passenger door for Lyle. Oliver stepped from his side and opened the door for Bill.

"Thank you for bringing us here and for providing us with such interesting and valuable information during the trip," said Lyle, with his hand outstretched to Oliver. He opened his wallet and gave him several bills.

"If you need my assistance again, please feel free to give me a call," Oliver replied as he gave Lyle his card and pocketed the money. "I wish you luck and God's blessings on your research. *Adieu.*" He tipped his cap, turned and opened the trunk for the doorman to retrieve their luggage.

That evening, after a delicious dinner within the terrace restaurant, they lounged near a piano in the extravagantly decorated bar. The French decor was rich in color and design. Great swirls of sculptured rock framed the windows and entryways. Rich draperies of three blue tones were hung artistically about the windows and doors. Marble statues of Napoléon, Catherine de Medici, Joan of Arc, Charlemagne, Charles de Gaulle, and other notable French citizens stood guard in out-of-the-way niches observing the political flavor of this century's nobles. Large palms and schefferas gave a calm and natural appearance to the room, as did the subdued lighting that radiated from beneath sofas, pillars, ceiling corners, and the mirrored bar.

"One more round and then we had better call it an evening," said Lyle, as he signaled for the waiter.

"That sounds good for me," responded Bill, giving a healthy yawn and stretching his arms leisurely.

"It's been a very full day, a lot to absorb."

Lyle agreed as he ordered a second round of drinks. His watch showed that it was about 10:30 P.M. and they had yet to plan for the next day. He also wasn't quite sure what to think about Ben. He had not answered his phone and it was beginning to worry them.

"Tomorrow, Bill, let's go over to Ben's house and see if something unusual has occurred there. Of course he may just be out with a friend this evening and not available."

"I'm for trying to locate him tomorrow," replied Bill who was having a great time humming along with the lady at the piano. "I don't think we should just sit around."

Bill was a man of action and always eager to get on the road. He liked resolving problems and coming to the core of seemingly difficult situations. Lyle was sure he would be an asset on this adventure.

That night, Lyle was awakened gently by the sound of voices singing. It sounded similar to the voices he heard at home after the evening mass at St. Scholastica. A chill crept through his flesh and he began to remember his dreams of the Knights and their battles. He recalled reading about the conflicts they had with the Moslems and how, when everyone else fled the Holy Land, they alone remained to defend the temple and the other sacred areas important to the Church.

Alone. It must have been extremely difficult and yet it showed a deep strength that was nurtured in them by their faith. Lyle felt a deep desire to know these men better and to understand the calling that seemed to envelope their entire being forever.

5

Lyle awoke the next morning with the sun shining in his face. He yawned lazily and rolled over toward the nightstand and looked at his watch. The time was 7:30; past time for him to be up. He lay there in the comfort of his bed and marveled at the interior of their room. Lyle was certain it had once given privacy to some notable world leaders as they rested from the affairs of state. The room was approximately the size of four of his classrooms, with windows covering the entire wall that opened onto a ten-foot-wide balcony. Long, rose-colored velvet draperies hung in the corners and two sections on either side of the balcony door. Several French contemporary paintings of favorite sites like the Eiffel Tower, the Conciergerie, Notre-Dame de Paris, the Arc de Triomphe, and the Pantheon were displayed upon the ornate white and purple wallpaper. The furnishings of the room were constructed of dark walnut and obviously created by one of the finest carpenters in the city. Two large dracaenas stood by the balcony door, stationed there as if they were proud sentinels for the guest. Outside, there were also several dracaenas and potted red geraniums that beautified the area. Lyle smiled to himself and slowly climbed out of bed. He loved this extravagance, even though he wasn't sure it would be healthy for his budget over an extended period of time. Still he would enjoy it while the moment lasted.

After he had showered and shaved, he awakened Bill. They had planned on having breakfast early and then taking a taxi across to the French Quarter on the Left Bank to see Ben.

"What a night," exclaimed Bill as he jumped out of his bed and went over to the front window to gaze at a perfect view of Place de la Concorde and, beyond that, the River Seine.

"Would you look," Bill called over his shoulder to Lyle. "There is a monument to the execution of over one thousand Frenchmen. You never know what can transpire when deep-seated passions are stirred in the hearts of these people."

"Yes, quite a number of men and women died in this area during the Revolution and the White Terror that followed. More recently, the Germans brought slaughter to Paris and blood ran once again in the streets of this gay city," Lyle replied, as he joined Bill. He handed Bill a cup of steaming coffee that had just been delivered to the room.

"I think that Paris has experienced more violence than any other civilized city throughout its history, don't you agree?" asked Bill as he sipped the steaming brew.

"Only Rome could come close to the amount of strife that would swell up in people as they sought to expand their families, lands, and country. It must have been a terrible and yet an exciting time to live." Lyle headed for the inside balcony with Bill close behind him. Employees were beginning to stir about in the areas below, dusting tables and adjusting lounging furniture for the guests.

"I'm not certain that I would have enjoyed living during the Renaissance period," said Bill as he finished his coffee and placed the cup on the balcony table. "Anyway, let's get ready for the day and then go down for breakfast; I'm starving."

Lyle proceeded with dressing, choosing to wear his new white sneakers, jeans and beige corduroy jacket. He looked into the mirror and combed his hair, wondering to himself that he still looked good despite his close call with death just two days ago. He picked up the telephone and tried once again to reach Ben, but there was still no answer. If Ben was out running around, he really would be furious. He was glad they had notified their relatives last evening about their survival from the plane crash. Lyle didn't want Madeline to worry about him while they were on this expedition. She had seen the crash reported on CNN and was devastated by the thought that her grandson might have been killed. Father Marcos seemed interested in Lyle's story concerning all the coincidental occurrences since he had left Minnesota. He asked again that Lyle notify him if there was anything that he could do to assist with the operation. Then before hanging up the receiver, he gave Lyle a special blessing for protection from the evil forces that seemed to be hounding the trip.

By 8:45, they were having breakfast in the hotel coffee shop adjacent to the main lobby. Quite a number of the hotel guests were up and beginning to think about where they would be going that day. Lyle could overhear bits of conversations between couples concerning various attractions about the city and whether they would be able to accommodate everything on the agenda or wait until the following day for another excursion.

Outside again and under the entry canopy, Lyle asked the bellman to obtain a taxi for them. The employee took a few steps forward and raised his hand toward a couple of waiting cabs parked about forty feet away. The first one started his car and brought it under the canopy. "*Plaire*, take us to 15 Rue des Ecoles, it's located in the French Quarter," said Lyle politely as they got into the taxi's back seat.

"*Oui, monsieur*, I know where it is," answered the cabby politely and maneuvered his car onto the busy street of Des

Champs Elysées, the base once of a wall about the city of Paris. The morning traffic was very active and horns could be heard as people tried to arrive at their destinations as quickly as possible. City buses were already crowded with tourists and businessmen on their way to work. The sky was partly cloudy, but that did not prevent the sunlight from peeking out and spreading cheer over this happy city. Everywhere, friendly people were chatting together and showing hospitality to each other.

The cab crossed the river and headed east on the river road Anatole France; then onto Quai Voltaire; then Quai Malaquais, etc. Lyle had never seen one street with so many names and wondered who comprised the planning board for the city design.

"There on the left, you will see the Cathedral of Notre Dame," said the driver proudly. He slowed down and pointed toward Cité Island and the church that illuminated the horizon. It was beautiful, and both Bill and Lyle hoped that they would be able to enter the famous building before they left. The cathedral was Romanesque in style. Two solid square towers headed a massive body that extended behind. Many round arches and sculptured porches adorned the church and provided quiet areas for silent meditation. Large gray marble pillars supported the mammoth roof and lofty stained glass windows that looked prayerfully out upon their beloved city. The church stood tall, strong, and quiet as it surrounded itself in the arms of the gently flowing Seine river.

They moved on again down a semi-quiet street that was lined with ash trees and parked automobiles. The leaves were still in their infancy and had not as yet seen the fullness of life. The homes that were built here during the past century showed modesty in architecture and constructed so that land was conserved between them within the city's once protective walls.

The cabby slowed as he approached his destination. Peering out his side window, he finally said, "Here we are, 15 Rue des Ecoles."

"*Remercier tu*," Lyle said as he gave the man 20 francs. Bill got out of the taxi and headed for the building. He was curious about the conspicuous absence of the professor and hoped that there hadn't been foul play.

As they approached the entrance of the large house, Lyle noticed a side panel with eight names and bell buttons. Glancing down the list he saw Ben's name and pushed the proper button. After several minutes without an answer, they decided to go inside and see if they could locate the apartment. Lyle, surprised that the door was slightly ajar, gingerly nudged it open and they quietly entered the lobby.

Ben's apartment was probably located on the third level because the first number of his apartment address was a three and the stairs leading upward seemed to indicate to them that this was the way to proceed. The carpeting on the stairs was well worn but clean. The walls and general upkeep of the building were also very well taken care of. As they approached Ben's door they slowed down cautiously and listened for sounds inside. The last thing they wanted to hear were cries of agony or voices that were fearfully demanding. Hearts pounding in their heads, and holding their breath—reminiscent of their plunge into the Atlantic—they quietly tried to turn the knob on the door. It rotated easily beneath the grip of Bill's strong hand. His knuckles were white and damp with perspiration as he slowly opened the door into the apartment.

The room, darkened by drawn curtains made the air ominously quiet as a tomb. After his eyes had adjusted to the dim light, Lyle glanced about the living area. He quickly determined that things were not right. Furniture had been knocked about the room, as if a bull had been turned loose. Pictures on the walls were either hanging crookedly or lying broken upon the floor. Shattered glass lamps made walking about the apartment hazardous and the crunching sound beneath their feet made their presence audible.

Lyle's pounding heart was driving the blood from the heart up the carotids into the brain, making his head throb until he thought his eyes would explode from their sockets. He was beginning to perspire heavily and had to use his jacket sleeve to wipe droplets from his forehead before they could sting his eyes. The air, stifling, very warm, and filled with stale smells, suggested that the quarters had been closed and dark for too long.

"Lyle," whispered Bill in a strained voice. Lyle turned toward Bill and nodded for him to speak.

"I don't think anyone has been here for awhile, but to make sure let's split up and check the other rooms. Here's a stick if you should need it." He handed Lyle a chair leg that was lying beneath their feet.

"Okay," answered Lyle, "you go to the right and I'll start to the left. Yell if you need help."

"Oh, I'll yell all right, and that won't be all. Try not to leave your fingerprints anywhere," said Bill with a bit of irony in his voice.

They both turned and slowly moved in their appointed directions with sure and steady steps. Club upraised, Lyle pushed open the first door and looked into a bathroom that had towels strewn about the tile floor and magazines dumped into the white enamel bathtub. The medicine cabinet was emptied into the sink, and the linen closet was totally wrecked. Obviously, whoever was here was looking for something, Lyle realized as he poked his stick into a mound of clothing near the corner.

Bill had entered the master bedroom and started to investigate the contents of the dresser that had been emptied on the floor. He then turned and knelt to peer beneath the bed. *There might be a body hidden anywhere*, he figured. The closet was ruined, as was the bedside stand. Bill continued filtering through debris hoping to find a clue that might lead to an explanation of Ben's whereabouts. Surely, the hostiles might have dropped something that would provide a hint as to their identity and what might have happened here. He rubbed his neck and straightened his back.

"Bill."

Lyle's low voice was coming from the hallway near the front door.

"Quickly, I hear somebody coming," Lyle uttered in a hushed voice that barely reached Bill's ears. Bill cautiously crept toward the place where he had heard Lyle and peered around the corner of the doorway. Lyle, crouching with his stick raised in his right hand, was looking toward the entrance, seemingly ready to strike a blow upon the newcomer.

"Lyle, what is it?" quizzed Bill as he came up behind and knelt to the left. The area was still dark and extremely difficult to see clearly. They had decided earlier not to open the draperies or turn on the because it might cause suspicion or alarm someone was watching outside.

"I can hear footsteps coming up the stairs! I've not heard any doorbells, so I'm assuming someone either knows the place or . . . "

"It could be the thugs, returning to recheck everything," suggested Bill with jaw firmly set and fist clenched. He was certain that be could disarm any man and make a permanent impression upon a hostile body. Many were the times in his previous expeditions when he had been forced to combat adversaries who were ready to overthrow and seize his property. It had not happened then and would not happen now if he had anything to say about it. He had never killed anyone yet, but there might be the first time, if necessary.

Both Bill and Lyle could now hear the footsteps sounding closer and definitely progressing toward them. Muscles taut, nerves tuned to a fine edge, eyes steadily watching the door, both men waited breathlessly as the footsteps came even closer. Both were beginning to understand without a doubt that their mission was becoming extremely dangerous. Silently they prayed that God would be with them.

The footsteps stopped at the slightly opened doorway and then the door slowly began to open, letting in light from the stairway. A long shadow stretched itself upon the floor and became ever longer and more menacing as the door widened. Then, without a word or warning, Bill leaped forward toward the form. Hand raised and with body rushing, he threw himself upon the figure.

A groan emanated from the body as it landed with a *thud!* on the floor. Bill quickly scrambled to gain control of the flailing arms and kicking legs before taking a sitting position on top of the intruder.

"Who are you?"' demanded Bill in a fierce voice that was intended to intimidate. A muffled cry came from within the heap and the person again tried to struggle against the bondage. Bill reached for where the shoulders might be and shook them vigorously. Again a muffled sound, and then a feminine scream broke loose.

"My God," exclaimed Lyle as he came rushing forward and knelt beside them.

"That sounded like a woman to me," announced Bill with relief in his voice.

"Let's unwrap her a little and see what she is doing here." They pulled off the scarf and trench coat that had covered the face and upper torso of their captive. Beneath, they discovered a beautiful young woman with long dark hair. She appeared to be in her late twenties and relatively well off, considering her clothing and classic sculptured face.

"*Bonjour*! Who are you?" Bill asked in his best French. "What are you doing here?" The girl slowly gathered herself together and sat up after Bill had released her from his grip. She raised one hand and brushed back the hair from her face, then looked about calmly. It was apparent that she was not going to let this unusual situation upset her.

"My name is Marie de Molay," she replied with a strong voice despite a slight quiver from her bottom lip. Lyle felt a small shiver run down his spine; his scalp prickled. The dark silence of the room suddenly seemed to come alive and envelop all of them in its black embrace. Lyle noticed the fire in her eye and the strong but beautiful lines of her face and decided that she must be the daughter of nobility. Was there a possibility that she was of the lineage of Master Molay, the leader of the Knights Templars? There was an air of determination about her, one that convinced both Bill and Lyle to give her a chance to defend herself.

"Come, let's go inside and close the door," suggested Lyle as he stood and offered his hand to Marie. She reached up and took it, pulling on it gently as she rose to her feet.

They re-entered the apartment and closed the door securely behind them. Lyle went across the room and set the sofa upright. He motioned for them to sit down. There was silence again in the room and Lyle listened attentively to the sounds around them to determine if there was anyone else out in the hall who might come suddenly bursting in upon them.

"Now, tell us why you are here," questioned Lyle with a firm but gentle voice. Both he and Bill had positioned themselves across from her.

"I'm Marie de Molay," she repeated again, and this time with greater confidence. "I'm a friend of Professor Ben Sully. I've not been able to reach Ben by phone for a couple of days so I decided to come over to his place and see if anything was wrong. Obviously, I was right, by the looks of things!"

"What is your relationship with Ben?" queried Bill, who was sitting on the edge of his chair.

"He is a close friend of mine and we've done some work together," she replied as she straightened her clothes and hair. Bill got up and crossed the room to retrieve a candle that was lying beside an overturned table. Bringing it back to where the two were still sitting, he reached into his pocket and brought out a packet of matches. He lit the candle and placed it on the table beside Marie.

"I also am an instructor of history at the Paris University and I have worked closely with Ben on different projects. He has permitted me to assist him with the organization of some materials and information that we have come across."

Lyle thought that she seemed honest, but was skeptical because of all the recent strange incidents that had occurred, which were potentially life-threatening. Perhaps Marie worked for some of these hostiles and was here to investigate their activity and determine just what he and Bill had and knew?

Marie looked hard and long at Lyle. Then she picked up the candle and held it closer to Bill's face. Slowly, she turned the light toward Lyle until the flame was but a mere twelve inches from his face. She studied him for several seconds and then returned the candle to the table.

"I've seen you two somewhere," she said, thoughtfully. "Yes; it was a dream I had two nights ago. I was standing on a beautiful hill that overlooked a valley with lush green trees. In the distance there was a black castle on top of a very large hill. Everything was so peaceful, I remember, then there appeared an army coming across the valley toward the castle. Out in front of the force were several knights dressed in white cloaks with striking red crosses on the front and back. There came another army from the castle and the two met in the valley with all the fervor of battle. The knights in white were magnificent, slashing with their swords, and then taking aim with the lance they were able to hold off or destroy much of the enemy. After the battle was over and the enemy had retreated to their fortress, I went down to the battlefield with a group of monks who were singing as they approached the wounded. *'Ave mundi spes Maria. . . . Ave mundi spes Maria. . . .'* The music filled the heavens and floated over the hillside till it settled at the feet of the slain. I bent down to help a couple of fallen knights, my tears spilling onto their cloaks. As I turned their almost lifeless faces toward me, I . . . ," she stammered and paused, obviously not wanting to proceed with her story.

"Please continue, okay?" asked Lyle, reaching his hand toward hers. His body and mind were alert with every fiber of his being, causing both his heartbeat and breathing to increase. *He knew of the scene that she was describing!* It was the same dream that he had had in Duluth, the night after he had received the manuscript from Ben.

"The faces I saw resembled yours," she whispered and then placed her hand over her mouth. Her face had gone pale in the semidarkness, and all were momentarily frozen in silence.

"It's just a dream, Marie," whispered Lyle as he tried to shake off a strange feeling that was growing in him. "But I'm sure that there must be some reason for you to be here with us. Do you know who we are?"

"No, not for sure," she replied, looking hesitantly at

them both. "Ben did tell me that there were two friends of his who were coming from America to assist in some research."

"Yes, I am Professor Lyle Longsworth from Minnesota, and this is my friend Doctor Bill Burley, from New York. We were on our way to meet Ben when our airplane went down on the northwestern coast of France. It is a miracle that we survived. We were pulled from the water and rescued by a strong stranger who just happened to be on the coastal shore for the weekend."

Lyle stood up and began to walk about the room. "It looks like Ben was kidnaped and the thugs ransacked his apartment. Do you have any idea who may have done this, Marie?"

"No, not for sure," she answered hesitantly. "Ben did tell me about a couple of men who stopped him on the road recently and threatened him. I didn't want to believe a thing like this could happen, especially in these modern times. Do you think these men could have been involved with this?"

"It's my gut feeling that they were part of it," interjected Bill. "I'm sure they were after the manuscript."

"Yes, the one Ben sent you," added Marie, as she also stood and started to look about the room. "I'll see if there is any of our material left here. We had a file of information that was going to be useful in the search for the Templar gold."

Marie went into the library and Bill quickly followed her. Lyle proceeded to search though the kitchen for clues and after several minutes came back into the living room.

"Find anything?" he called as he peeked outside through the drawn curtains.

"Not a thing," Marie replied as she also came back to the living room. "All the research we had is either gone or destroyed. If they have it, I don't think it will be useful to them though."

"Why is that?" asked Bill, as he also emerged from the library.

"The most important information and connection we had to the gold is in the manuscript that Ben sent you, and also with a friend of ours at St. Nicholas des Champs."

"What is this place?"

"It is an old church that was built in the twelfth century by the Benedictines of St. Martin des Champs. Father Hugues and Ben were in the midst of reconstructing probable activities that occurred at the time of the Knights Templars' arrest and executions," said Marie with a smile beginning to show on her face.

"Do you think Father Hugues might share their information with us?" asked Lyle eagerly.

"Maybe; at least we can try," answered Marie hopefully.

Lyle wondered what they should do about Ben's abduction. Should they notify the police and become involved in a serious criminal affair while they were in a foreign country? It might not go too well with them, especially if the police found an important historical journal in their possession.

"Bill," questioned Lyle, "how shall we handle telling the police about Ben's disappearance, and the condition of his apartment?"

A frown came across Bill's face and he slowly rubbed his chin. "It's my experience that when one is traveling in a foreign country, it is imperative not to tangle with the law, or do anything to attract unnecessary attention. Usually, if you're arrested and detained, you are guilty until proven innocent. The judicial process outside of the United States can take a very long time, sometimes a lifetime."

"What shall we do then? We can't just *not* report this," stated Lyle emphatically.

"I've got an idea," interrupted Marie. "Lyle, you and Bill should go back to your hotel and I will notify the police of this incident. I think it would be advantageous for both of you to maintain a low profile when it is possible. Meanwhile, see if you can arrange an appointment to meet and talk with Father Hugues at St. Nicholas."

"What do you think Bill?" asked Lyle.

"Sounds like Marie has a great idea; couldn't have devised a better one myself."

"Okay, that settles it," Lyle said as he reached into his billfold and removed a guest card for the Crillon Hotel. "Give this to the bellman and he will bring you to our room. Can we expect you about seven o'clock this evening?"

"Yes, I should be finished with the police reports by then. I don't plan to tell them anything that might put your plans in danger."

Marie reached down for her coat and Lyle stepped up quickly to assist

"Now go swiftly and God be with you," she said as the two men looked once more about the apartment. Lyle wanted to be assured they hadn't left any signs of having been there, and he proceeded to wipe off a few objects that they had recently touched.

"Go, go," repeated Maria as she pointed toward the door.

"Yes, as you say," Bill answered grudgingly and turned to leave. Lyle was right behind him and turned to wave before closing the door. He noticed that Marie had bowed her head and had clasped her hands in front of her, as if praying for her friend Ben Sully. He instinctively liked the girl and could understand why Ben trusted her with his research. She had a level head and an understanding, analytical mind. It was good that his friend had found someone beautiful to work with.

Lyle and Bill took a taxi from the heart of the French Quarter back to the Crillon. It was about three o'clock and they already felt as if they had completed a full day's work. Lyle's heart, still in his throat, thought about the police possibly of becoming involved with their project. And then, he also hoped he wouldn't be spending too much time looking over his shoulder for those thugs. Wouldn't it be just peachy if he and Bill were kidnapped some dark evening as they were exploring old ruins? He was unsure how he would react if he were threatened with losing his life. If that cold steel blade should touch his neck, and his arms were stretched high above his head, how long could he keep from telling all he knew?

The taxi pulled under the hotel canopy and the attendant arrived quickly to open the door for them. Lyle snapped out of his nightmare, paid the driver and headed into the hotel.

"Bill, what do you think about visiting the lounge and having a little refreshment?"

"That sounds like something the doctor might order," replied Bill with a wide grin. "Don't worry too much, Lyle; things haven't become so terrible yet." He slapped his friend heartily on the back and laughed.

"Yet? You say *yet*?" Lyle grimaced. "I pray things don't get any worse.

They entered the lounge and settled themselves in a comfortable leather half-circle sofa. The cocktail table was a half-moon marble top, with a candled lantern. Each ordered his favorite drink when the waiter arrived. Then they settled back against the softness to let their bodies relax.

"When we arrive in our room," stated Lyle as he

munched on a few peanuts that were on the table, "I'll try to contact Father Hugues and make an appointment for tomorrow."

"I bet he will have some interesting information. I just hope he won't be uneasy about sharing it with us."

"Yeah, maybe I should do one other thing that might assist us. Maybe we should contact Father Marcos in Duluth. He told me before I departed to let him know if there was anything he could do. He might telephone Father Hugues and give us a letter of introduction, so to speak. That might help to break the ice for us." Lyle inhaled deeply, letting out a tired sigh. This type of activity was unusual for him and he was certain that was why he felt exhausted. He was glad that Bill was accustomed to adventures of this nature and had the fortitude for such negative situations.

They relaxed a short while longer and then departed for their room. Arriving at their door, Bill inserted the key into the lock. The click indicated that the door was still secured, but Bill still pushed it open cautiously. He went slowly and methodically around the room, checking under and behind everything. He then opened the bottom dresser drawer and took out Lyle's briefcase.

"Everything appears to be in order, Lyle. Even your treasure is safe," Bill said, as he placed the case on the sofa table. "Do you mind it I study more of the manuscript while you are on the phone?"

"Not at all," answered Lyle as he removed his jacket and laid it across a chair. He walked over and picked up his computer from the case. He set it down near the phone and plugged the computer into both the phone jack and electrical system. He then opened and turned on the Hewlett Packard laptop and clicked onto "Productivity" and then "Addresses." Father Marcos' number was easy to locate in the computer memory. Then he went onto the Internet and was able the locate the Paris telephone directory, where he found the number for the St. Nicholas Rectory. He wanted to do the contacting of important individuals through this computer because it contained a special program called "Confidentiality" and would not allow taps, bugs or other leaks of information to occur. He also wanted to use a new program on this trip called "Data Examination," which would analyze formatted data that was entered, examining for the closest and most similar probability factors. He hoped that DEX would test them against their own conclusions and assist them in making logical decisions as to their next course of action.

"*Bonjour*," said Lyle as he heard an answer on the other end of the telephone line. "I'd like to speak with Father Marcos if he is available." It was about 11:00 P.M. Minnesota time, and he hoped Father would still be reading by the fireplace.

"Hello, is that you Lyle?" came the familiar voice of his friend "What kind of trouble are you in now?"

"You won't believe what's been happening, Father," replied Lyle with the sound of dismay in his voice. "We went over to see Ben Sully today but he was not to be found. His apartment had been ransacked beyond belief and all his material stolen."

"I don't believe it," gasped Father Marcos, "What is going on? There is more danger than we had previously thought. What are you going to do?"

"Well, we're not discouraged yet. Bill is handling the situation admirably and today we got to meet a friend of Ben's. A woman by the name of Marie de Molay."

"Molay, did you say?" repeated Father Marcos, "You don't suppose she's any distant relative of Master Molay, leader of the Knights Templars?"

"Why, Father," said Lyle with a bit of humor sounding

in his voice, "you haven't been studying about the Middle Ages, have you?"

"Well, I thought I must if I was going be of any assistance to you men," replied Father, "Anyway, what happened with the girl?"

"She said that Father Hugues of St. Nicholas had been working with Ben on this project and that he has material that would be helpful to us if we can obtain it. I'm going to make an appointment to see him tomorrow and I thought it would be helpful if you could make contact with him and pave the way for our meeting. This might help ease the abruptness of the situation. What do you think?"

There was a pause at the other end of the line and Lyle wondered if he had exceeded his boundaries in asking Father to assist in this manner.

"I think something can be arranged, Lyle," answered Father Marcos. "Do you have the telephone number where Father Hugues can be reached?"

"Yes, here it is," Lyle said with relief in his voice. "86-55-05-99; shall I repeat it?"

"No, I've got it. Give me an hour before you make your call to the rectory."

"Yes, I will—and thank you very much. Also," added Lyle with a touch of softness in his voice, "give my love to my grandmother, if you see her."

"Yes, I will do that; God be with you on your adventure, my friend," replied Father Marcos.

"Thank you, Father, and good-bye."

"Good-bye, Lyle, and give my best to Bill."

Lyle hung up the receiver and clicked "OFF" on his computer. He had a feeling that everything was going to work out and decided not to worry about it anymore. Of course, he would take extra precautions from now on, in their investigations and their travels. He looked over at Bill who was absorbed in the reading of the old manuscript. Perhaps he could find some clues in the message that was written over six hundred years ago. Lyle tried to relax and project himself mentally back to the years when the Knights were of noble purpose. The struggle they must have had against the French government, fighting off growing invasiveness into their organization. The members of the Church who had turned against the heroic Templars and contrived with King Philip must have been spiritually starved to have forsaken Christianity for the sake of pleasing the present ruling power. How the Templars must have ached when they discovered members of their own faith turning against them in such a diabolical way.

An hour had passed and Lyle was ready to place the call to Father Hugues. The phone rang several times before a feminine voice answered.

"*Bonjour.*"

"*Bonjour, madame,*" replied Lyle, hoping his French was understandable. "May I speak with Father Hugues?"

"*Oui,* I'll get him for you," she replied. "May I tell him who is calling?"

"Lyle Longsworth."

Lyle took a deep breath and braced himself for the conversation with Father. He hoped that Father Marcos had been able to reach and notify him about this call. It was important that this man see them and share information that he and Ben Sully had been working on.

"*Bonjour,* Professor Longsworth," came the voice of Father Hugues. "Are you the friend of Professor Sully?"

"Yes, I have come from the United States upon Ben's request and am now in bit of a jam with some things that have recently occurred. Would it be all right if I, Dr. Bill Burley and Marie de Molay come and talk with you tomorrow, or as soon as possible?"

"I think that would be in order, Lyle," responded Father Hugues. "I fear something has happened; I too have been unable to reach Ben."

"Yes; that and a few other occurrences have caused us to become alarmed and cautious."

"I received a telephone call from my bishop a short while ago," explained Father Hugues. "He asked that I provide assistance to you in your search for information. I would be happy if you all would come over. I could see you directly after the 5:00 P.M. mass here at St. Nicholas. Would that be a good time for you?"

"Yes, that is a perfect time," answered Lyle, with the sound of relief coming to his voice. Father Marcos must have pulled a big string to obtain such an immediate confirmation of their request. Lyle returned the phone to his receiver and disconnected the computer from the line. It would be best to keep these conversations quiet. He then took time to enter all the information that had happened to them since he had left Minnesota into DEX. He wished he had completed this earlier; so much had happened and he was afraid that he might forget some important clue in the recollection process. He vowed that from now on he would be more diligent about such details. He glanced over at Bill who was still absorbed in the manuscript. Wasn't he ever going to come up for air?

* * *

As the sun faded from the countryside, the lights of the city began to flicker across the skyline of business and the residential districts. Not all was well with the world. Outside away from the warmth of homes and loved ones, were the devices of evil men. Lost to the memory of trust; forgotten by dear friends and meaningful family; there were men skillfully plotting to commit yet another injustice that would bring them momentary pleasure.

So it was, in the lower level of a mansion on the outskirts of Paris, that Monsieur Jacques Gerard and several of his companions had gathered to discuss current matters. The room was large and filled with an assortment of stolen artistic creations. They were not placed reverently about as if to display their beauty, but roughly stacked together seeming to await further decisions. A large table in the center of the room was set with a variety of food and drink. Smoke filled the air as the men sipped liquor and discussed their day's activities.

Obviously, as leader of the organization, Gerard was sitting at the head and paying great attention to what a member of his group was telling him. He smiled and brushed his hand across his mustache.

"I've just received the message that Professor Ben Sully is being taken care of and that this evening we will be apprehending his girlfriend," said Gerard as he stood and raised his arms for all to be silent. "With the American men out of the way," he leered wickedly, "we will be close to eliminating everything that will stand in our way of finding the Templar gold."

His men raised their glasses in a salute and hailed his genius. They were both respectful and afraid of Gerard. They worked for him because he was one of the best art smugglers in the world, and his collection of historical artifacts was estimated to be worth billions. His exploits ranged from the buying and then dismantling of some of the most famous mansions in the world, to the highjacking of art transports. It was also reported that museums were not impregnable to his men and that insurance against such losses were beginning to reach maximum levels.

There had been several close calls with death, but this only served to spur Gerard onto greater risks. It was his defiance of law and order that made his men admire him. A man without conscience, a man without a soul. He had long ago severed the ties with decency and had given himself over to satisfying his own desires. Moderate in physique; dark bushy hair and eyebrows framed the thin white line that encircled his piercing, stone-gray eyes. They seemed to be windows into the evilness of his character, and often this was an unnerving characteristic for many individuals. He frequently wore dark sunglasses to hide the hideousness of his features so that he would not frighten anyone unnecessarily.

Gerard was glad that an old acquaintance had given him information regarding the discovery of the ancient manuscript in the cellars of St. Martins in the Fields. It was only by accident that this journal ever left the grounds and that the Professor had possession of it. Nevertheless, soon it would be his; and with it the Templar gold.

The night grew cooler and dreadfully dark about the mansion. Northerly winds began to stir through the evergreens and dark clouds moved to cover the stars. No one moved about the grounds. Had they been secretly warned about imminent danger? Somewhere there seemed to be a lonesome moan. Or was it just the breeze attempting to enter closed shutters?

6

Marie had finished providing the French police with information about Ben's abduction and the circumstances that brought her to his apartment. The police seemed to be very understanding but told her that frequently when individuals disappeared and it was assumed that they were kidnaped, they suddenly appeared miraculously somewhere. The chief of police insisted they would do everything in their power and authority to locate her friend and bring the villains to justice. He seemed sincere and honest, but maybe she was just impressed with his handsome appearance and sparkling navy blue uniform. Nevertheless, she gave them her business and home telephone number, told them that she would be available to answer further questions if need be and left for her apartment.

She arrived at her residence after a short drive though the busy afternoon traffic. It was located north of Paris near Saint-Pierre-de-Montmartre. After parking her restored 1963 Austin Healey in front of the house, she collected her belongings and went inside. The two-level flat was a charming residence for a college professor and very femininely decorated with flowering plants in the windows. She had moved away from her parents just two years before after insisting that she must become more independent. Her father was reluctant to see her leave his protection since she was the only child and had lived a sheltered life. He, a wealthy man, a business entrepreneur, had succeeded handsomely in a thriving import venture. His close friends called him Sir

Molay with reverence in their voices and bowed slightly when entering his presence. The extraordinarily beautiful family estate was located near St. Martins in the Fields. Marie remembered Ben warning her once that she should be careful because evil men might kidnap her and demand large sums of money from her father. Still, she wanted to live independently and become a successful professional woman, one who would earn respect in her own right.

Marie checked her mail and then her answering service for messages. One message was from Father Hugues and she sat down near the phone to return his call. Though just twenty-three, she had the intelligence of a more mature woman; and though beautiful, she tried to never let this factor interfere with her judgment. She brushed back the dark brown hair that covered her right cheek and ear. Then removing her pearl earring, she placed the receiver to her head and dialed his number. After four to five rings, Father Hugues answered.

"*Bonjour.*"

"*Bonjour,*" replied Marie. "You telephoned me, Father?"

"Yes, Marie," came his answer. "I'm worried about Professor Sully; I've tried to reach him and cannot. Do you know what might have happened?"

"Yes, Father," Marie said with a voice that wanted to falter but wouldn't. "I've just been to his place and something awful has happened." She related the entire story to him, telling him of the encounter that she had with Ben's friends and their conversation. Father Hugues was horrified and gave a low groan of disbelief. She told him of their plan to meet later that evening and then of coming to see him tomorrow if he was willing to share some information with them.

"Oh, my dear," said Father Hugues, tenderly. "I'm

afraid for you now. You must find a place of safety until this situation becomes secure again. Is there anywhere you can stay for a while?"

"Yes. If you think it is necessary, I can return to the home of my parents," she replied. "They will be more than happy to have me with them temporarily, or indefinitely, for that matter."

"Good. And yes to the previous question about seeing your friends tomorrow. I'd be most anxious to visit with all of you."

"I've already talked with Professor Longsworth a short while ago and am beginning to see the problem." Marie was standing now and peering out of the curtains toward the street. The area in which she lived was rather delightful. There were many contrasts in culture and all seemed to live together harmoniously. The "Butte" was a charming village with cobblestone streets; blocks of stone steps, and courtyards filled with stone containers of petunias, poppies, roses, and geraniums. Ivy laced the terraces of the residential homes that were sanctuaries for both pilgrims and night-life revelers. This community was once the location of the powerful Abbey of Montmartre that was owned by the Benedictine Sisters during the 12th century and housed at one time forty-three mother superiors. The quarters were also once used by the King of Navarre and then four centuries later by King Henry IV when he was attacking Paris. In 1794, after living locations were altered and the name of the hill was changed to Mont-Marat, the last of the abbesses was guillotined and the convent destroyed. Their flint quarries were soon abandoned and the grain business forgotten.

"We'll see you then, Marie; okay?" asked Father Hugues patiently, interrupting her thoughts.

"*Oui, Père,*" she answered with relief in her voice, "and

I will go to stay with my parents."

As Marie replaced the receiver, she thought of the hard lives that the Benedictine Sisters had endured during those early years. Not only were they accountable for living a Christian life, but they were responsible for assisting the people of their community. It must have been painful for them to see the convent desecrated and the enemies of the church tearing at the doors of God's Holy Order. Marie loved the church and all the sacraments that communicated more fully the worship of God. She sorrowed inwardly at the coldness of present civilization and its disregard of holy persons and meaningful rituals. Someday, she hoped, people would come to realize the need for Christian principles to be present as a foundation of all social structures.

Marie turned away from the window and went into the bedroom to gather her belongings. She would probably have to take enough for several days, she thought, as she retrieved her suitcase from the closet. Fortunately, she didn't have anything in the apartment that needed care except the plants and she'd telephone her neighbor about watering them. She felt a deep anxiety for Professor Longsworth and Dr. Burley and the trouble that was apparently lying ahead of them. She had tried to warn them at Ben's apartment, but she didn't want to scare them excessively because the research was so important and it had to be continued.

She glanced at the clock on the dresser. It was almost 6:30 P.M. and she had to move rapidly if she was going to arrive at the Crillon on time. The warmth of the sun had already departed from the windows and Marie noted that there seemed to be a chill in the air. She moved slowly now about the apartment, checking to see if all was in order and making sure the windows were securely latched. The street lights had come on with the approaching darkness and the last snow bunting was finding a place to spend the night. Only a few cars could be seen moving about and occasionally a lone pedestrian was also seen, wending his way homeward. It was the close of another busy day and the world would have another rest before it would begin spinning once again. Such is the cycle of things in this world and this cycle revolves within other cycles until there appears such a magnificence in God's universal plan that it entreats us to worship Him. Marie caught herself daydreaming again as she sometimes did and hastily finished the last touches of her packing.

She sometimes wondered why she was so mystified by the saints and the history of the Church. There were occasions when she could almost reach out and touch a moment or feel the passions of past heroes. Then there was Ben, her university friend, who seemed very much like herself and she totally enjoyed the times they spent working together on the Templar investigation. There seemed to be a kinship between them, a fathomless spiritual bond which drew them together and provided unlimited answers for questions which arose. She knew they would always be friends and prayed that somehow God would spare him from all evil and harm.

Marie was unaware of the activity outside her home or the scheming which brought the men of M. Jacques Gerard to her residence. She did not know that lurking inside a nearby parked car were individuals who would attempt to abduct her either from the apartment or as she proceeded outside. Gathering one suitcase and her garment bag, Marie reached to turn out the lights and close the door behind her. The few steps to the landing were no trouble to handle and she thought it would be simple to navigate them successfully to her auto. Suddenly, her handbag hit the floor and she jumped at the noise. Struggling to regain her hold on the luggage, she bent over to retrieve the handbag—when the hall lights went out.

"Oh no," she exclaimed in frustration. Fumbling about in the darkness, Marie tried to locate a switch, but to no avail.

"Well, I'll just have to make it to the car anyway," she said out loud as it talking to an accompanying friend. Approaching the outside door, she grappled with the latch and finally succeeded in opening it. The door swung wide and permitted her to move outside with luggage still in arm.

Silently, as if guided by a great hand, an enormous cloud began to move across the evening sky. The light of the milky moon and sparkling stars was suddenly gone, leaving an unbelievable void. Then as in concert, the lights of the village were darkened as if an eclipse had transpired. The air was deathly quiet and the spring breezes were hushed by the same dark hand. Not a sound trespassed into this unknown realm or dared to interfere with this awesome plan.

Marie was stunned by the suddenness of the blackout and wondered if she could blindly navigate her way toward the car. *I must make it*, she thought, *if I am to arrive at the Crillon on time. The men will think I'm not trustworthy if I don't show up.* Slowly, she inched her way forward. Each step feeling for the next. She knew that her auto was parked directly in front of the house and if she proceeded straight ahead, she would surely arrive there. The jet blackness of the night was something Marie had never before experienced and she wondered why it was occurring at this time. There, she could feel the curbstone with her foot. Now just a few more inches and she would find her car. Suddenly, a sharp pain shot through her ankle and she felt herself drop sideways. *Darn*, she thought, *I must have twisted my ankle.*

The waiting strangers were dumbfounded by the abrupt lack of light and unbelievable darkness. It was impossible even to see their hands in front of their faces. One of them struck his lighter, but the flame was immediately engulfed by the malignant blackness. Stunned, they sat there in silence, not daring to embark further into their treachery.

Marie painfully loaded her belongings into the Healey and placed the key in the ignition. Her ankle was throbbing with pain and she hoped that she would be able to drive without difficulty. Turning on the headlights, she saw objects around her for the first time in several minutes. She carefully pulled out onto the street and proceeded to head toward the Place de la Concorde.

* * *

Lyle and Bill were beginning to worry about the whereabouts of Marie. The time was 7:30 P.M. and there was still no word from her. Lyle had just called down to the doorman and checked to see if she had made an appearance, but to no avail.

"You don't suppose that something has happened to her?" asked Bill, with a bit of anxiety growing in his voice.

"God, I hope not," replied Lyle. His eyes told of his great concern and his thoughts kept silent the forebodings that were beginning to grow.

"Well, I'm for giving her a call and then if nothing positive happens in the next thirty minutes, we should get a cab and go over to her residence," stated Bill firmly. He didn't like the idea of leaving the woman alone after such an ordeal as they had experienced earlier that day.

"Okay," answered Lyle as he stopped his pacing and

sat on the sofa. "We'll telephone in fifteen minutes, and if nothing, we'll go over to her place in thirty minutes."

Just then the entry bell rang and both men jumped to their feet. Bill walked swiftly to the door and opened it. There stood Marie, looking happy although slightly mussed with her luggage in hand.

"Marie!" exclaimed Bill as he reached out for her.

"You won't believe what I've been through," Marie stated excitedly as she hobbled into the room and found her way to a chair. "This is just awful." She told them about the telephone message from Father Hugues and about her plans to stay with her parents for awhile. Then she related her experience when leaving the house and the unutterable darkness that she had to contend with. Lyle smiled sympathetically and took her coat from her.

"What happened to you?" asked Bill worriedly, coming toward her and stooping down to inspect her leg.

"I think I twisted it in the darkness," she replied, grimacing as he gently examined her ankle.

"The complete darkness that you experienced must have been for some reason," said Lyle as he hung her wrap in the closet. "I'm convinced of that much. I'm also glad that you're going to stay with your parents for awhile. Father Hugues is right about the possibility of danger. We have already contacted him and have a meeting arranged after the evening mass tomorrow. Meanwhile, I think it would be better if you stayed here with us until that meeting. I can arrange for an adjoining room, if that's okay?"

"Yes, of course you are right," replied Marie with relief. She stood and walked gingerly out onto the balcony. The evening activities below were just beginning and the sounds of a nearby chamber orchestra filled the air.

"I'm sure she has a slight sprain in that right ankle. If she wraps it with ice this evening, it should be better in the morning," said Ben quietly to Lyle as they watched her.

"Have you had dinner?" questioned Lyle as he joined her. He hoped that she hadn't stopped anywhere before arriving here.

"No, I haven't," she said and turned toward him. It was good to have a man around again. There was a feeling of safety in being in the presence of two strong men.

"Good, I'll make the necessary arrangements for the other room and you telephone your parents about the situation. Then after a little freshening up, we'll help you to the restaurant for supper."

The dinner together that evening was enjoyable for the three of them and although they wished Ben could have been part of their company, they now shared a deeper fellowship between themselves because of the profound loss. Each in his own way prayed that their friend would somehow miraculously reappear and solve this unexplained act of violence. A room had been arranged for Marie and she would be returning to her parents' home tomorrow after the evening meeting with Father Hugues. They discussed the course of events; the likelihoods and probabilities of the case without any sure conclusions about which way to turn. One thing they were sure of; someone was after them and the manuscript. Someone who would do them harm if it were possible.

Bill was relishing his dinner of sirloin steak and vegetables when he looked up at them and remarked, "You know, in the manuscript written by Pierre Dubois it mentions the pursuit of the Knights westward from Paris, but it doesn't say anything about finding clues later on in the search. The authorities must not have discovered anything as to their whereabouts, or Pierre would surely have mentioned it in his notes, don't you think?"

"Yes, I'm sure you're right," said Marie with some eagerness returning to her voice. The past twelve hours had certainly put a damper on the investigation and had distracted them from their main objective. "Father Hugues has more information for you tomorrow and I'm sure you will be excited about it."

"You can't tell us anything about it now?" asked Bill in dismay. He was impatient to get on with the search and disappointed that Marie was withholding some potentially important information from them. Still, he didn't want to forget about Ben.

"Father Hugues made me promise not to say anything to anyone and I couldn't break a promise to him," she replied in a tone suggesting true sorrow. "But I can promise you that you will be pleased with the information. Ben and I discussed it about a week ago and feel that it is a significant discovery and will be meaningful to this investigation."

"Well, I suppose that another twenty-four hours won't hurt anything," Lyle said with unconvincing resignation. "Let's have a pleasant evening and a rewarding day tomorrow; then we'll find out more when we meet with Father Hugues."

Marie sipped on a glass of young Beaujolais while enjoying the atmosphere of the outside restaurant. The other patrons were dressed well and having a wonderful time celebrating in the exquisite atmosphere. The orchestra, made up of twenty-six instrumentalists, had chosen some beautiful selections from Mozart's repertoire. The "Overture" from *Don Giovanni* was one of Marie's favorites and then the Overture to *The Magic Flute* had to be reckoned with, but a somber look fell across her face when the orchestra finished their performance with *Lacrimosa*, the sixth sequence from Mozart's Requiem. Tears filled her eyes as she absorbed the music into herself.

"*A day of tears is that dread day, on which shall rise from ashen dust to judgment true each guilty man.*" The elevated notes seemed to move her spirit onto a higher level of sensitivity and thoughtfulness.

"*Then spare this soul, O God, we pray, O loving Savior, Jesus Lord, grant Thou to them Thy rest. Amen.*" For a while she was above the celebrating people and in a world of her own, a world where only God and the angels lived.

Lyle noticed Marie's eyes moisten and a distant look come over her face. *She must be transformed by the symphony*, he thought kindly. It was good to know other people appreciated such uplifting music, as he did. There was a deep inner beauty to this woman that went far beyond her physical loveliness. Her apparent appreciation of these great masterpieces showed her wisdom and maturity very well. He was beginning to feel a closeness to her that quickened his heart and sent a pleasurable feeling racing though him. He would try to protect her in the days and critical situations that lay ahead.

The remainder of the evening was uneventful and pleasantly quiet for them all. The following morning, they met at the coffee shop at 9:00 and had a breakfast of wheat cereal, orange juice and toast. They had decided to visit a few of the important historical sites around Paris during the morning and then go to St. Martins in the Fields after lunch before seeing Father Hugues at St. Nicholas.

Bill, Lyle, and Marie were well rested and refreshed for the day. Without seeming to be overly concerned about safety, each in his own way was observant of the people in their immediate vicinity. They needed to be on their guard, and very cautious with individuals who appeared suspicious in nature or activity.

The taxicab driver they hired was more than pleasant

when he learned they desired to be escorted about the city for several hours. Bill could just see the dollar signs click by in his eyes.

They visited the Conciergerie, an exquisite castle that had seen many noblemen incarcerated within its monumental walls. This was the place that Marie Antoinette, Robespierre, Madame Du Barry, and André Chénier along with several thousand other prisoners had spent their last days. Lyle shuddered at the thought of so many people dying. Why was it that when a government changed its leaders, there had to be revolution and such utter destruction? When were civilizations going to learn how to live peaceably with each other, especially with one's own countrymen?

The three of them moved on to see the Palais de Chaillot then to the Palais de l'Elysée. It was 1:30 P.M. when they stopped at a sidewalk restaurant near Grevin and ordered a small lunch. As they were resting their tired feet, Lyle thought he glimpsed a stranger with a dark mustache watching them from across the square. He took a quick deep breath and studied the people in that vicinity more carefully, but the figure did not reappear and Lyle rested easier.

"It would be wonderful for you both to attend the mass this afternoon at St. Nicholas before we visit with Father," stated Marie as she folded her napkin on the table. She glanced at Bill and smiled.

"I'd love it," replied Bill and looked over at Lyle who was finishing the last of his iced tea.

"I've always wanted to attend a mass in Paris, especially one at that location," Lyle answered enthusiastically. "I've been dying to visit some of the cathedrals of France and would welcome this opportunity."

"We have just enough time if we leave now to visit St.

Martins in the Fields. It is less than a block from there to St. Nicholas," said Marie with a winning smile. It was hard not to agree with her when she was so charming.

"Well," stated Lyle as he signaled for the waiter, "let's pay our check and be on our way."

After Lyle had given the young man sixty francs, Bill waved at their cabby, who was patiently waiting by his taxi.

The car traveled along at a moderate clip in the city's traffic and arrived at the front entrance of St. Martins. Lyle paid the fare and then dismissed the cab driver for the day. They would find another way back to the hotel when they had finished their business with Father Hugues. They might be tied up for several hours and the waiting time would be too expensive.

"The Benedictines first owned this place, with its original chapel, in the fourth century. It was dedicated to St. Martin, the Bishop of Tours, in the twelfth century. The large walls were constructed about the grounds for privacy and protection." Marie, leading the two men forward as if she were their tour guide, pointed at the high wall in front of them and then motioned toward the gateway.

"On this side is the actual wall that was built centuries ago."

They arrived at the gate and checked in at the admissions booth. Entering the courtyard, they were impressed at the selection of beautiful roses and flowering azaleas geometrically arranged in plantings throughout the grounds. Large cobblestones were artistically placed in the walking areas and were notably smooth after centuries of treading feet had polished them.

"Over to your right was the monks' refectory, built in the thirteenth century by a young man dedicated to the Benedictines, Pierre of Montreuil. It is now the library," stated Marie as she led them into the former church.

"The church and buildings of the priory were once Romanesque, but there was a change to the Gothic architecture in the late seventeen-hundreds. In fact," she added, "the Conservatory was created by the Convention of 1794, and installed in this priory five years later."

"Why did the Benedictines leave it?" asked Bill as they looked in awe at the inner structure of the church. The marble pillars were strong, stretching majestically toward the domed ceiling. The space that was once filled with rising incense was now filled with Foucault's pendulum, suspended from the once-beautiful roof. Marbled aisles that had felt the knees of the faithful now held exhibits of locomotion such as automobiles, airplanes, and motorcycles. Lyle gazed upward at the stained glass windows and marveled that these were still so well preserved. How his heart ached at the thought of these hallowed halls being desecrated by objects of man's invention. It seemed like a mockery to God and to the dedicated individuals who had spent so much time building a place of worship.

"That is another story, my friend," replied Marie, as she wiped a tear that was forming in the corner of her eye.

They walked on throughout the museum, taking in all the articles of discovery that man was trying to record in history and give himself credit for the accomplishment. There was a variety of trains; agricultural machinery; science that evolved from test tubes and mathematics; automata; and an impressive collection of horology. Lyle glanced at his watch and noted that it was 4:30 P.M.

"Well, my dear friends," he said, "it is time that we head for St. Nicholas."

"Oh yes," Marie glanced at her watch, "let's return by the way we came." She turned to lead the way out.

They entered St. Nicholas through massive, carved oak

doors and were immediately in the presence of one of the most inspiring wonders in Paris.

"This church," whispered Marie reverently, "was built in the twelfth century, also by the Benedictines of St. Martin in the Fields. It was to be used by the monastery servants, neighbors, visiting dignitaries, and other travelers as a place of worship. It was rebuilt in the fifteenth century, and enlarged during the following two centuries. The Revolution rededicated it to Hymen and Fidelity; can you imagine?"

"It appears to be Romanesque, although there are signs of the Gothic creeping in," murmured Lyle as he stared at the double line of pillars extending forward toward the altar.

"Yes; this is one of three churches left in Paris that are predominantly original Romanesque structure."

Lyle, amazed at the architecture which had to have been inspired by God, marveled at the vaulting in the aisles behind the altar. The design gave way to semicircular arcs and then continued on toward skyward points. The sides of the pillars exposed to the nave had been fluted by one of the most delicate hands of the century.

Marie led them on around to briefly visit the chancel and chapels that contained a number of valuable paintings from the seventeenth, eighteenth, and nineteenth centuries. They were impressed most of all by the painting of a retable by Simon Vouet of the sixteenth century and the painting of four majestic angels high above the altar by the seventeenth-century sculptor, Sarrazin.

It was then they noticed that voices were singing softly in a side chamber and people were starting to take their places in the church. Quickly, Marie led the way to a vacant pew and entered. Lowering the bench, they knelt in silent prayer as melodic sounds permeated the atmosphere. The acolyte was lighting several candles in front and in one side nave. Lyle felt a growing sense of wholeness as he knelt, here in a church that was centuries old. He would once again experience the revelation of God through the sacraments and participate in sending prayers to heaven as so many had done before him. He seemed to feel the presence of others, those unseen spirits, joining in the prayers that were ascending to God. The singing voices echoed through the sanctuary and re-echoed as the singers blended each phrase entry into the next. It was as if there was a conductor present who led the singers in the melodious swells. Then Lyle recognized what they were singing; it was a chant that he had heard before. He felt gooseflesh begin to crawl over his body; his scalp prickled, and his hands began to shake ever so slightly.

"Alleluja, beatus vir qui suffert." The melody of quiet ecstasy that acquaints you with itself and remolds you into a fresh individual more closely connected with God. The chant went on and they could see the monks beginning to file into the choir loft behind the iron grille. They were clothed in dark robes with hoods drawn over their heads and their arms folded reverently. *"Alleluia, beatus vir qui suffert."* And the singing continued as the celebrant proceeded down the center aisle toward the altar.

The Mass was beautiful in all its majesty and praise. All three of the visitors felt uplifted and closer to God as the Mass consecration transformed the bread and wine into the Body and Blood of Christ. After the celebration had ended, Marie stood and turned to leave the sanctuary. She paused for a moment and genuflected toward the altar, then proceeded toward the sacristy. Lyle and Bill followed her example and together they continued on until Father Hugues was located.

Entering a room to the right of the altar, Marie looked about for the priest.

"Father Hugues," she exclaimed happily as she spotted him. He was in the process of removing his robe, and turned toward her.

"*Bonjour!*" he responded with a broad smile and a twinkle in his eye. He was a tall gentleman with silver gray hair and tan skin. He looked to be approximately sixty-five years of age, and very intelligent. Lyle was usually correct in his evaluation of people but did not let them know that he was analyzing them; this is would be a mistake.

"Father Hugues," said Marie with a gesture toward her companions, "these are the friends of Ben, Doctor Bill Burley and Professor Lyle Longsworth. They have come here from the United States to do research with Ben, and have encountered some trouble."

"Yes," stated Father Hugues kindly, "I understand the problem. Let's go down into my private library where we can discuss the situation." He turned toward the outer door and opened it. The others followed closely behind and Lyle closed the door to the sacristy after them. Father then led the small company across a courtyard and through a door in an adjacent building. The entrance was heavily structured with black iron and weathered oak. A small window inserted near the top contained a Celtic cross imbedded in leaded glass, and the strong latch sounded loudly as it locked behind them. They descended a long flight of stone steps that stretched into a wide corridor. The darkness was lit by many white candles along the way and provided enough light to see where they were stepping. After what seemed a long distance from where they had entered this portion of the building, they followed Father Hugues through a large doorway and into an immense room. Father Hugues found the light switch and sudden brightness filled an enormous library. The walls were lined with books, from ceiling to floor. Several tables in the center of the room contained stacks of history books and bound documents.

"I think I will light a fire in the fireplace, if you don't mind," said Father Hugues as he turned toward the far center wall. As he gathered wood and kindling together, the others made themselves at home. Lyle proceeded to peruse through some of the books that were stacked on the table while Bill started to browse among the commentaries that lined the shelves.

"Well, now." Father Hugues had pulled up a heavy leather armchair and was resting himself comfortably. "Come, let's get acquainted, and tell me everything that has happened."

The others also pulled up some chairs and seated themselves near him. The fire was warming the coolness of the room and soon they were at home while they related the incidents that occurred over the past several days.

"I've ordered some tea," stated Father Hugues as he rubbed his hands together. "It should be arriving here directly."

"You read the manuscript that Ben sent to me?" questioned Lyle as he leaned forward in his chair.

"Yes, it is very interesting," replied Father Hugues. "I do trust you men and I know Marie, so. . " He got up slowly and went over to the fireplace. He touched a portion of the mantle. The entire structure moved slightly and then the fireplace slowly swung backward until only a narrow passage could be seen ahead. He entered and disappeared from view for several minutes. The room became deathly quiet as the three friends looked at each other in amazement. Not a sound disturbed the stillness.

Then slowly Father Hugues emerged with a leather-wrapped journal in his hands. They all expelled a long breath as though they had been holding it all the while he was gone. He quickly pressed the lever on the mantel again and returned to his armchair. Suddenly there was a knock on the door. Lyle jumped up from his chair.

"Don't be alarmed," said Father quietly and with reassurance in his voice. "I'm sure the housekeeper has arrived with our tea. Would you please see to it, Marie?"

After Marie had received the tea tray, she placed it on a table nearby and proceeded to pour them each a cup.

"What we have here, my dear young friends, is a collection of letters that were written several hundred years ago by a small group of Knights Templars."

Lyle felt his heart begin to race, and he again jumped to his feet. Was this possible? Every fiber in his body was alive as he leaned over the shoulder of Father Hugues and peered down at the journal.

"You may look at it more carefully if you'd like," Father said as he handed the packet over to them. Bill was immediately on his feet and by the side of Lyle. Together they sat on the brown woolen rug near the fire and began to examine the yellowed pages more carefully.

"You will find it interesting, just as Ben and I did." Father Hugues smiled and began his version of the message as it might relate to them.

"There were twelve Knights Templars who escaped the sudden, deadly onslaught of King Philip's soldiers. They were fortunate enough to have been visiting St. Martins in the Fields on business the day that their Temple was surrounded and captured. The Benedictines soon discovered what was transpiring nearby and suggested that the Knights stay in hiding at their monastery until danger had passed." Father Hugues took a long sip of his black tea and continued.

"The site of their temple is about seven kilometers from here, to the east. It was later totally destroyed and there is a small monument there now which is surrounded by a park. The Templar Prison is another five kilometers, but it was also razed in 1808 in order to prevent pilgrims from converging on that location to worship. The government then erected the Statue to the Republic and created lovely gardens about the area."

"It was a miracle that these Knights happened to be at St. Martins," exclaimed Bill in astonishment.

"Yes," continued Father Hugues, "it would seem so. After a few weeks with the Benedictines, they began to understand from outside reports that the invasion into their quarters was extremely serious and that the government of King Philip intended to devastate the Order by falsely accusing them of a variety of crimes that included the denial of Christ; sacrilegious acts upon the crucifix; obscene affection; disbelief in the sacraments; idolatrous practices; and the absolution of sin.

"It was then arranged for the surviving Knights to leave Paris and take with them some of their financial assets in order to preserve them. The head abbot helped them make contact with another Benedictine Order on the coast of France, the Abbey of Jumieges. It is desolate now, but still remains a peaceful location for meditation."

"Yes," interrupted Bill, "We traveled near that place on our way to Paris. I'm now sorry that we didn't stop to get a closer look."

"Anyway," Father Hugues leaned forward in his chair, "the Knights Templars set off one night by carriage and horses. They arrived, according to one letter, safely and immediately went aboard a merchant ship that was owned by a friend of the Templars. I believe his name was Lord Chancy. They set sail for Spain because of their connections there and the opportunity to lose themselves in the mountainous areas."

"Do you know where they landed?" asked Lyle as he stood to stretch his legs.

"The last letter in the packet indicates that they landed to the east of Santander; and from that point nothing more was ever heard from them."

"Do you know of any Benedictine Monastery there or any Templar castle?" questioned Lyle eagerly as he stood with his back to the fire and warmed his hands.

"The Spanish do have on record that there is a ruined Templars' hostel located near Castro Urdiales on the northern coast. They might have landed at this point, but after this they just disappeared into history," replied Marie as she drew her chair up closer. She had been listening quietly until now, but the mention of Spanish territories perked her participation.

"The interesting part of the story is one report that was received from the Benedictine Abbot of St. Martins after the Knights left." Father Hugues deliberately stalled and looked at each of the guests carefully. "They had with them several chests of gold."

Lyle, Bill, and Marie looked at each other. There was an extended period of silence in which each examined his heart and thought of reasons why they should or should not pursue this quest.

"Now that I've told you this," asked Father Hugues, "are you going to continue on and try to find the treasure?"

"I think I would like to continue," replied Lyle as he looked at Bill.

"I'm still in," said Bill determined as ever and now on his feet ready to go.

"I'd like to go also," interjected Marie as she stood by Bill. "I know I should stay here and help look for Ben.. "

"That would be a great idea," interrupted Lyle, "you have a knowledge of the Spanish language and the country, that would be a wonderful asset. What do you think, Bill?"

"Yes, I'm for letting her come along. The men who have abducted Ben are still here and probably trying to figure ways to get their hands on her. She would be safer coming with us. What do you think, Father?"

"You're probably right, Bill," said Father Hugues as he stood and joined the circle near the fireplace. "I do think it would be good for you to hire a muscle man, if you don't mind my putting it so delicately."

"Absolutely," responded Lyle emphatically. *But where are you going to find a muscle man?*

"What about the driver we had?" asked Bill, punching Lyle's arm as if to awaken him.

"Yes—you mean Oliver? I think I still have his card in my pocket," replied Lyle as he began searching through his wallet. Then almost immediately he held a small white card in the air and exclaimed, "Here it is, I've found it. He would make a good bodyguard and also a driver for our trip south. I don't know about you Bill, but I'd prefer going the distance by motor vehicle."

"Say, that sounds like a plan. All the way to Spain in a Rolls-Royce; now that's the way to travel and I wouldn't mind letting planes alone for awhile either," Bill said with a chuckle.

"Is there anything else we need to know or do before we leave Paris?" asked Lyle as he looked directly at Father Hugues.

"No, I can't think of anything," he replied thoughtfully. "I'll keep current regarding the whereabouts of Professor Sully and will let you know how things are here when you periodically check in. By the way, that computer of yours will sure come in handy." He paused for a moment and looked at Marie.

"Marie," Father Hugues held out his hands toward her

and took them into his. "God will protect you, of this I am sure. These men, Lyle and Bill, will take care of you," and as he turned he raised his hands above their heads. "The peaceful blessings of the Lord be with you and may His guardian angels be watchful of your steps." He folded his hands in front of him and smiled graciously.

7

The evening at the Crillon was spent arranging a multitude of details for the trip south. Lyle connected his computer to the telephone system and placed a call to Oliver. He related the experiences they had since they last saw him and told of the recommendation that Father Hugues had made regarding getting some muscle to assist them. Lyle noted the pause on the other end of the line and wondered if he had insulted the man.

"Strange that you should ask me to do this," Oliver said with a quiet voice. "I can remember another time that I was involved in this type of activity. I was extremely good at it and I'm sure that I can be a benefit again."

"Great," replied Lyle with relief. "Can you be here tomorrow morning about 9:00?"

"Yes, I'll be there and the auto will be ready for your trip."

Lyle smiled at the others as he replaced the receiver. They were busy arranging their belongings and checking through last minute details for the trip ahead. Marie had already telephoned her parents and explained to them the necessity of going away with Ben's friends. They were moderately upset but soon began to understand the reason she wanted to leave Paris for a while. Her father, Philip de Molay, insisted that she take special precautions and offered to send along extra men with them for protection. Marie smiled as she explained that they were going to have enough extra men along, and her father seemed temporarily satisfied.

Lyle and Bill pored over maps of France and Spain, plotting their route so as to make good time on some of the main highways. They also wanted to see some historical sites while they were traveling through the countryside and made notations of special locations on the map.

"I think we can make this trip in two or three days," stated Bill as he began to calculate mileage on the computer.

"That should put us into Bilbao, Spain, on Tuesday if all goes well. Or Bilbo, as the Basque people pronounce it." Lyle was beginning to feel excited about continuing on with their exploration. He wondered it they could slip unnoticed out of Paris and have an uneventful trip. Would there be hazards along the way? Would Ben be found? Were they ever to locate the Templar gold? His mind was spinning as he thought of all the possibilities that lay ahead. *Come now*, he told himself, *get hold of yourself or you won't be worth anything to this investigation.* He checked his luggage over and then made sure that current data had been entered into DEX and then punched SOLUTION.

It took the computer a few seconds to file and crossfile. The word READY appeared with a colon. Lyle entered one question: PROBABLE LOCATION OF TEMPLAR GOLD? and then sat back in his chair to wait for the results.

He jumped slightly when a message flashed on the screen. HIDDEN BENEATH THE GRANDEST SKY AND COVERED BY YEARS OF PROTECTION.

What was the meaning of this? *It must be a game that had been introduced into the program*, he thought as he entered, CONTINUE PLEASE.

Another few moments elapsed and then another message. PROBABLE LOCATION OF TEMPLAR GOLD IS IN SPAIN WITH FRIENDS OF THE KNIGHTS TEMPLARS.

Lyle sighed tiredly as he disconnected the computer and put it away. He would have to enter more information in order for it to assist them in any meaningful manner. Their own conclusions about the location of the gold was logical enough, but it was good to have another opinion, even though it was from a computer.

The evening passed quickly for the three as they enjoyed dinner while listening to the hotel's orchestra. Each seemed wrapped in his own private thoughts concerning the recent past and the potential events that lay ahead. Each sincerely desired to fulfill their dream of locating the treasure and genuinely hoped that it would come true.

That night and the next morning went as planned. Their preparations were rewarded with smooth sailing and they were soon on the road in Oliver's Rolls-Royce heading south, away from Paris. Paris, the city of intrigue, grandeur and the glory of days past. A city that holds a complexity of ideas, emotions, and personalities in history and in present conditions. *France's complicated history holds the key to many secrets*, thought Lyle as he gazed back at the beautiful city silhouetted against the pale blue sky. The men, women, and children, some of whom had become great in this world's eyes, lived and died here. People—thousands and millions of people—came and went in this land, each leaving a mark in the pages of time. Even though there had been much political conflict and many brutal deaths, still the attitude of the French people remained filled with national pride and good will for their fellowman. Lyle reckoned that growth toward true civilization was not always easy, and least of all just.

*   *   *

The evening grew cool as the sun began to descend in

the western sky and into the dark Atlantic Ocean. In the year of our Lord, thirteen hundred and seven, from the balcony of the Abbey of Jumieges that overlooked part of the English Channel, one could see the great Atlantic that lay beyond. Sir Norbert of Thames was resting against the white granite ledge and pondering everything that had recently occurred to the Order of the Knights Templars. Their miraculous escape from King Philip's soldiers was still enough to cause even the bravest Knight to shudder in disbelief. *What had gone wrong?* Sir Norbert thought, as he took a deep breath and glanced over his shoulder to see who was approaching. His shiny brown hair glistened in the sun's last golden rays and the armor about him sparkled brightly. He was thankful for the assistance from the monks of St. Martins in the Fields and for the men here who had readily agreed to aid them in their time of distress.

"Here you are, Sir Norbert," called Father Abbot Francis as he came around the corner from the inner corridor. Father was approximately five feet tall and somewhat plump with a pleasing disposition. He had lived at Jumieges since he went into the monastery at the age of fifteen and had enjoyed the life of contemplation that was dedicated to God. Although deeply disturbed about the government's hostile activities against the Templars he was not totally surprised. There had been talk within the province of Burgundy that the Order might be in serious trouble with the King. Burgundy was the home, or the birthplace, of the Holy Order and the people took pride in the Templar activities.

Father Francis looked upon this brave Knight with tender sympathy in his eyes. He would do everything in his power to see that no harm would befall these men.

"Father, I'm glad you consented to have us stay with you." Sir Norbert knelt before the abbot and kissed his hand. He reverently bowed his head and waited for the priest's hand to rest upon his shoulder.

"Please stand up, my son," said the abbot with great love and admiration. *This courageous Knight shouldn't be kneeling before me; it is I who should be at the feet of this great warrior*, he thought.

"I want you and your associates to make yourselves at home," continued Father Francis. "There is a ship that will dock here tonight, and there is a good possibility that you may gain passage. I hate the thought of your leaving France, but under present circumstances, I think it would be the best plan. What are your reflections?"

"You're right, Father," replied Sir Norbert after a few moments; then he continued with sadness, "I will talk with the men and get their opinion."

They looked toward the sound of boots on the stony walk that led up from the courtyard. There, emerging from the dusk and fog that had started to settle around the bay, came the Knights, tall and strong in their armor. They had once again placed their white capes with the red cross in front and back over their bodies; the capes with the insignia of the Order that had once sent a joyous thrill running through bystanders. Heads were held high in pride, and the carriage of their bodies showed strength of person. They slowly approached the two and stood before them in respectful silence.

"Men," stated Sir Norbert as he looked intently at each of the eleven knights, "you remember the twelve disciples of Christ? How when he was departing from us, he gave instructions for them to go forth and teach people of His love; to assist those individuals in distress and to be an example of Himself on this Earth? Well, the time has come when we must go forth, from this, our beloved homeland, to another country. We know not why this thing has occurred to our order or why Pope Clement seems to have forsaken us, but we shall be faithful to our vows and always be upstanding Knights of the Temple."

"Where do you think we should go?" asked Sir Charles, stepping forward. He was a man of many years, but the gray streaks through his hair made him appear distinguished rather than aged.

"Father Francis tells me that there is a ship due in this evening. We shall see to where they are bound and make a request for passage."

"Why, Father Francis," questioned Sir Joffre, "doesn't the Pope come to our aid? He has been living in Avignon for several years now and is a part of the French culture. You would think that he could influence the government in favor of the Order."

"I don't know why Pope Clement is not able to assist you in this matter. Perhaps only time will tell us the reason why some occurrences happen the way they do, and after we understand all the factors surrounding the case we will be better able to judge the incident." Father Francis hung his head and for a moment there was complete silence as all the men wondered what the future would hold for them.

"Sirs," a young Benedictine monk said from the doorway, "we are serving dinner in the Hall and would like for you to dine with us."

The Knights, led by Father Francis and Sir Norbert, made their way into the Hall and seated themselves around a large wooden table. Clean straw had been placed on the floor and the other monks had already assembled themselves about another table. The room was bare except for one large, intricate Benedictine tapestry hanging on the wall behind the head of the table, and several large candles placed in the room. One of the monks stood and offered grace and they began to enjoy a dinner of wild roasted duck, browned potatoes, cooked carrots and baby peas. Not a word was said through the course of the dinner and after everyone was finished they all stood and again the thanksgiving prayer was said. Slowly the monks filed out of the Hall and into other parts of the abbey. Father Francis motioned for the Knights to follow him and then proceeded to leave by a side doorway.

"You men can make yourselves comfortable in this room," he stated, motioning toward the chairs, tables and beds that were located in various places about the large room they had entered. "This is one of the guest drawing rooms and is available for you as long as it is needed."

Later that evening, Father Francis and Sir Norbert greeted the ship as it sailed into the Abbey's harbor. After most of the passengers and some of the seamen had disembarked, they went up the gangplank to locate the notable Martin Marillac, whom they had learned was the captain. They found him at the helm, giving some last-minute orders to the first mate, and they patiently waited until he had finished before approaching him with their request.

They discovered that this was one of Lord Chancy's vessels, which was bringing in a shipment of furs from Norway. It had been at sea for several months and the men were elated to see land again. After discussing the urgent situation and the plight of the guests that were at the Abbey, the captain graciously consented to allow the Knights to take passage with him. He had wanted to depart for Spain the following day, but when he learned about the critical nature of their request, he decided to make haste and leave that night.

The Knights of the Temple gave their farewells to the monks and Abbot Father Francis of the Benedictine Abbey. Then, with tears beginning to glisten in their eyes, they took one last look around the moonlit countryside. This was the land they loved, the land for which they had shed their blood, the land that had given them birth; and with God's help they would see this land again someday. They followed one of the seamen down the steep stone stairs of the monastery; across the courtyard that was filled with evergreens and rosebushes to a carved archway at the top of another long flight of stairs down to the harbor landing. They were silent as they waited for permission to come aboard and by moonlight they were able to see their belongings loaded. Among these belongings were five chests of gold that were to be taken to their next headquarters and guarded until further notice came from their leaders.

The sea is the place to be when the soul yearns to find rest. The Knights had many things to think about as they searched their minds and hearts for solutions, reasons, and future planning. They had time to think about themselves, their leaders, their brothers and the plight of the Order. So much time that they began to worry too much and then they decided that work was the solution. Over the next several days, the Knights sailed the Atlantic Ocean while making themselves helpful about the ship when it was possible. The seamen wanted their guests to rest and enjoy themselves. The Knights wanted to be busy and prove their worth.

Most of the weather was beautiful for sailing this large ship with three mastheads. Then on the fifth day out the wind shifted and a gathering of dark clouds could be seen. The watery waves began to increase and the ship started to surge to and fro with each passing. White caps could be seen on the tops of the watery giants. Great showers of water were thrown across the deck, soaking the men on board. A dense, gray fog started moving in upon them and the course ahead was becoming dangerously obscure.

"I want you Knights to go below to the mates' quarters," said Captain Marillac loudly over the noise of the angry ocean. "This could really get nasty and I don't want to lose any of you."

"We will obey," shouted Sir Norbert through cupped hands. "Let us know if there is anything that we can do." The men followed him forward, to the lower quarters where they set about finding a place that would be safe from flying or falling objects. The room was about eight-by-six feet and contained a couple of bunk beds, along with one desk and three wooden chests. A rope of wide diameter was nailed to the wall about the room for holding onto when the sea became savage. There were also two small windows that looked out aft, and a lantern that swung hazardously from an upper beam

"I can only hope that this will not be a violent one," said Sir Norbert as he peered out of the window and into the blackness that seemed to be swallowing the ship. The men were quickly finding secure places to sit or stand so that the motion of the rolling vessel wouldn't throw them to the floor. Loud sounds of banging were heard on deck as large barrels and crates hit the floor above. These noises were interrupted by the howling of the fierce wind and the smashing of the waves against the wooden hull.

The men were now hanging onto posts and ropes with both hands as they were thrown forward, sideways and backward. The lantern broke loose from its tie and crashed to the deck sending a mass of flames coursing across the floor. The men quickly grabbed the nearest object they could find and began beating the fire desperately before it could do any damage. Trying their best to maintain their footing in the confusion and turbulence of the storm, they lashed at the flames until they were extinguished.

"My God," choked Sir Joffre, who was trying to re-assemble the lantern, "What is going to happen next?"

"It almost seems like God has forsaken us, doesn't it?" asked Sir Charles as he brushed his clothing off and secured his position.

"It may seem like that," replied Sir Norbert patiently, "but I'm sure these are only God's trials and that He is still watching over us."

"Why didn't Pope Clement come to our aid?" asked Sir Joffre again. He still was very perplexed about the political circumstances that prevented the head of the Catholic Church from intervening on their behalf. As a Knight who had many times defended the innocent and the helpless, he understood the commitment that one has when vows are taken. To him it seemed inconceivable that a leader would let his people, whether citizens or knights, be destroyed.

"I don't understand it either," interrupted Sir John of Galary. He stood on his feet amid the fallen debris and faced Sir Norbert. He was about six feet tall with broad shoulders, of a rugged appearance, with a dark, bushy beard. He had spent thirty-five years with the Templars and revered every moment with them. Theirs had been a life filled with conservatism in their style of living and in the methods they used in dealing with the people. Their love of God and for their religious institution had deepened; the Pope was seen as the head of this institution and was reverently loved by the Knights. This made it all the more painful and difficult for them to think that he might have abandoned them.

"Perhaps something has gone wrong with the conditions at the Vatican, and Pope Clement is in trouble," suggested Sir Norbert as he struggled to maintain the balance of the men. The sides of the ship continued to be hammered by beating waves that seemed at any minute to cave in upon them.

"Maybe that's the problem," responded Sir John with sadness. "My heart feels as if it has been broken. I pray that his Holiness is well and that this condition we're in has had nothing to do with him." His eyes began to glisten and his voice quavered. "We can go on, although it does feel as if we've been separated from God and the Church."

"This may be a dark time for us," said Sir Norbert confidently, "but I'm sure God has not forsaken us. Let us be strong and try to make the best of our plight." He paused for a second and looked at the men seriously. "Do you again renew your vows to accept Christ, and to follow the teachings of the Holy Catholic Church, and do you renounce sin and the Devil? Do you vow again to serve the brotherhood of the Knights Templars and so live until the day we all die? Do you so swear?"

The room was deathly quiet except for the rattlings of the ship and rumblings of thunder within the storm.

"I do," replied Sir John.

"I do," stated Sir Charles with confidence.

"I do," agreed Sir Joffre in a strong voice.

"I do," answered Sir Rostand of Rouergue. Each of the Knights repeated the words and each placed his hand across his heart. They stood there for a few moments as the meaning of the words sank into their hearts and cleansed their souls. There would be no more doubting from them. They would continue on with their goals and serve in the manner which they knew best.

Outside the harsh winds began to abate and the frantic jostling of the ship stilled. Sir Norbert peered through the wet cabin window and could see in the distance a parting of the threatening dark clouds. The bright light from the sun was beginning to break through and send rays down upon the troubled waters. The rain had subsided and a freshness filled the air as Sir Norbert opened the window and allowed the clean air to permeate the room. This was a new day, he thought. Tomorrow they would face the challenges that lay ahead with renewed confidence and be assured that all would end well.

* * *

The Rolls-Royce traveled on over the rolling hills toward central France. The air was clean and fresh in the late morning. An early morning shower had freshened the trees, grass and spring daisies that honeycombed the landscape. Lyle, Bill, Marie and Oliver had traveled in silence for the past several miles and only now began to stir about.

"We must be getting close to Bourges, the Berrichon capital," said Bill examining the map that was in his lap.

"Yes," replied Marie, excitedly pointing out of the car's window toward a steeple in the distance. The flat land was broken only by a few rolling hills that were beautifully covered with enormous wheat fields that stretched forever into the distance. They had just passed through some of the most fertile vineyards that Lyle had ever seen, and this change in the landscape was breathtaking.

"Saint-Etienne is one of the greatest Gothic cathedrals in France," said Marie. "It was built by Jacques Coeur in the fifteenth century. As we pass you will notice most of the architect's keen design in harmony with the facade's five intricate portals. There are also five chapels that are linked to the chancel, which overlooks the archbishop's beautiful gardens. The chancel is directly beneath the spireless tower."

"It sounds glorious," stated Lyle as he continued to stare out the window and across the landscape.

"There is one item in the cathedral that impresses me greatly," said Marie reverently. "Inside, on the central portal, is a monumental sculpture that depicts the Last Judgment. Jesus is surrounded by angels carrying the utensils of the Passion, and St. Michael is using the balance to ascertain souls that will be ready for the Resurrection. It is so impressive."

They rode on in a peaceful quietness, each enjoying the comfort of the auto and the serenity of the countryside. Marie went on to inform them that the entrepreneur Jacques Coeur not only was responsible for the cathedral, but was involved in building most of the financial enterprises of the area. He had also built a fortress about the town that resembled old Gallo-Roman ramparts. Inside, the palace was elegant, as was the courtyard and attractive balconies. Many of the houses in the town had been restored to their former beautiful appearance and once again portrayed a peaceful articulate time of life.

They were approaching the province of Auvergne when Oliver suggested they stop for lunch near the capital of Clermont-Ferrand. It was about 2:00 in the afternoon and he could tell that his passengers were getting restless. Besides, he wanted a chance to show them one of his favorite sites.

Oliver turned the Rolls off at Chateaugay and headed for the town's fourteenth-century castle. There they got out and leisurely stretched their arms and legs. The town was nestled among high rolling hills and displayed a quaintness of years gone by in its houses, streets and native attire.

"This is beautiful, Oliver," exclaimed Bill as he came alongside of the driver.

"They have a wonderful restaurant here and serve some of the finest wine in France."

They approached the quaint little outdoor café and chose a table that overlooked the castle nearby and the lovely gardens surrounding it. Upon the hillside, one could see the meticulously groomed rows of grape vineyards. The lush green leaves and deep brown vines spoke of rich soil and nurturing rains. The happiness of the people in the area spoke of peaceful living and pleasant homes with families.

There were other visitors at the café and all seemed to enjoy sampling the area's renowned Côtes d'Auvergne wine.

"Let's have a glass of their famous wine and a wedge of their delicious Cantal cheese with homemade bread and fruit," suggested Oliver as he glanced over the menu. "You won't believe this, but the wine cellars are located on the ground level of this castle. It was once the home of a great military gentleman who built it in the fourteenth century." The gay blue and white umbrellas moved slightly in the spring breezes, as did the castle banners on top of the corner towers.

"This is all so great," responded Marie as she looked across at Lyle and Bill. "I will agree with your choice of refreshments; how about you guys?"

"Let's do it," they replied in unison and then laughed.

Oliver signaled for the waiter, who arrived quickly with tray and paper in hand.

"Bonjour, Madame et Messieurs," he said politely as he brushed the table off with a cloth.

"Bonjour," replied Oliver, and proceeded to place the order for them in French. Marie told them about Spain, the land they were headed towards.

"We're traveling into an area now that was once the route of many pilgrims as they traveled west to Santiago de Compostela. There they visited and did penance at the tomb of St. James. He was one of Christ's disciples who was murdered in A.D. 44 while in Jerusalem. His remains were then transported back to Spain by a few of his friends. King Alfonso II ordered the building of a beautiful temple above the saint's tomb which then became the focal point of pilgrimages across Europe."

"Marie," asked Lyle as he listened intently to her story, "Why did the people venerate him?"

"He was dear to them because he had traveled throughout their land after Christ left this world and had performed many miracles, helping to bring Christianity to their country. After his death it was reported that St. James could be seen as a white knight on horseback, wielding a fearful sword against the Moors who had invaded Spain. The Christians saw it as a sign that God was with them, and they were successful in many wars and conquests that followed."

"Yes, that's right," agreed Oliver as he sipped his wine. "His temple tomb was enlarged in the year 1075 and is now called a Cathedral. Pope Calixto II bestowed one of the greatest privileges to the See of Santiago de Compostela; he designated a holy year in honor of St. James and gave one year's indulgence and absolution to those who worshiped there."

The afternoon breeze whispered softly through the nearby maples. White cotton clouds were beginning to appear against the brilliant blue sky and the chirping of song sparrows could be heard in the area. Lyle was intensely absorbed with the moment and with the history he was receiving about this land. He loved the richness of days past and the efforts that had been given to build society and develop culture.

After finishing their lunch, they returned to the auto and again headed south. It took them approximately thirty-five minutes to arrive in Clermont-Ferrand and Oliver drove them by the Gothic cathedral that had been built of black lava in the thirteenth century by the architect Viollet-le-Duc. Oliver told them that the stained glass windows in the chapels had taken four centuries to complete. Portrayed in distinct rich colors was the life of Christ and His saints.

Close by was the eleventh-century basilica of Notre-Dame-du-Port, also created from the same black volcanic stone which was reportedly as strong as granite but much simpler to work with. Oliver told them that they would be passing some of the volcanic areas on the way and would be able to see some of the old quarries.

They continued to travel on into the early evening, excitedly talking about the land and its history. Emperor Nero, Julius Caesar, Napoléon and others arose in the conversation as if they were currently causing a stir in world politics. Oliver apologized for not being able to take them by Le Puy, for it truly was a city from which to gain inspiration and a deeper relationship with God. There a large statue of the Virgin Mary was erected on a tall point of lava, Rocher Corneille, that stands about four hundred and thirty-three feet above the city. This gigantic, rust-colored statue was made from the melted-down metals of the cannons that were taken from the Russians after the Crimean War. Napoléon had given the military weapons to the Bishop of Le Puy for the purpose of decomposing them and making the statue. Next to it, on another pinnacle, was built the twelfth-century Chapelle Saint-Michael. The architecture of the church had been influenced by the Muslims. It was elaborate in its adornment and contained a trefoil arched haven and minaret bell tower. Originally, during the days of the Romans, this hill was first dedicated to the god Mercury. Oliver told them that this location was on the main route for pilgrims making their way to Santiago de Compostela; multitudes of people tarried there to worship. The people of the area are still very religious, Oliver continued; they greatly revere the Holy Virgin and Her Child. It is said that no other place in the world celebrates Mary more and that numerous observances occur here in honor of Christ and His Passion.

The area has a large number of convents, monasteries and churches, with religious hospices for the poor and infirm. The most outstanding celebration of the year occurs around Easter, beginning with services on Maundy Thursday. Laymen of the White Penitents fraternity reenact the Passion of Christ through the streets of the city and on toward a distant hill. The spectators become so overwhelmed in their devotion and love for Christ that one would truly think that they were actually reliving that historical event. Tears of love and suffering course down the faces of the believers, and souls are once again reunited with Christ.

They proceeded on past Issoire, St. Fleur, and Rodez, and onto Toulouse and the Pyrenees Mountains where they began to look for a hotel to spend the night. The day had been intensely interesting but the constant awareness of strangers who were out to do them harm, made an evening's rest seem even more necessary.

They entered the town of Saint-Bertrand-de-Comminges, off the main highway, and drove along a winding road that led toward the top of a hill. The small village overlooked lush green pastures and the opposite side was back-dropped by the snow-capped Pyrenees.

"Isn't this the loveliest town that you have ever seen!" exclaimed Bill, leaning forward and motioning toward the small, colorful and well-built houses that lined the cobblestone streets. Everywhere in the town, people had planted flowers in every container that could be found and had placed them artistically about the area. Poppies, petunias, daisies, and baby's breath were arranged decoratively about the shops and homes. A few people were moving about in the late afternoon, closing their stores and preparing to return to their homes for the night.

"Ask that gentleman over there near the café if there is

lodging in the town," said Lyle, pointing to a man who was removing the tablecloths.

"Yes," Oliver said as he maneuvered the Rolls toward the nearby curb.

After Oliver had turned off the ignition, he got out and proceeded over to the man. The stranger seemed friendly and after a short conversation, Oliver returned to them.

"He says that it is possible to stay at the St. Bertrand Cathedral guest house, if there is still room," reported Oliver as he climbed back into the driver's seat. "He said something about a car with four men heading that way just thirty minutes ago."

Lyle turned to Bill and Marie with a worried look. *It couldn't be,* he thought. *Who knew that they had left Paris already?* Lyle started to open his mouth but Bill interrupted

"Lyle, I don't think those men are concerned about us. They were probably just traveling businessmen." He sounded confident and it seemed to put everyone at ease.

"Well," said Lyle, after considering their options, "let's go and see it there is still room at the inn." Everyone laughed and the tension seemed to dissipate.

Oliver followed the main road to the edge of the town and then made a right turn up the hill. The rough dirt road wove back and forth as it led them steadily upward near two large oak trees that arched over the roadway. Then they saw the high walls of the Romanesque-Gothic cathedral and the twin spires reaching toward the evening sky. There was a huge double gate entrance through which they drove and entered the courtyard of the sixteenth-century religious sanctuary.

A monk came toward them from a side doorway and Lyle got out of the car. They met and shook hands.

"My name is Professor Lyle Longsworth," said Lyle respectfully. "These are my traveling companions." He motioned toward the auto and they got out.

"Welcome; my name is Father Johns. I am the priest who manages the cathedral and the cloister." His voice was kind as he spoke, and Lyle wondered how many monks lived there.

"There are twenty-four of us and we enjoy the company of guests that stop by."

Lyle wondered how the priest knew what he had been thinking.

The evening air was chilly as the sun's last rays lit up the cathedral's tall spires. From across the courtyard, from the church's doors and windows came melodious musical sounds that were familiar to Lyle. The beautiful sounds of Gregorian chant floated from the chancel and seemed to warmly embrace them. The peace of the countryside was elevated by the sounds echoing around the stone arches just as they had for centuries. The cool shadows seemed to turn warm and the group stood transfixed as they absorbed the music.

"You wish a place to stay for the evening," inquired Father Johns as he aroused Lyle from his thoughts.

"Yes, if it would be possible," replied Lyle, turning toward the priest again.

"We have rooms in the guest hotel area that have been used for many centuries. Are you on your way to Santiago de Compostela?"

"No, we will not be going that far," Lyle answered politely as he followed the priest toward the entrance from which he had emerged. He beckoned for the others to follow them.

They were led through a lobby area and up one flight of stairs to a corridor. The stone walls were cool but dry and several tapestries depicting French culture were hung decoratively. A ruby red rug ran the center of the hall that went by several closed doors. Father Johns stopped at the fourth one on the outer side and opened the door.

"This room is for a lady," he said smiling at Marie. "You will find everything you need. These rooms were upgraded with running water, showers and toilets a few years ago. We are now in the twentieth century.

"The next three rooms are for each of you," he said, pointing toward entrances that were ahead of them. He glanced at his watch and offered, "If you would like to join us for dinner, we will be in serving in thirty minutes. The dining hall is just to the right of the lobby."

"Thank you, Father," said Lyle, "We will be there." Father Johns turned and left them to settle in.

Each went into his room, Lyle choosing the one next to Marie's. Oliver told them that he would bring in the luggage while they freshened up. Bill began to explore around his room. One large window to the west overlooked the remarkable Pyrenees Mountains that were the first sign they were getting close to Spain. The mountain range was a natural barrier between the two countries and were gentler than the Alps. Landscapes were composed of rolling fields, babbling brooks, and a few snow-capped peaks. Deciduous trees lined the low areas as the scenery sloped upward. As far as Bill could see, there wasn't any sign of life and he wondered if the region was still relatively unexplored.

He moved on about the room, closely examining the stone walls and the integrity of the masonry work. It was hard to believe that these walls were so intact. The mortar was minimal as the stones seemed to be perfectly cut and fitted for each other. In the center of the wooden floor was a multicolored Persian carpet, and the bedspread was a rich blue velvet that matched colors from the carpet. The old lamps in the room were made of dark iron and the wooden bed and chest from well-worn but highly polished oak.

"Bill," came the voice of Lyle from the corridor. "Are you ready to go to dinner?"

"Yes, I'm coming."

They were the only guests at dinner that evening along with Father Johns. The dining room was small but gracious in its size. It also overlooked the distant mountains and was very comfortable.

"Tell me where you are from," asked Father Johns as he passed the vegetables.

"Bill and I are from the United States and Marie and Oliver are from France," replied Lyle.

"It is good to see friendship between countries. I have never had the opportunity to visit America, but I hope to someday."

They continued their dinner in polite conversation. Lyle was hesitant about revealing too much information concerning their adventure because of the potential danger. Instead, he gave the impression that they were traveling to a convention in Madrid, and were stopping at various historical sites along the way.

After a pleasant evening by the fireplace and a glass of brandy they said good night to the Father and retired to their respective rooms. They were more tired than they knew and secretly hoped for an earlier bedtime than usual.

Lyle took a quick shower and then removed his computer from his briefcase. He entered current data and then signed off. Pulling back the bedspread, he stretched comfortably beneath the sheets. Then he opened the manuscript again and began to search for clues through the old worn pages. The bedside lamp lit the room with a soft white light and after a while Lyle felt his eyes begin to close. He relaxed in the dimness and didn't notice the scent of the sea that began to permeate the room. A strange, bluish mist began to fill the air, creeping across from the open window. Emerging from the misty past appeared the distant shores of Spain. Along the sandy beach marched numerous men in armor with spears and swords drawn for battle. Their dress was blackened and their faces dark. A white castle stood magnificently on a hilltop in the distance, and beyond, the sky was filled with dark, billowing clouds that loomed menacingly.

Suddenly, from between the cliffs came a brigade of Knights, bearing the red cross upon their white capes. Lances readied for battle, swords drawn, they charged down upon the invaders. There was a clashing of steel upon steel, and cries of the dying filled the evening air. Muscle was pitted against muscle as the fervor of the battle reached its peak. Horses wheeled under the orders from their riders and obeyed every command instantly. One Knight was outstanding in his attack and brought down the enemy with every stroke of his sword. His face had a youthful appearance though it was mostly hidden by dirt and sweat that streaked down upon his cape. His brow was creased and his lips pursed. He wheeled his horse about again and again, putting his sword into the enemies' hearts with a surgeon's skillful stroke.

At last the enemy was routed and the Knights gathered themselves together and proceeded toward the castle. The young Knight stopped long enough to retrieve the banner from the hand of a fallen enemy and then led the Knights toward the open doors of the castle.

The Spanish lord stood at the entrance with his court behind him and together they cheered the approaching Knights. The young Knight dismounted his white horse, and drew near to the lord and, with the banner of the Moors in hand, he knelt down on one knee before the nobleman and placed the flag at his feet. The Spaniard raised his hands above the young man and proclaimed him their hero. Then quietly and with respectful hands, he bent forward and placed his royal cape about the shoulders of the young Knight. The people of the castle opened their arms and their hearts to the Knights that evening and celebrated with them over the defeat of the infidels.

The blue mist in the air and sea scent began to lift as the Knights began their march along the coast, leaving behind joyful citizens and blood-stained sand. The room became warm once again as the embers of the fire flickered into flame and the breezes of the sea calmed.

Lyle slept on peacefully and did not notice that the quilted cover had been drawn about his shoulders and that the lamp had been turned out.

8

The early morning light awakened Marie from a sound and refreshing sleep. She showered and dressed quickly so that she could enjoy the fresh morning air in the courtyard and explore the grounds about the church. Closing the outer door of her room quietly behind her, she walked softly down the corridor and stairs, then on through the lobby until she was standing in the brilliance of the sunrise as it shone upon the cathedral's walls. The only sound that broke the silence was the song of a purple finch in the balmy fresh air. The song seemed to be coming from around the side of the cathedral and Marie decided to find out whether she could locate the bird. She progressed slowly among the trees, glancing frequently up into the branches and among the leaves that overshadowed her. The grass was still dewy from the night's refreshment and moist droplets could be seen on the green blades.

Then she heard the low sound of voices ahead of her. Cautiously, she crept on, eyes searching for the source. She entered into a garden area filled with evergreen shrubs and a few daisies that lined the pathways. There at the far corner of the garden was a grotto with a white statue of the Virgin Mary beneath a covering dome of multicolored stones. In front of her were half a dozen monks on their knees, heads hooded. Their voices spoke in unified, harmonious tones and their fingers gently followed the beads of the rosary.

"Hail Mary, full of grace, the Lord is with thee . "

There was such reverent love in their voices and great humility shown in their bowed forms.

"Blessed art thou among women, and blessed is the fruit of thy womb, Jesus."

Marie felt her heart fill with warmth and love. She stood there in awe and a great peacefulness passed from them to her. Slowly she knelt in the dewy grass and began to recite the words with the monks, as the rosary became a part of the air they breathed. There was a timeless calm about the cloister that seemed like the presence of God incarnate was living here among them.

"Holy Mary, Mother of God, pray for us sinners now and at the hour of our death. Amen."

All about the garden there was quietness. The birds had even ceased their songs and all seemed to be meditating upon the words and the Holiness of Christ.

As Marie quietly left the dedicated monks who lived there, she hoped that other travelers would come and stop a while to rest and pray with them.

The Rolls-Royce was moving again after their light breakfast with Father Johns. They looked back in wonder and marveled at the cathedral as they slowly drove down the hillside. Lyle wondered silently where the gentlemen that had arrived before them had disappeared to.

The highway to Pau curved around low hills of grain, and pastures with grazing sheep. To their left they could see the snow capped Pyrenees Mountains following them along in the distance. They appeared like a strand of pearls lining France's southern border.

As they arrived in Pau, Lyle instructed Oliver to make a left on N 134-E 07. It was the route that would take them over the mountains. Oliver stopped the auto to refill the tank and Bill asked the attendant about the road conditions ahead. Soon they were on their way again; all were refreshed and the Rolls began running smoothly again along the blacktop. The hills started becoming steeper about thirty miles away from the city, and the valleys less shallow. Lyle had always loved the mountains and had frequently vacationed in both the Canadian and American Rockies. This experience brought back wonderful memories. The height of the terrain seemed to lift him in spirit, for he always felt renewed after spending time in elevations that were above the tree line. It seemed to him that the air became more clean and fresh nearer to God.

"The station attendant said that it should be clear sailing over the top today," said Bill, interrupting their thoughts. "He mentioned that there was one report of weather coming in from the coast, but he didn't think it would arrive here today."

"It's so beautiful now," exclaimed Marie, "I'm sure it will be clement."

The altitude seemed to be increasing as the Rolls's engine began to accelerate. A clear mountain stream followed the road; but at times it seemed to be flowing in the opposite direction. *It was strange*, thought Lyle, *that situations containing hard facts could be so deceptive at times.* It was like an optical illusion.

The mountains appeared to be growing taller and the valleys more narrow as they passed between. Great boulders could be seen jutting out of the earth and reaching toward the sky as if someone with a mighty hand had heaved them upward? The covering earth and greenery were stripped away as their hard core was exposed to the elements. Clusters of birch and spruce were gathered in low places and about these lived the delicate spring flowers of the mountains. Bluebells, wild roses, daisies and violets grew at the foot of rocky cliffs, and groves of brush. The sky was as blue as the Sea of Cortez and white clouds drifted lazily eastward.

"If I'm right," said Marie, interrupting the silence, "I believe that it was through this pass that both the Romans and the Visigoths entered Spain, conquering the nation many years ago. It's hard to believe that they could have scaled these steep mountains on foot and horseback with all the military equipment that they carried with them."

"It does cause one to marvel at their perseverance and fortitude, doesn't it?" asked Bill.

"Spain has had its share of conflicts and wars during the past three thousand years. First, they were inhabited by tribes that crossed over from North Africa, and then multitudes migrated in from Italy, France, and Britain between 3000 B.C. to 900 B.C. Then in the seventh century B.C., the Greeks began to trade with the country and build towns in the new land. This civilization brought a great deal of culture and richness to the inhabitants. Craving world power, the Romans spread into Spain as they did in other neighboring countries. The final conquest was the Cantabrian War of 29–19 B.C. It had taken the Romans about two centuries to conquer this fearsome land. Rome was almost bankrupt and many of the soldiers refused to participate in foreign engagements with Spain any longer."

"Marie," questioned Bill as he turned and looked at her, "how did the Spaniards fare under the Romans?"

"Actually they fared quite well. Latin became the pervasive language for the upper classes and everyone quickly found that the Roman customs were agreeable and the laws were equitable. There was economic trade between countries and soon Roman citizenship was offered to all. Christianity was brought to this country by Paul of Tarsus and also by James, the disciple of Christ. By the time that Constantine was in power, Christianity had become the one religion embraced by the Roman Empire. Civilization advanced greatly under the influence of the Romans. Cities with bridges, aqueducts, roads and massive walls were constructed to strengthen their homes and communities. Highways were built throughout the country to make travel easier. Education was established for students to delve into classics, philosophy, literature, and the sciences. All considered, this time was to be one of Spain's brightest, and the country prospered. Then in 401 A.D., the Visigoths came over the Alps and destroyed Rome. Tribes from this Germanic race crossed over the Pyrenees and plundered homes and land in Spain. They killed mercilessly and took booty from the countrymen. It took only five years to overthrow the Roman rule and then they set up their own regime."

"I bet they had a hard time fitting in down there," interrupted Lyle.

"I actually don't know how they won the war," Marie replied, smiling thoughtfully. "They were only 200,000 Visigoths, and the Spanish numbered into the millions."

"It was probably the overthrow of key military headquarters," interjected Bill. "Then the country people, without leadership, just did as they were told."

"Yes, you're right," Lyle stated. "Communication in those days was only by word of mouth and it had to be carried by horseback which took weeks. So by the time everyone knew what was happening, it was already over."

Marie was gazing out of the auto window, thinking of the scenery. "It's like you're living happily, when all of a sudden you open your eyes and see a black cloud coming over the mountains." She pointed toward the eastern sky, well above the snowy peaks. A large mass of dark clouds had gathered and seemed to be growing rapidly. It wasn't five minutes before the whole sky had darkened and the wind had picked up noticeably.

"Don't tell me that we're going to get a storm up here," said Marie disgustedly. "We were supposed to have fine weather over the top, remember?"

The snow fields near the crest were quite visible and Oliver pointed to a road sign informing motorists that the elevation was 5,500 meters (about 7,000 feet). All had managed to keep their ears open by chewing gum and swallowing frequently.

The wind was beginning to blow nearby surface snow across the road and it was difficult for anyone to tell exactly if it was coming from the clouds. The auto veered strongly to the left as Oliver struggled to keep it in the proper lane against the fierce winds. The whistling of wind could be heard and Lyle began to worry about them heading into trouble.

"I'm beginning to be quite scared," stated Marie as she gripped her seat. "Aren't you guys somewhat frightened?"

"I might have been frightened this time last year," recalled Bill calmly, "but I'm sure there is Someone up there," he pointed toward the heavens, "who is watching over us and will protect us."

"You can say that again," blurted Lyle with a smile. "After the plane accident that we survived, there will never be another situation to make me doubt that God is nearby. You just have to trust in Him and let His peace fill your being when night is the blackest."

Marie looked into Lyle's eyes and saw that there lay deep within his soul a profound love for Christ and a strong faith that would keep him steadfast in the mightiest of storms.

The snow had started falling now and was being picked up by the blinding wind that was swirling around them. They were above the tree line and the landscape appeared barren and dismally isolated. The mountains had surrendered to the white snowy veil; the winding road ahead was disappearing from view. Oliver slowed the auto in order to avoid accidentally running over the edge. He did not want to take them into the nearby river or down a long hillside into a woods.

Oliver had turned on the auto's heater and the windshield wipers were trying to keep the front windows clear of the accumulating snow. They could see nothing on the outside. Oliver brought his vehicle to a stop. They had not seen any other automobiles on the road in the past hour and knew that the likelihood of someone coming upon them now was nonexistent.

"We'll just wait it out," said Bill patiently, not wanting to sound worried.

"We can wait for a while but if this continues all night, we could freeze to death," whispered Marie, also not wanting to put fear into anyone's head.

Oliver had turned on the interior light and tried to keep everyone comfortable. He opened the bar, offering them soft drinks, some salted peanuts and a blanket that was stored under the back seat. They accepted graciously and enjoyed the snack while continuing to watch the raging winter storm. Enormous sheets of blowing blue-gray snow cascaded in undulating folds from the mountainside, creating large overhangs and periodically brilliant streaks of misty sunlight would break through, highlighting a rock or cavern.

After what seemed like a couple of hours Lyle began to get restless. "I wonder how much snow has accumulated out there?"

"Well, let's check it out," Bill quickly responded as he moved toward the side door and pushed open the latch. The door seemed hard to move and it became apparent that there was massive drifting around the auto. The wind whistled sharply about the open door and brought heavy gusts of snow inside.

"It must be about two to three feet deep," said Bill, brushing his clothes off after closing the door. The wind's howl was becoming fiercer and a coldness was beginning to creep into the auto despite the heater. *We might sit here and freeze*, thought Lyle as he gazed out into the frigid night. He was sure there wasn't going to be anyone out in this weather now. He had to think of something to do. *Please God*, he prayed silently, *help us out of this situation that has become so desperate.*

"Lyle," declared Oliver, from the driver's seat, "I'm going out to see if I can locate a house or gas station ahead. We cannot just sit here and wait for this blizzard to quit."

"You can't," exclaimed Marie with a look of horror. "It would be suicide. You wouldn't get back."

"Please," Oliver held up his hand in a gesture for her to be silent. "I think that I might be able to locate some help. I remember once, several years ago when I was skiing in the area, that there was a gas station and hotel somewhere in this vicinity. I have to try."

"Good luck," Lyle said quietly, not wanting to show anxiety, "We'll keep our fingers crossed and hope you will return soon."

The others also wished Oliver a safe trip as he exited the Rolls with his coat pulled tight about himself and a woolen hat jammed over his ears. He was grateful that he had just happened to bring along a pair of boots and gloves that were tucked under the front seat.

Within seconds Oliver disappeared into the evening's darkening landscape and blinding snow. The fury of the snowflakes immediately filled his path and nothing but the wailing gale knew of his whereabouts. Time passed endlessly as the three passengers sat in hopeful but stunned silence. Could this be the end of their exploration in Spain? Was the Templar gold forever to remain hidden?

Two hours later, Bill let out a shout of joy. "Look, I see something coming, out there, in front of the auto." He was excitedly pointing through the front windshield.

They strained their eyes to discover what he had found and could see nothing, then both Lyle and Marie saw it. A light was moving slightly to and fro, inching forward. They were mesmerized as they watched, hoping that it was someone coming to their aid. Would the snow prevent rescuers from locating the auto in the wild, blowing drifts? *Maybe I should open the door and shout to the strangers approaching*, thought Lyle, as he clenched and unclenched his fists.

The point of light was steadily coming closer when suddenly it disappeared and after several minutes had elapsed Bill made a move toward the door.

"I'm going out to see if I can locate them," he said bravely. He opened the door and vanished in the howling gale. Lyle could barely hear Bill shouting above the wind and his voice seemed puny against the enormous storm's fierceness.

Then abruptly, there were three men at the left side windows. The light they were carrying streamed into the dimly lit interior and sent a warm glow over Lyle and Marie. Bill opened the door and the three entered.

"Thank God you've arrived," exclaimed Lyle as he shook hands with the two men. "Where is Oliver, the man who left us to look for help a little over two hours ago?"

"We didn't see anyone else." answered one of the strangers. "My name is Thomas Berard and this is Robert Craon," he said, nodding toward his companion. "We're Americans so we're accustomed to this kind of weather. It occurs all too frequently during the winter around Denver."

"We saw your lights over two hours ago from our hotel window and when you didn't arrive we decided that we should search for you," added Robert as he rubbed his hands together. "Maybe Oliver has found our hotel and will stay there until we all return."

Lyle gave a look of despair across to Bill who shook his head in disbelief. They all silently prayed that Oliver hadn't gotten lost in the storm.

"Turn off the auto and follow us," said Thomas as he tightened his coat. "Wrap yourselves up warmly. I'll lead the way and break trail. Robert will follow at the end of the line."

Lyle, remembering what it was like to live through blizzards in northern Minnesota, was unsure about them leaving the auto. He had known of individuals who had frozen to death after getting out into these conditions, hoping to find help.

"We must be careful to cover all of our exposed skin," Bill said as he pulled out a couple of scarves for Marie. "Hands, noses, ears and feet are the most susceptible parts in these extremely low temperatures. Small blood vessels will constrict; they will then stop circulation and the tissue will begin to die. Also, make sure that you wrap yourselves with dry clothing, because the dampness will aggravate the process."

"I've found more gloves and caps," Lyle said from the front seat as he held up a supply of winter clothing. "One more thing before we go," he paused and looked at the men. "Once we get started we must not stop. This will be crucial in our survival as coldness accelerates when inactivity begins."

The group left the auto and stepped out into the raging wind. The blowing snow cut into their faces as they tried to arrange face coverings. It was hard to see one another, but they lined up behind Thomas and began wading through thigh-high drifts. Each step was laborious as they moved forward in the footsteps that were created. Thomas had the lantern and was careful to move slowly and deliberately with small steps, so that the others wouldn't have difficulty. The night air seemed to have reached thirty below zero, or so it seemed to Lyle as he clutched his coat about him. He hoped that shelter wouldn't be a considerable distance away because his clothing wasn't heavy and he knew that Marie's wasn't either.

Marie stumbled in front of him and practically sank from sight. Lyle bent over and reached down to help her up. The blinding wind and stinging snow smarted as he brought her to her feet again. She gave his arm a squeeze of thanks when righted and again resumed following Thomas. *She is unusually brave,* thought Lyle; she voiced not a sound of complaint or discouragement.

They stumbled on in the darkness and the frigid cold for what seemed to Lyle like a mile, when just before them they could see the lights of the hotel. Fighting their way across the last few feet of deep drifted snow seemed like an eternity. Aching legs and backs tormented each one as they staggered into the lobby and collapsed upon the rug. Snow was caked about their faces and layered into their clothing. Marie slowly began to remove her shoes and gave a small cry of pain as she slipped them off.

"Let me help you," said Bill as he knelt in front of her. He gently removed both stockings, then examined her skin carefully.

"Much more of this and you might have received frostbite, young lady! But you'll be all right soon," he added reassuringly. The skin on her feet was bright red but had no visible white spots. Bill dried her feet with his shirt tail and asked the clerk who had come from behind the desk to bring warm water and some towels.

"They feel somewhat numb," murmured Marie as she removed her coat and lay back on the carpet.

"That's the first sign of frostbite," replied Lyle as he came over and inspected her feet.

"She'll be okay," Bill responded assuredly. "We'll soak her feet in some warm water for a while and then keep an eye on them for several hours. If injury has occurred it will show itself in the form of blisters by tomorrow morning."

"*Buenos tardes*," interrupted a well dressed gentleman. "*Invitado?*"

"*Buenos tardes*," answered Marie, smiling up at him. "*Si*, we will be your guests for this evening or as long as the storm lasts if you will allow us to stay here."

"*Si, por favor*," he said with a smile that beamed across his face. He was approximately forty years of age, Marie figured. His hair was black and slightly curly with a few light gray hairs showing at his temples. He also appeared to be educated and well mannered. She wondered if he had seen Oliver as she looked about the room.

"I do speak some English and my name is Mark Fernandez." He motioned for one of his sons to retrieve belongings and place them in their rooms. Lyle followed Mark over to the hotel counter and signed them into the registry.

"It was a great deed that Robert and Thomas performed in coming out into the snow storm to find us," Lyle told Mark.

"*Si*, my two sons wanted to go along but the men wouldn't let them go. Please, you come and sit by the fireplace and we will get everyone some hot coffee and apple cider."

Mark showed the group into the parlor where a wonderfully warm fire was blazing. They made themselves comfortable in large lounging chairs and soon were sipping hot drinks that were offered. Marie began to soak her feet in a pan of warm water brought by the young boys and was relaxing contently. Lyle could still hear the winds howling about the corners of the hotel and again wondered about Oliver.

"Have you seen our friend, whose name is Oliver?" questioned Lyle, turning toward Mark.

"No, we've not seen anyone but you three," answered Mark with a frown beginning to show on his forehead.

"I don't think we ought to go searching for him," Bill interjected as if reading Lyle's mind.

"It's really bothering me, Bill," replied Lyle. He stood and began to pace in front of the fire. "Here we are, and our brave friend is probably freezing to death!"

Marie felt tears beginning to sting her eyes as she tried to finish her cider. Her heart ached for Lyle and his apparent sorrow at losing his friend.

"If we go out again, we might not find our way back here," said Thomas, coming closer. "I've seen storms like this before and I know with certainty that you will get lost out there. The only reason that we were able to find your auto was noticing your car lights. Then we had a particular direction in which to proceed. Oliver could be anywhere on this mountain."

The silence in the room was dreadful as each realized the gravity of the situation. There was nothing they could do and it was Bill who agonized the greatest. He had always been the brave and noble hero, wanting to come to the rescue of the unfortunate. There was a time that he almost lost his own life while hanging from a rope off a two-hundred-foot cliff in order to free his friend from a rocky cave. There was also another time when he jumped into the roaring Grand Canyon River to save a friend from going over a deadly twenty-foot-high rapid. He had never been afraid to fight the savageness in nature but gauged his movements so that strength and timing resulted in conquest. Always his actions were correct and his instincts came to his salvation time and time again. This time though, he knew in his heart and had a gut intuition that they should not venture into this storm. He felt a strong impression that it would be futile and that there was already an intervening force at work.

"We really don't know Oliver well," said Bill, interrupting the silence that seemed to have frozen everyone. "I think he has some survival skills so he might surprise us all and make it."

They calmly agreed with him and tried to put their hearts at peace. Soon they departed for their rooms and turned in for the night. Mark had assured them that if the storm had ended they would resume the search in the morning.

Lyle tried to sleep. He snuggled beneath the large feather comforter and listened as the winds howled around the outside walls. His prayer that evening was for Holy Mother Mary to encircle Oliver in her arms and protect him from the freezing temperatures and the dampness of the snow. He prayed for the peace of Oliver's soul and that God's will be done. As his eyes closed and the worry from his thoughts abated, he relaxed as he envisioned Mary kneeling beside Oliver and covering him with her cloak.

The morning came and Lyle jumped out of bed as he heard a clock ringing in the room next to his. He glanced at his watch. It was almost 9:00 and light had come to the hotel windows. Rushing over to the draperies he threw back the curtains and looked out over the countryside. It had stopped snowing and the warm sun was just beginning to break over the mountaintops. There was a pristine freshness in the air and the sky was a brilliant blue.

Lyle quickly dressed and ran down the stairs to the lobby.

"Hey, there you are," called Bill from the lounge. He was with Marie and sipping a cup of coffee.

"Why didn't you awaken me?" asked Lyle as he entered the room and waved a friendly greeting to Mark.

"You needed the rest; besides it gave Marie and me a chance to become better acquainted." Bill smiled at her and pulled up a chair for Lyle.

"As soon as you folks have some coffee and breakfast cakes, we will go out and search for your friend," said Mark from his table. His sons were just finishing breakfast and both jumped up.

"*Por favor, Papa,* "they cried excitedly.

"*¿Quieren ustedes?*"

"*Nosotros deseamos a ir, papa,*" The pleading look in their dark eyes certainly seemed to weaken the resolve of their father. Both boys appeared to be about fourteen years of age and were very respectful and helpful to their father. Their keen awareness of things about them was noticeable and Marie had been surprised when she overheard them discussing Spanish politics the evening before.

"*Si*, if you dress warmly and promise to stay close."

The two ran off and Mark stood up. He called for the waiter and came over to join the three friends at their table.

"Where do you think we should start looking for him?" asked Marie addressing Mark.

"We will go back to your auto and start from that point," replied Mark as he poured himself another cup of Spanish coffee. "Thomas and Robert have said they will assist in the search also."

"Which way do you think we should go from there?" asked Lyle.

"If we begin at the auto, we should fan out as we proceed up the mountain. He shouldn't have strayed too far off the road if he was following the flat pavement. Even though there was a lot of snow, one can determine by the terrain when the pavement ends and the irregularity of the landscape begins."

"When do you think a snowplow will be coming through the area?" questioned Bill as he arose and walked over to the window that overlooked the mountainous approach. He knew that finding Oliver was going to be very difficult and wished that there were more people to assist in the search.

"It usually comes through here by noon after a storm such as this one was," answered Mark.

"We should get started soon," stated Lyle, "or the snowplow might contribute to his burial."

"Oh, Lyle!" gasped Marie, "Don't say it that way. It sounds so morbid." She didn't want to think about the possibility of Oliver not returning to them.

"Yes, everyone get ready," said Mark as he stood and started toward the lobby. "There are extra coats, boots, mittens, hats and scarves in the room to the right of the desk. We'll be ready to leave here in thirty minutes. I'll go and find the other men. He turned and left the room. Lyle stood and assisted Marie to her feet.

"How are your feet?" he questioned sympathetically.

"They're just fine today. They must have returned to normal during the night," she replied as she stepped about the floor. "See, they don't bother me at all."

"Well, let's go see if they have any extra clothing that will fit us," said Bill as he turned away from the window and started toward the lobby. The others followed and soon they were well outfitted in attire that befitted the type of weather they were about to encounter.

The others arrived and soon they were pushing out the front door and across the snow-filled porch. The air was clean and crisply fresh as the breath from their nostrils steamed upwards. Snow had been packed heavily by the blowing winds as they waded thigh-high across the front yard and toward the main road.

They arrived at the main highway in approximately thirty minutes and began to follow the road downhill toward the location where the auto had been abandoned. The going was slow but methodical. Thomas was again leading the group, and Robert was bringing up the rear. By the time the trail had reached him the traveling was much easier than for those who were ahead. He had told Thomas earlier that they would break off after an hour and he would take the lead in order not to stress anyone intentionally.

They soon were able to find the auto by noticing the black roof shining in the sun. Lyle and Bill began to scoop armfuls of snow away from the driver's door so that they could peer into the interior. There was a chance that Oliver might have returned to his vehicle and be safe inside. But the Rolls was empty.

"Okay," said Mark as he motioned the others to come close. "From this point we will divide up into three groups. Thomas, Lyle and Marie in one; myself and my sons in another; Robert and Bill in the third group. Two groups will go to the left of the road and the other to the right. If you find Oliver or see anything that may be of help to us, sing out. Are there any questions?"

Everyone shook his head in the negative and then proceeded to head out in their respective directions. The going became even rougher as they left the main road. Rocks, dips and rises caused them to stumble frequently. Bushes and small tree clumps interfered with progress and the drifts became increasingly difficult as they used their bodies to plow ahead. Lyle was following Marie and Thomas as they headed off to the right of the road. Approximately two hours had elapsed since they left the hotel and still no sign of life anywhere. The air was strangely quiet and deathly cold. Bill and Robert had headed to the left along the edge of the road and off into the low culvert area. Obstacles were often unmanageable and they frequently had to return to a previous point of origin and take an alternate course.

"If Oliver had gone off the road and become lost, what would he have done?" asked Bill of himself. He had been on many a survival outing and knew that if one were smart he could outwit the elements. If he were Oliver, what would he have done in this situation? Probably, it would be most advantageous to find a cave or a hollow of some sort if he were lost, he thought. He put his gloved hand up in order to shade his eyes. Where was there a natural harbor? His eyes squinted against the bright sun as he scanned the horizon. Of course, Oliver wouldn't have been able to discover a safe spot deliberately, it would have to have happened only by accident. They struggled on through the snow, investigating each mound and feeling into each shallow crevice.

Suddenly Bill noticed a large rocky boulder that protruded out of the snow, just about eight feet from their path. Wiping the snow from his face and giving a kick to the drift that lay in his way, he headed toward the rock.

"Robert, I'm going over to investigate something," called Bill to his fellow searcher as he headed off in the direction of the large granite stone. He pushed on, breathing deeply as the work of pushing the snow aside became exhaustingly difficult. His heart began to pound deep within his chest, and he thought his lungs were going to burst as he struggled against deepening snow. Soon he was up to his armpits, but the thought of his not succeeding made him work even harder. Just two feet away, Bill was thrashing his arms madly at the snow, trying to make a path. Then he slipped on something slick and fell. He lay there for a moment, wishing that a miracle would happen; then he decided to start crawling forward, creating a tunnel in the snow toward the rock. He soon discovered that it was easier this way and he was also able to maintain his warmth. Slowly inching his way on, he abruptly came in contact with the hard surface of the stone against his head. He began to feel about its base and discovered that there was a large gap extending underneath. Turning to the right, he followed the stone wall a couple of feet until the space on the lower side started getting larger. The light in his tunnel was very faint but he could make out a gap that extended well beneath the gigantic granite rock. As he progressed forward on his hands and knees into the space he soon discovered that he was leaving the snow behind and coming onto dry ground. Reaching into his pocket, he pulled out a lighter and struck a flame.

"Oliver," he called, "are you under this wonderful rock?" He knew that this would be his wildest wish come true.

"Bill, is that you?" came a voice from the darkness.

Bill's heart jumped as he shouted, "Oliver, you son-of-a-gun! Come out here!" He was still holding up the lighter and its flame cast a dim glow for approximately two feet. Bill could hear the sound of movement and then before his eyes Oliver appeared. His face was weathered and ashen white. He was shivering as he clutched his arms about himself.

"I was wondering if you were going to attempt a search for me. Actually, I was thinking about proceeding out again myself to see if I could find the station I remembered." His smiling face looked good to Bill and they embraced each other awkwardly as they met in the cramped quarters. He was shaken by the thought that Oliver had actually been found in the many miles of this snow-covered region.

"Come, let's leave by the way I entered," said Bill as he turned and started to crawl back through his tunnel of snow.

As they approached the main road, Bill called out to the other searchers and soon they were together near the Rolls hugging and loudly proclaiming Oliver a miracle man. They started back toward the hotel just when the snowplows were starting their swing past the resort and were able to direct them to the half-buried Rolls. Oliver apologized several times for not being able to was locate help for them the night before. He explained that he knew he was lost and was unable to either return to them or go forward. A soft look came over his face as he related to them that something impelled him to crawl under the rock that he had accidently run into. He went under as far as possible and then curled himself into a ball. It was then that he seemed to feel an unusual warmth come over him. Lyle gave a knowing smile and didn't wonder at the answer to their prayers. Marie was beaming and in very good humor by the time they reached the hotel and while the men found snow shovels and returned to dig out the auto, she went up to her room and took a leisurely bath. It was good to be warm again.

The remainder of the day was spent relaxing about the fire and the retelling of heroic stories. Bill was by far the greatest of the storytellers and gave wonderful details of all of his expeditions. Mark had the cook bring warm pastries and coffee for everyone and they spent this time becoming closer friends.

Later that evening, Oliver brought the Rolls to the station and had it serviced. He wanted to be sure that it was in good operational condition by the time they left. The attendant said he would check over all the fluid levels, gaskets, hoses, belts and wiring to insure satisfactory working condition.

Lyle rested in his room's armchair late that night as he again started to read the manuscript that Ben had sent. He wanted to know more about the conditions of the time in which this aggression took place against the Knights Templars. It was certain that Pierre Dubois was truly involved with their demise. But why did the Inquisition become involved in the ordeal? Weren't they all working for the Church? He must ask someone who knew this period of history.

> *It is with great confidence that Guillaume de Nogaret and I endeavored to convict the Knights Templars of the charges that were brought against them. King Philip had suppressed Pope Clement's power and we had been given the signal to proceed with all haste and diligence. The Knights would not be able to stand against the accusations of.*
>
> *—denial of Christ—denial of the saints and the Virgin—*
> *—sacrilegious acts against the cross—obscene affections—*
> *—disbelief in the sacraments—worship of idols—*
> *—absolution from sins—*
>
> *We had been assured that the property of the Knights would be dispersed. Most of the wealth went to the King and some of his friends, but we also received sufficient monies as a reward for our services.*
> *This project wouldn't be impossible to manage. The King had done this same type of maneuver in exiling the Jews and the Lombards in order to suppress their affluence and gain control their wealth.*

Lyle despised Pierre Dubois and the others that were responsible for such atrocities. How could a country with such a progressive spirit bend to such utter inhumanity? He hoped that there would be something that he could do to avenge the Templars' pain and justify their beliefs. Well, tomorrow would be another day and with it the adventure would continue. Lyle closed the script and climbed into bed.

9

Marie and Lyle scrambled to get their belongings loaded into the Rolls, which was parked out in front of the hotel. Oliver was busily arranging the luggage and talking with Mark about the upcoming trip and what territory they would be heading into. The weather was still clear without a trace of clouds in the sky and only a whispered breeze cooling the cheek. Mark's young sons had just finished with their morning chores and were beginning to build a snowman in the front yard.

"*Señores*," said Mark with sadness in his voice, "it was a miracle that you came to stay with us and we shall never forget these days. You seem to be on an important mission and I wish you God's speed and safety." He shook each of their hands warmly and gave Marie a strong hug. She smiled shyly at him and then the others before climbing into the rear seat of the auto.

Giving one last look around at the snowy peaks of the Pyrenees Mountains and absorbing the beauty into his mind, Lyle also got into the rear of the Rolls. Oliver and Bill made one last check about and then got into the car. Last good-byes were said from the open windows and Oliver again pulled out onto the highway headed for the pass that was approximately one mile away.

Lyle felt relieved and thankful that once again everything was back on track and proceeding as planned. He remembered Bill telling him not to worry on adventures such as this because one couldn't predict what might happen or when. It was important to roll with the punches, so Lyle was trying to remain calm and enjoy the course of events. He gasped in wonder as the roadway afforded them a fabulous view of the valleys and hills below. The scenery was spectacular and filled them with awe and reverence. The sun was just rising over the eastern slopes, spilling brilliant rays of light across the undulating landscape. Hills slowly changed shapes and colors as the sun altered its position in the morning sky. A light gray mist could be seen rising from the lower valleys, then, changing, it created a soft pink haze upon the snow fields.

"We're entering Basque territory now," said Marie as she interrupted their thoughts. "These people are amazing. Their civilization dates back before the year 778, when Charlemagne, the powerful King of the Franks, tried to conquer their lands without success. They were severely beaten and forced to retreat through the Pass of Roncesvalles. Soon after this, a segment of the Basque people decided to form an independent state and named it Navarre. That is the area into which we are now heading."

"I've heard that these people are dangerous and roam about these hills in bandit groups," interjected Lyle as he adjusted his position and loosened the neck of his shirt.

"They are considered to be quite fierce and sometimes impossible to deal or negotiate with, but you couldn't find a more devoted or protective people than these," answered Marie. Her voice had a proud ring to it as she continued. "They are considered to be the most Catholic of Catholics in Spain. They consider their religion an important part of their lives and keep it in the forefront of all activities. The state lost its status in 1841 after the King of Spain decided to unite the country for the sake of military strength and defense of their borders, economic exchange, and reduction of redundant government services. Needless to say, there were many who did not take kindly to this because they felt the government was going to attempt insidious changes into their way of life. Then in 1979, the Statute of Guernica gave the Basques independent government; nevertheless, pressures still continue for even greater autonomy for the people. So, you do occasionally encounter some of these groups as you travel through this area. But," she said thoughtfully, "I don't think they will bother us, because we are not a part of their government."

"I've read something about these people starting a Basque nationalist movement but the people of Navarre won't have anything to do with it," said Bill from the front seat.

"You're right, the people of Navarre are afraid to join willingly with anyone for fear of losing or being overcome by a stronger force."

"I admire them for their courage," said Lyle. "They have held their civilization together for many centuries and have accomplished the feat of nurturing a productive community."

"Anyway, the people of these mountains have had a most interesting life." Marie paused for a moment and gazed out at the scenery. "We're still traveling upon some of the ancient trails that saw many pilgrims pass on their way to either Rome, the Holy Land, or Santiago for worship. With their passing they brought with them their designs and culture. The pilgrims persuaded the Spaniards to erect many churches from Galicia to Catalonia. These structures were designed to be Romanesque so that the pilgrim would feel comfortable in a foreign land and so that there would be continuity in Christendom."

"They couldn't have chosen a more pleasing architectural design," stated Bill.

"We're going to be arriving in Jaca soon," continued

Marie as she reached for a soda from the auto's cooler and leaned back comfortably against the soft leather seat.

* * *

Back on the outskirts of Paris, Gerard got up from his tough black leather chair and strolled angrily toward the window. Parting the curtains, he looked through squinted eyes across the dry grounds and wondered if they were ever going to have rain. He didn't want to pay money for the gardeners to water the lawn and gardens unnecessarily when the skies could provide it free! The brightness of the sunny day hurt his eyes and he reached into his jacket pocket for his sunglasses. There was a knock at the office door.

"*Venir dans.*"

The heavy door opened slowly and Louis entered cautiously. He was Gerard's closest associate but chose to remain at a respectful distance. *His large, strong frame and dedication to me makes him an indispensable commodity,* thought Gerard as he motioned for Louis to come in.

"*Maître,* there is a man by the name of Abdel here with an important message for you."

"*Oui,* yes, let him in," replied Gerard impatiently as he retreated to the leather chair behind his desk. He would like to see this man, for he was the one who had first notified him about the discovery of the manuscripts. Abdel was in a key position to learn of important information. He was one of St. Martins in the Fields' groundskeepers, and he knew about Father Hugues' activities.

Abdel entered the darkened room and walked carefully over to the desk. He held his hat in both hands and looked beggarly in his sheepish unkempt appearance. Greasy hair and pasty skin made him seem even more like a disgusting bloodsucking parasite.

"Well, what is it you want?" demanded Gerard. He was

in no mood to dally around with this scum, although he didn't want to completely sever his ties with this source of information.

"I've got more news for you, *monsieur*," stammered Abdel as he shifted his weight from one foot to the other.

"Well, spit it out, *mon ami*."

"I've just heard that Father Hugues has seen the two men from America and that he has sent them on to Spain with Ben's friend Marie."

"*Quoi?*" exploded Gerard as he jumped to his feet and slammed his fists onto the desk. This explosion startled Abdel and he cringed backwards. One never wanted to deliberately remain in the same room with Gerard when he became enraged.

"LOUIS!" he yelled as he stormed about the room, knocking over and kicking at the German shepherd that lay by the fireplace. The dog yelped and disappeared behind the sofa, wanting to be away from his master's fearful outburst.

Louis peaked around the door and quickly entered.

"Louis, the Americans are not dead," Gerard growled as he faced his man nose to nose.

"They couldn't have escaped that plane crash," answered Louis with a confused look. "How could they have escaped? Everyone was reported to have perished." He looked across at Abdel and said angrily, "You must be mistaken, how could you come here and give us such false information?" He strode across the room and grabbed Abdel by the collar. Raising him off the floor, he began to shake the little man vigorously. Abdel swung out against Louis with his arms and fists but couldn't begin to strike him.

"You liar, I'll fix you."

"Wait, Louis," Gerard interrupted the struggle. "Let's see what this scum has to say for himself" Gerard took

Abdel by the arm and pushed him roughly onto the sofa. "Now tell us again; the truth this time or I will allow Louis to pull your fingernails out."

Abdel began to shake all over and tears started spilling onto his grimy flannel shirt.

"*Plaire, plaire.* It is the truth, I swear on my mother's grave," choked Abdel as he wiped his nose on his sleeve. "I overheard this information as I was passing the office door of Father Hugues yesterday afternoon. I wouldn't lie to you, sir." He looked up pathetically at Gerard who was glaring down at him.

"If they escaped that crash," said Louis, "it must have been a miracle."

"Rubbish," bellowed Gerard as he turned toward Louis. "Why haven't you and the others been able to get Ben to talk?" His face was dark with anger as his nostrils flared.

"We've been trying everything on him, but he won't cave in."

"Well, we're going to modify our plans. We're going to take him and travel to Spain. We must find these people pronto." He turned back to Abdel and said with a softer tone, "Thank you for giving us this information and now you may go." He reached into his pocket and brought out a roll of bills. Fingering off four, he handed them to Abdel and waved him towards the door in dismissal.

Abdel rose quickly and left the room before Gerard would have a chance to change his mind.

"Let's go see how Ben is doing," said Gerard, thinking that it was time for some action.

The two made their way through the main corridor of the old mansion until they arrived at a door near the rear. Louis retrieved a key from his pocket and unlocked it. He then proceeded down a circular flight of stony stairs that were darkened by the lack of proper lighting. Gerard followed closely and together they arrived in a large room that was lighted only by kerosene lanterns. The air smelled strongly of stale dampness and foul mildew. Water dripped from the ceiling and slippery black moss grew on the stone floor.

"Over here," said Louis as he motioned toward the far wall. He picked up one of the lanterns from a table and began to approach the location where he had left Ben. The light flickered more strongly now and its beams fell upon the figure of a man hanging by his arms. Large iron chains had been attached to his wrists that held him suspended inches from the ground. His head was slumped and on his bare chest were tiny rivulets of blood mixed with sweat trickling down from his battered head and neck. Barefoot and unconscious, Ben was no longer able to respond to their threats.

"Ben," said Gerard, slapping Ben across the face. "Wake up and talk to us."

"Shall I throw some water on him?" asked Louis.

"Get Joe and Nimes down here, then take him down. I want him cleaned up, dressed and ready to leave with us in three hours. I've got to make several telephone calls and pack. See that you fellows prepare also."

"Yes, boss," answered Louis as he turned to the telephone on the nearby wall.

"Be at the rear entrance and have him presentable!"

* * *

The Rolls glided gracefully along the asphalt highway that curved through the Spanish countryside. The beautiful green valleys were marked only by colorful villages and cottages that lined the way toward the coast. Sure enough, they were able the spot the Romanesque churches and hermitages of orders without much difficulty. Marie told them that north of Xavier was the Leyre Monastery, Navarre's center for spiritual growth during the 11th century. Kings celebrated there and gained strength from the order and from communion with God for their leadership. Gorgeous Romanesque architecture sprang up from the earth and struck magnificently at the sky. Rough mountains surrounded this haven and only the peacefully blessed, in searching of a closeness with God, would find the time to manage the winding road to the location. Presently, the Benedictine monks have restored it after its abandonment during the last century and it once again sparkles brightly in the midday sun for all those who come.

They arrived in Jaca shortly after noontime and Marie pointed out their beautiful cathedral that stood silhouetted against the mountains.

"This one is supposed to be the most lovely of all the cathedrals in Spain. It has original Romanesque frescoes and the purest, most meticulous stone work that was ever erected. Its domed cathedral ceiling is awesome and the stained glass pictures of Christ and the saints come to life when sunbeams shine through them."

"We should stop at the El Parque for lunch if it is open for business," interjected Oliver while the Rolls waited at a traffic light. The streets were filled with visitors moving about eagerly, trying to locate the most important treasures of the town. Colorful attire fitted the local men and women as they showed their wares and customs of the area.

"Good idea, Oliver," said Bill as he stretched and tried to straighten his clothing. Marie and Lyle quickly agreed and Oliver knowingly turned right at the corner. Two blocks down he pulled the Rolls up to the entrance of the restaurant and the doorman motioned for a boy to take the auto. The exterior of the facility was nothing extraordinary, but as they entered the interior they quickly realized that they were in for a treat. The menu consisted of Aragonese cuisine and other dishes that were typical for the region, such as *chilindron* or *magras con tomato* and peaches in wine.

Luncheon conversation was pleasant as they discussed their last few days and what the disappearance of Ben meant.

"Do you think we'll ever see him again?" asked Marie as she laid down her fork. She couldn't seem to swallow when the memory of Ben emerged into her thoughts.

"I think that somewhere, somehow, he will reappear when the time is right," reassured Bill as he patted her hand.

"I'm going to contact Father Hugues as soon as we arrive in Santander. He may have heard something about Ben by now and perhaps he has discovered who is darkening our trail," said Lyle with confidence returning. He did feel better now after beginning to take sustenance, and once again envisioned hope for their project. He smiled at Marie who was studying his face. Their eyes met for a long moment and he felt a blush creep upward from his neck. *She is beautiful,* he thought, as he averted his eyes downward. His heart pounded and his breathing became shallow. *Why was she affecting him so?* There was a feeling of closeness towards her that was illogical and hard to explain. He knew that she belonged to his friend Ben and that he had no earthly right to imagine the situation otherwise. He took a deep breath and touched the napkin to his perspiring upper lip.

"Do you think that the Templars could have arrived this far down into Spain?" asked Bill of Marie, breaking the silence.

"I don't know, it's a possibility."

"Father Hugues stated that the ship which left the Abbey of Jumieges probably went to the seaports east of Santander," recalled Lyle thoughtfully. "I think we should start there and ask persons who are connected with historical institutions. There might be some information or clues that may be kept in their archives."

"You're right, Lyle," responded Oliver excitedly. It wasn't often they saw him this way and looked at him quizzically. "I also have a strong hunch that they landed near the ports of San Sebastian, Laredo or Santander. Frequently, there were large cargoes of Spanish wine and wool shipped from their harbors to northern countries during those years."

The others leaned forward eagerly.

"The ports along the Bay of Biscay were, according to some reports, the jewels of the Spanish emperor's kingdom. This was the closest possible location for them to escape after the orders from King Philip were given."

Bill nodded his head. "From this general location we will determine the best direction to go next."

The others agreed and after Lyle paid the waiter they returned to the auto and headed towards Pamplona, the city of the bulls.

* * *

Abdel staggered along the darkened streets of Paris, aimlessly wandering alone and not caring where he might end for the night. His senses were dulled from whiskey and his body sick from a fever that he had been carrying for weeks. Food had not touched his mouth for several days and he wondered if his wife would recognize him anymore.

The blackness of stone stairs to the right beckoned him to rest awhile and he allowed himself to sink into the void, striking the concrete hard. Taking another drink from his bottle, he stretched his legs out. Why were they cramping so badly? He couldn't understand them becoming so weakened and unable to hold him up properly. He reached down with one hand and felt for his knees. He felt again. Perspiration broke on his forehead and he grabbed at his legs with both hands. His legs weren't there! Or at least he couldn't feel them. Shock and disbelief surged through his head. *What was happening?*

"You are damned, *mon fils*," came a man's voice from somewhere in the darkness.

Abdel jumped and looked about wild-eyed and shaken.

"You are going to die," the voice was stronger and penetrating into the very soul that Abdel had remaining. A sudden feeling of utter abandonment overwhelmed him as he realized that everything was coming to an end. This was it; he had committed the unpardonable sin and was going to be punished for it. Why had he become so greedy and joined forces with the likes of Gerard and his friends? How could he have committed such a betrayal as eavesdropping on his friend Father Hugues and then selling the information for a few francs?

Abdel started to shake violently as the realization of death flooded his being. He began to sob uncontrollably and with his last thoughts he remembered a song that his mother used to sing: *"Amazing grace, how sweet the sound, that saved a wretch like me."* Could there possibly be salvation or at least forgiveness from the priest he had offended? He silently vowed to God that if he could make restoration, he would never again slip into this awful state. He would never again associate with men whose characters were questionable. A moment passed, and he slowly reached down to once again feel his numb legs. *Thank God*, thought Abdel, *they've returned for one more walk to the confessional.*

Abdel located a taxi and had the driver take him directly to St. Nicholas so that he could find Father Hugues. The night was starless and the only brightness that lighted the city was from the street lanterns or an occasional passing auto. Abdel's head pounded and his heart ached as he thought of the upcoming meeting with the old priest. Father Hugues didn't deserve this act of hostility, after all of the kindness that he had previously shown him.

The taxi arrived at the cathedral and Abdel gave the cabby his last bill. He looked toward the church and noted that the only light was coming from the priest's area. Could it be that Father was still up?

He knocked on the door and waited for the sounds of someone coming. *It must be approximately midnight*, he thought, as he shuffled his feet on the doormat. Straightening his clothes, he waited for the door to open.

"*Bonjour*, Abdel," Father Hugues said kindly.

* * *

Oliver had just turned onto the highway leading west of Bilbao. It was lovely to see the ocean and it made his heart joyful to be near water again. He loved the fragrance of the sea and the lifestyle of those who made their living from employment with sea activities. The sun was approaching its final position in the sky before setting and he wondered if they were going to make it to Santander that evening.

"This is gorgeous," Marie stated as she pressed her nose against the window.

The fishing boats were coming in for the evening and fishermen were gathering their nets together for storage. Large baskets of fish were hauled ashore by assistants and their children were milling gleefully about the laborers, hoping that they could be of some service.

They passed family beaches that were dotted with red, green, yellow, and blue striped umbrellas, all making the area quite festive. *No doubt they were enjoying a dinner of a local fresh catch and sipping on some local wine,* thought Lyle as he absorbed the beauty. The sand was refreshingly white and immaculate for the sunbathers who had been there that day.

"Keep your eyes open for any sign of old docks and stone buildings that may have been erected during the thirteenth century," said Lyle as he studied the map "We should be getting close to the Templar landing location."

"I hope that there is something still standing," stated Bill hopefully.

"If all those cathedrals, monasteries and government office buildings that we've seen over the past few days have stood the test of time, then there should be some significant remnant of an old building remaining along here now."

Everyone was looking out of the auto's window, straining their eyes to be the first to get a glimpse of a Templar hostel. The coast had some rocky areas that appeared every few miles. On these expanses a few stone houses or a restaurant was built, making an exquisite setting for some landowner.

"Look there," exclaimed Bill, pointing up along the coast to a white castle near the water.

Suddenly Lyle felt his heart jump in his chest. The castle!

"Hey Lyle, what's the matter? You look like you've seen a ghost!" said Bill as he leaned over and took Lyle by the arm.

Lyle's face was ashen white and he couldn't say anything, but only stared in the direction they were pointing.

Oliver pulled the auto over to the edge of the road and turned off the engine.

"What is it?" he asked.

"You won't believe it, guys," Lyle began after taking a deep breath. "I had a dream two nights ago when we were at St. Bertrands." He told them of the extraordinary dream, remembering all the details as he went along. The group was silent as he related his story, believing every word. When he finished he looked at them and asked, "Now, what do you think, now that we've seen this castle? *It's just like the one I saw in my dream.*"

"There's no doubt in my mind," said Oliver, thoroughly convinced that Lyle had experienced a revelation. "I think we're on the right trail."

"You must have had that dream for a reason," murmured Marie who was dumbfounded and eagerly awaiting Lyle's word.

All were thoughtful for several minutes and then Bill interjected, "Your dream of a white castle must have been a prewarning for you to look for it as we traveled. This must be the location for us to start our search for Templar information." He was serious and Lyle nodded his head in agreement.

"Yes, that's right. Let's proceed on to Santander and stay there for the night. Tomorrow we can inquire around and then return to this area."

"I'm for that!" responded Bill and Marie in unison.

"I think that would be a great plan" Oliver now said. "We've had a very tiring day and a night's rest will be important if we want to think clearly tomorrow."

Oliver pulled the auto out again onto the highway and headed for the next major city. The traffic was moderate and didn't pose a problem for driving. The sun was just beginning to set in the west when they arrived on the outskirts of Santander and people were starting to either close shop or were dressing to attend dinner at the local casino, which was well-known throughout Spain.

"I've got reservations at the Real Hotel," said Lyle as he

looked about the area. "It's supposed to be near the beaches."

Oliver swung the Rolls down the street that led toward the ocean. A mist was coming in from the water, and the street lanterns were coming on with the fading of daylight.

After rounding the last corner near the ocean, Oliver pointed out, "There it is, the Real. It is really REAL." He chuckled to himself and the others laughed. It was an elegant hotel that appeared to date back to the early part of the century. Lavish architecture and beautifully curtained windows made the hotel very attractive. Lyle was glad that he had chosen this place upon Father Hugues' suggestion.

After they registered and settled themselves, they enjoyed a dinner of seafood, garden salad, hard rolls and white wine. They all decided to retire early, and bid each other a good night—except for Lyle and Bill, who decided that they would try to contact Father Hugues in Paris.

"Bill, come to my room for a short while. I think it is important that we communicate with Father Hugues this evening," Lyle had an urgency in his voice that Bill hadn't heard before.

"Sure, sounds like a wonderful idea."

They entered Lyle's room and he went over to the closet and removed the leather briefcase from the top shelf. The time was about 10:00 P.M. and he hoped that Father Hugues was at home.

Connecting the computer to the telephone system, Lyle dialed the residence of the priest.

"*Bonjour*," came the voice of Father Hugues.

"Hello Father, this is Lyle."

"Lyle. Am I ever glad to hear from you. Are you all right?"

"Yes, we just arrived in Santander and have registered at the Real Hotel."

"Was your trip uneventful, that is to say, you didn't have any difficulty, did you?"

"It couldn't have been better." Lyle went on to tell him about his dream and their coming across a castle that appeared very similar.

"Sounds like you're on the right track."

"Have you heard anything of Ben?"

"No." Father hesitated and then continued, "I just finished talking with a fellow who works on the grounds, and he has related a shocking story to me Lyle."

"Tell me, don't leave me in suspense," said Lyle motioning Bill to come over and listen in. Lyle clicked on the word "EAVESDROP" and the computer screen opened a file that was able to type out the words that were said over the wire.

"I have information which was given to me in the sanctity of the confessional. It concerns the gravest of sins, but the penitent was so stricken with remorse that he asked me to notify Marie, you, Bill and Oliver. Please understand that under the seal of the confessional I cannot give you his name and must ask you and the others to maintain strict confidence."

"Yes, we won't let the information go further."

"There is a crime syndicate that is located here in Paris that deals in stolen art. It is headed by a man named Gerard, who is reportedly quite ruthless and has stolen millions from galleries and private estates."

"Is he the one who entered Ben's apartment and apparently kidnapped him?"

"Yes. This gardener was working for St. Nicholas and was the leak about the information on the manuscript. He confessed to me this evening after coming from Gerard's place this afternoon. The man was somewhat drunk and had sustained an awful injury to his legs. He thought that this was a curse brought upon him by his wickedness and decided to come clean."

"What was this afternoon business about with Gerard?"

"That's the really bad news, my friend," began Father Hugues.

"Well, we might as well hear it," replied Lyle as he gave Bill a painful look.

"This man overheard me tell my secretary about you guys and the mission you were on. He went immediately to Gerard and related the story to him. As he was leaving, he heard Gerard tell his right-hand man that they were going to head straightaway to Spain in pursuit of these men and they were going to take Ben with them."

"My God," exclaimed Lyle as he looked at Bill in disbelief. "So they're coming down here. Well, I'm glad to hear that Ben is still alive."

"What would you have me do?"

"Keep your ears open for any further information regarding what these men are up to."

"Yes, I will; and you take care over the next few days. I pray that there will be some way for Ben to escape."

"Me too," answered Lyle with sadness. "We're going to move quickly about the area tomorrow to establish the 'point of entry' that the Templars might have taken and then proceed from there."

"Good. Give my love to Marie and hellos to the others."

"Thank you, Father, for the information."

"Keep in touch with me, okay?"

"Of course. Good-bye for now."

"God bless you all." Lyle heard the receiver click and the computer read "TERMINATED."

"Well, we're in for a good time now," kidded Bill as he strolled over to the window. The bright moon was out and reflecting light off tiny fishing vessels on the dark water.

"I wonder how the folks are doing back home," he said as he turned toward Lyle.

"I was just thinking about them myself."

"I can just hear Laura now, if she knew what kind of trouble I was getting into. She'd be telling me how I was nearing the end of my nine lives or that I was coming to the end of my rope. She gets so angry when I get close to danger."

"This is the first time that I've undertaken such an adventure," said Lyle as he entered the telephone number for Father Marcos. "I want you to know that I appreciate your coming along with me. I knew you'd be the right guy to ask. Now I'm just going to fill Father Marcos in on the latest happenings and see if he has any suggestions. Then I will contact 'DEX'."

The telephone rang several times before Father Marcos answered. He was surprised and pleased to hear news of their activities and that everyone was safe.

"I'm relieved to hear that your journey is going well."

"Yes it is," replied Lyle confidently. "We've arrived at Santander, Spain and will search the area for information about the Templars tomorrow."

"Have you come close to Castro Urdiales? It's a small village on the coast."

Lyle looked at his map and located the spot where they had seen the castle. "Yes, it's near the location where we spotted the castle that I saw in my dreams."

"That must be the Castle of Santa Ana. It is beautiful, as I remember." Father paused and then said, "Well, there is the Gothic Church of Santa Maria located nearby on the small fortified peninsula. It is quite beautiful and you must pay it a visit. There is a Bishop by the name of Father Jon Damasus who presides over the parish, whom I met once while traveling through Spain. Visit with him if you can. I think he might be able to shed some light on the subject in which you're interested."

"Yes, we will and thank you for the information. By the way, how is my grandmother doing?"

"She's doing very well, and I'm keeping an eye on her while you're away."

"Give her my love and tell her to take it easy on those bridge partners."

"Will do, and you folks be careful with your investigations about the place."

Lyle couldn't tell him about the latest kink in their plans, that one of the worst criminals in Spain was coming after them. Besides, he really didn't want them to worry more than they already were.

"Good-bye for now," said Lyle.

"Good-bye to you and may God bless," replied Father Marcos before hanging up.

Lyle disconnected the computer and placed it back into the briefcase with the manuscript.

He joined Bill by the window and gazed out over the night ocean. They had come far on their quest and obviously they had been under the protection of God's angels. The days ahead could be tough but Lyle had a feeling that their little group would be all right. Just as the stars were held in their intended places in the heavens by an unseen power, so were they protected and guided along their journey.

"Well, I am going to turn in and will see you about 7:00 in the morning at breakfast," said Bill, interrupting Lyle's thoughts.

"Okay, good night." Bill closed the door after him and Lyle again turned to the window and looked out at the night. Somewhere up there, beyond the barriers of the universe was God's heaven, he contemplated, with all its magnificence. The power that placed all the worlds in their proper spheres and then arranged for them to rotate on a schedule without colliding, must be an awful power to relate to. Yes, it was his God that had created this universe and it was He who created and cared for them. Lyle's anxieties started to dissipate and a peaceful calm filled his being as he turned away from the window. He didn't see the star that shot across the heavens, and then slowly disappeared into the outer universe, leaving a white cosmic trail behind, but he did feel the awesome power that controlled the world and confidently knew that God was everywhere.

10

The next morning at breakfast the four sat around a table in the dining room and were discussing the day's activities. The room was filling up rapidly with customers and they hoped there would be enough privacy for their deliberations.

"I've made a list of all the possible locations to visit and I would like to suggest that we split up and cover this town first. Then we can return to Castro Urdiàles," said Lyle as he brought out his note paper and pen. He told them of Father Hugues' conversation and warning. Marie gave a shallow cry of glee and then let out a groan of disappointment and distress. She was happy that Ben's whereabouts was known, but agonized over the thought that he was in the hands of ruthless men.

"Oh, poor Ben. I bet they've done some harm to him.

"You're right, my dear," interjected Bill. "Men of that nature are known to try and beat information out of people."

"If there's a chance that he can be rescued, I'm going to attempt it," blurted Oliver as he flexed his muscles. "They won't fool around with me very much."

"I hope there will be an opportunity," said Lyle, "but for now we will concentrate on locating our objective. We must try to make good time if we are to stay ahead of Gerard and his men."

"Okay," responded Bill eagerly, "give us our assignments and we will begin work, that is after I finish this cup of coffee and apple fritter."

Lyle pushed aside several items on the table and made room for an area map. Giving each a piece of paper with notations written on them, he said, "Now, orient yourselves to where we are and where you will be going. Inquire around quietly, do not attract unnecessary attention. Return here when you have found something, or at least by noon. Is everyone okay with that?"

"I am," answered Marie, eager to be gone.

"I'm ready," agreed Bill, standing on his feet.

"I'm gone," as Oliver turned and left the room.

"Boy," laughed Bill, "he's certainly taking this job seriously."

Marie glanced at her paper and then studied the city map carefully. Standing, she slipped on her light gray trench coat over her white slacks and sweater. Her dark hair cascaded gracefully over the shoulders and her dark eyes sparkled brightly in anticipation about the prospect of locating some meaningful data. Nodding politely to Lyle and Bill, she turned and exited.

Marie's assignment was to investigate the local courthouse and try to find information concerning the past land holdings of the Knights Templars. She felt confident that she would be able to manage this task and strode with assurance across the town square. The morning sky was filled with a gray fog that was rolling in from the Gulfe de Gascogne. In the distance she could hear the mournful sounds of a harbor foghorn as it cast a somewhat eerie atmosphere over the countryside. There was a cool dampness in the air and Marie was glad that she had worn a coat. She could barely make out the buildings in the town square through the mist and then spotted a structure that looked as if it were a government seat. The courthouse was located at the opposite side, a magnificent structure that was probably a couple of hundred years old, thought Marie as she approached and studied the people who were gathered about the entrance.

The fragrance of the sea was in the air and she remembered the time that her father had taken her on a sea voyage with him when she was sixteen. Those were the days when life seemed full of surprises, and wonderful things were waiting around every corner. Her father had created a wonderland filled with enchantment and it wasn't until her days in college that she began to realize that not everything in the world was honest.

She smiled at the men who were eyeing her curiously and they smiled back in a timid yet gregarious manner. They seemed pleasant and were probably conversing about the day's upcoming activities. Stepping aside, they let her pass up the stairs and through the large doors that then led onto the entrances of various legal offices.

There was one door that had the sign "LAND" over it and she went over and opened it. Looking around inside she spotted a counter with a clerk standing behind, thumbing through the pages of a book. Walking closer, she bravely cleared her voice and said, *"Perdon, senor."* The gentleman glanced up and looked at her quizzically.

"Si, mayo yo ayuda tu?" he said in Spanish. His eyes glowed radiantly and his white teeth sparkled behind the beautiful smile. *A truly handsome fellow,* thought Marie as she blushed and returned his greeting.

After placing her bag on the counter she continued in Spanish, "I'm wondering if your office still maintains land records from several centuries ago. Specifically, I'm interested in the twelfth and thirteenth centuries and the estates that belonged to the Knights Templars."

The gentleman looked at her for a moment with a puzzled expression. He turned around and walked to the bookshelf on the opposite wall containing hundreds of hardback ledgers. After searching through them for a few minutes, he turned and walked back to where she was waiting.

"The information you are looking for is not located in the records that we have here." He noticed the disappointment that crossed her face and proceeded. "There are however, quite a few old cases filled with records in the basement if you would like to search through them. I can help you if you'd like."

"*Si*," Marie answered, happy to learn that her endeavors weren't ending too soon. "My name is Marie Molay. What is yours?"

"Don Juan," said the young man, opening the side gate for her to enter. She smiled to herself and followed him to the rear door. They entered a small staircase that was dimly lit and started down into a musty smelling basement. The wooden steps creaked and each step forward was beginning to become more frightening. Cobwebs brushed against Marie's cheek and quickened her heart. Was she trying to be too brave on this adventure? Was she heading into a situation that she was going to have trouble getting out of? Marie's mind was racing when they finally arrived at the bottom and Don swung open a door that ground noisily on its hinges. Reaching upward, he pulled a hanging chain and a bulb lighted a large room that was filled with numerous shelves, cardboard cartons and wooden boxes.

"Let's see if I can locate the material that coincides with the years that you are looking for," said Don, beginning to examine hand-written notations on the ends of the containers. Marie waited as he slowly went down the first row and then started to inspect the cases in the second row. There was a layer of dust over everything and spiderwebs hanging from the shelves. She was sure that nobody had been to visit this room in centuries. The notations were in Spanish and not easy to decipher through the smears and dirt. Minutes went by while the two were engrossed in the search.

"OH, OH!" yelled Marie as she jumped back and began to slap herself about the head and upper body. "Help," she called. "There's something on me!"

Don came running from around the corner and began to search her over, trying to find the offending creature.

"*Tener* still," he commanded and she froze in her tracks. Moving slowly behind her, he picked up a book that was lying on a nearby shelf, and carefully raised it and brought it down swiftly, knocking a large hairy black spider to the floor. Marie hurled herself back toward the door from where they had entered and waited for Don to put an end to the creature's existence.

"There!" he stated emphatically as he brought his foot down again and again on the flattened body. "He won't be going anywhere anymore," He walked over to her. "Are you all right? It didn't bite you, did it?"

"No, it didn't bite and I'm okay. How are you doing on your search?"

"I think I'm getting close to the location. Come and look." He turned and led the way back to the area where he was examining one of the wooden boxes near the floor.

He looked at the front of the box again. "Yes, I think this may be the one. It has the dates A.D. 1100 to A.D. 1200 on it." He pulled the carton off the shelf and began to pry open the lid with his pocket knife. After some work, the wooden boards fell to the floor and the contents were exposed, lying as they had been left several hundreds of years ago. The paper had turned yellow and was brownish along the edges. Marie carefully lifted a sack that was tied with a piece of cloth and sat on a crate beside the box. Gently, she untied the package and began to leaf through the material. She was careful not to break any of the brittle pages and was filled with unimaginable ecstasy as she thought of the years that were represented here.

"We've been talking about sending these boxes over to the museum," said Don as he interrupted her reflections.

"*Si*, that would be an appropriate thing to do."

Suddenly her heart jumped and she laughed with glee. "Here it is! A paper titled 'KNIGHTS TEMPLARS'." Marie held it up and together they studied the small ink scribbles that had been made on the paper so many years ago.

The property of the Knights Templars shall be without taxation by the government which controls the lands of Spain. These noble men shall be respected and great honors shall be bestowed upon their heads for all the assistance they have provided to the kingdom in dealing with its enemies.

The Castle of Santa Ana is their headquarters and there they shall abide safely and without trouble from anyone.

Signed on this day, June 13, 1153 by His Lordship and King Alfonso I of Castille.

There was a sharp sound behind her, as of lightning striking an object, and both of them immediately looked in the direction of the light bulb. The light was flickering, first threatening to be extinguished and then again stabilized into a steady glow. There wasn't anything else around and Marie glanced back at the clerk. "I hope your electricity doesn't fail."

"I hope not too. Maybe there is some faulty wiring," puzzled the man. He proceeded with his search through the pages and then suddenly exclaimed, "Here is something!" He paused and studied the writing carefully. Then he opened a large atlas that was lying nearby and thumbed through its pages. He was undoubtedly searching for some location.

"Here," he announced, pointing at a spot along the northern coast. "There was a Templar Castle or Hostel near Castro Urdiales. It was called the Castle of Santa Ana. Unfortunately, it has been desolate for many years, but you can still imagine the beauty that once existed when you see it."

"*Si,*" said Marie, "I think we saw that place yesterday when we were driving here. Is there anyone around that might know of the Templars and what became of them?"

"I don't know," hesitated the clerk. "You might try the church nearby, the Church of Santa Maria. Bishop Jon Damasus is there and could probably assist you. I've heard that the church keeps some records in its archives and there is a chance that you might locate what you're looking for there. Remember," he said as he looked at her in a kindly manner, "the Knights Templars were a benefit to Spain and we should like their reputations to remain pure."

"*Gracias*, we have every intention of doing just that," said Marie and extended her hand in a farewell shake. "Could I get a photocopy of these two pages?"

"*Seguro.*" he replied as he picked up the papers and pushed the box back onto the shelf. He had been most helpful and it pleased her that her impression of the Spanish people was as she remembered it.

As she exited the main room upstairs with papers in hand, she noticed a man with dark sunglasses standing in the corner, staring in her direction. His hat prevented her from detecting the color of his hair and she hurriedly pushed on through the doors in a hasty departure, giving Don a farewell wave of her hand.

There was still time to examine the remainder of the town square and Marie, thinking that she should stroll around to see if perhaps the stranger in the Land Office might follow her, started walking more slowly. She settled into window-shopping, stopping frequently to study paintings that were created by local artists and original clothing that was made by Spanish designers. There was an air of holiday all around with colorful hangings in store windows and flags flying in the breeze. Tourists were spending the day visiting various spots of interest about the city and then spending their dollars in the evening at the world famed Grand Casino del Sardinero. She glanced over her shoulder frequently to see if anyone was following her, especially the strange man.

Santander had been the provincial capital since the eighteenth century, when the French inhabited the area and rebuilt it after a fire destroyed the major portion of the city's center. Marie learned from a resident that the area supported a major university and that there was an annual international music festival which attracted thousands of foreigners. Nearby, on the Peninsula de La Magdalena, was the summer palace for nobility that was visited annually by the royal family. It had been constructed for the bride of Alfonso XIII in 1912 and was later donated to the University.

Marie finally made her way back to the Hotel Real and met Lyle as he was coming from the opposite direction. She looked about once more but did not find the man that she had seen at the Land Office, so she joined Lyle with a bright smile on her face.

"Hi, how did you do?" she asked, as she reached for the door.

"Not great," he replied, moving ahead to open the door for her. "The university is large, but I did manage to find some interesting information in their library."

"Wait till we're all together," she interrupted and entered the lobby.

They were the first to arrive back from their expedition and chose a table in the lounge where they could watch the hotel door. A waiter approached quickly and asked if they wanted anything.

"Just a glass of iced tea for me," Marie said as she removed her coat.

"I'll have the same," stated Lyle, "and could you bring us a few peanuts?"

The waiter nodded and returned in a few minutes with their request. Marie noticed that he seemed unusually interested in them and was beginning to feel uncomfortable when Oliver and Bill appeared.

"Hey, everyone's back," stated Lyle with pleasure, "and on time."

"Let's order some lunch while we review our information," said Bill, rubbing his stomach.

Everyone agreed and Lyle motioned the waiter to return. After placing their orders, Lyle asked for a report from each when they were alone again.

Bill told of his visit to the museums and the interesting display of ancient artifacts that attracted many tourists. There was a collection of clothing, armor and weapons that were used by knights from the eleventh to the thirteenth century. He had asked a museum assistant about information concerning the Knights Templars and was shown a large collection of materials such as armor, banners, books and tapestries that had once belonged to them.

"I noticed a small leather-bound volume and asked if it would be possible to look at it closer. He thought it would be okay and allowed me to examine it."

"Was there anything important?" asked Lyle excitedly.

"It seemed to be a record of the Knights' activities in

this part of Spain. It listed lands that had been procured or that were given to them. Gifts from different dignitaries were listed and programs such as hostels for pilgrims and the defense of Spanish territories that they were involved with for the king. There was no mention about the arrest of the Knights that had occurred in France, or of those few that had fled into Spain. There was also no conclusion in the record that would indicate they were leaving the territory or dissolving the Order."

"That's too bad," said Oliver as he sipped on his lemonade.

"Oliver, did you come across anything?" questioned Lyle.

"I walked along the coastal area and talked with the locals who were busy with their fishing materials. Unfortunately, they couldn't go out on their fishing expeditions because of the heavy fog, but they were still busy preparing for the moment that it lifted. They certainly enjoy their work. Anyway, after questioning several concerning their knowledge about the Knights Templars, I began to get the feeling that they were uncomfortable talking of the subject. They would look at each other suspiciously and then shake their heads."

"You remember that the Knights did not have the same fate in Spain as they did in other European countries," Bill said. "Perhaps they continued to live on in their Order, assisting with the local armies in detouring the enemy and providing for pilgrims." Bill had an interesting thought.

"They might have continued to function quite well here, but they also might have changed their name in order to prevent the French from locating them," said Lyle.

"Maybe the Spanish wanted to protect them and that is why everyone seems reluctant to say anything," suggested Marie.

"Is that the impression you received when you went to the courthouse?" asked Lyle, looking at her intently.

"Yes, I did get that sense," she replied with a touch of satisfaction in her voice. She retrieved the photocopies from her bag and related the sequence of events to them. In closing she told of the strange sound that they heard in the basement and about the man who was watching her from the corner. Lyle appeared suddenly anxious and asked her if she had noticed him following her.

"No, I walked about the city quite a while too and didn't see him again or anyone else that looked suspicious."

Lyle then told the group about his experience at the university. It was recommended that he search for information in the library and he did so, but with little success. There was of course information on the Knights Templars, their life and demise, but no other material concerning their status between the thirteenth century and now.

"Well, I think that Marie has the most logical information to follow. Also, Father Marcos recommended that we talk with the same bishop at the church of Santa Maria. It's lucky that we were planning to return to that location anyway," announced Lyle as he motioned to the waiter for the check.

"Let's take a few minutes to freshen up in our rooms and then meet in the lobby. Oliver can bring the Rolls around to the entrance, okay Oliver?" asked Lyle as he nodded in the driver's direction. Oliver responded affirmatively and they departed the lounge.

Lyle entered his room and went to the closet to pick up his briefcase. The door was slightly ajar and Lyle stopped suddenly, his heart beginning to beat quickly. Was there going to be someone behind the door? Not another encounter! This was starting to aggravate him. Angrily, he threw open the door and looked about the area while standing poised, ready to strike out at any intruder. No one appeared. He looked carefully, high and low, to see if he could locate anyone. Nothing was revealed. He felt somewhat easier and noted that his pulse was beginning to slow down. Retrieving his briefcase from the upper shelf, he turned, crossed the room and laid it on the bed. Then he returned to the closet to obtain a clean white shirt. He didn't notice the outer door close slowly or hear the click of the latch as it locked.

Oliver had the Rolls in front of the hotel when Lyle joined the others. The weather had deteriorated into a heavy downpour and lightning could faintly be seen through the northern fog bank. Under the umbrella of the doorman they left the hotel lobby and climbed into the auto. The time was about 1:30 P.M. and they knew there would be plenty of time to investigate the old Templar Castle and visit Bishop Damasus at the church, if he was available.

The drive back to Castro Urdiales was pleasant and yet produced some anxiety for the group. Thunder could be heard in the distance and the driving was tedious for Oliver as he strained to visualize the road ahead through the pouring rain. Other autos were using headlights and Oliver quickly turned his on for maximum visibility. Silence permeated the atmosphere as the travelers were enveloped in their own thoughts, hoping that their trip would be without incident.

They arrived in Castro Urdiales about two hours later; the rain was beginning to subside. There were still sounds of thunder rolling in the distance and an occasional flash of light as the electrical storm moved away. All were straining their eyes to catch a glimpse of the Templar Castle and then, suddenly, there was a sign pointing the way to the coastal area.

"There, Castle of Santa Ana," said Bill as he pointed to a small white sign that was partially hidden among some juniper bushes.

Oliver turned the auto down a narrow graveled road and headed out onto a peninsula. Ahead of them they could see a clearing in the trees and then, there it was, the Castle! It rose upward from the top of a hill and out of the fog, giving everyone chills as they gazed upon it. Overlooking the beautiful Cantabian beach and though somewhat dismantled by time, the castle seemed to possess an unspoken power over them. After a few moments, they got out of the auto and started toward the former home of the Knights Templars.

"Doesn't it look ghostly?" Marie interrupted the silence that had settled on all of them.

They looked at each other with eyes that spoke of curiosity.

"Follow me," said Oliver as he started up the path that led toward the main gate. His stride was confident and bold as he entered the castle walls. The others followed and soon they were investigating rooms, hallways, arches, stairs and other structures that had been left standing. Obviously, there were no small artifacts left lying around the grounds. They had probably already been obtained for museums and private collectors.

After an hour of searching about the old castle, Lyle found himself on a balcony overlooking the sea. The stone railings were still marked with the carvings of some medieval stone mason and were quite attractive. He gazed at the walls that had been erected by the Knights and began to wish that he could have known them personally. He admired their strength and their devotion to the Order's sworn word that they would defend the people of the Church.

The fog was beginning to settle in again and the upper

portions of the castle were starting to disappear into the gray mist. Lyle strained his eyes at the tower and longed for a chance to help redeem these fearless men of God. Then across the miles of sandy beaches came a sound that he remembered well. The voices of the monks from Santo Domingo De Silos, giving the countryside a moment of holy blessing with their melodious music. Lyle was stunned as he listened, afraid to move for fear that he would break this precious spell that had him entranced. Then his eyes saw a movement along the ocean's beach. There, coming on horseback, dressed in armor and wearing the white cape of the Templars, were several Knights riding toward the castle. Their banners held high for the wind to catch the colors and their faces beaming with good news for the master.

Lyle was mesmerized in ecstasy as he idly wondered if Bill, Marie and Oliver were catching this magnificent display of the Knights. As they began to fade into the foggy terrain, Lyle reached out his hand over the balcony as if trying to forestall their departure. The last wisp of a crossed cape disappeared and along with it the music that had so hauntingly held him. He moved slowly and carefully away from the edge as he heard Bill calling to him. Giving one last glance toward the ocean, Lyle could hardly wait for their search to continue.

"Hey," came the voice of Marie as she spotted him coming toward them. "Have you seen everything, or at least what you were looking for?"

"Yes, I've found what I was searching for and feel even more confident that we're on the correct route."

"I do too," replied Bill.

"Yes, I've just had the most wonderful feeling come over me and I can't explain why," said Marie.

Lyle noticed Oliver smiling and wondered if he too had experienced something unusual.

"Well, let's head on over to the Church of Santa Maria," Lyle suggested as he headed for the gate and their auto.

The Gothic church was located about five hundred feet from the castle, and its lovely French sculptures could be seen through the incoming fog. The unfinished towers, for some unknown reason, were like the Notre Dame Cathedral of Paris. The church looked down upon a harbor where fishermen made their living and tourists spent hours enjoying the warm sun. Lyle wondered if the Knights had assisted in the erection of the church, and if they had worshiped there.

Oliver stopped the auto in the parking lot located at the foot of the hill and they proceeded to wind their way along a cobblestone path that led to the entrance. The damp green grounds were dotted with several tall black spruce and appeared very picturesque as they gradually faded into the fog at higher levels. The church's stained glass windows were glowing with radiant colors despite the darkness, and singing could be heard coming from within.

"It's about 5:00 and I imagine that mass will be starting soon," said Marie as she approached the huge carved wooden doors.

"It's okay with me if we attend mass," stated Bill as he opened the door and the group entered. "I just hope that we'll be able to locate the Bishop."

The four entered the sanctuary after genuflecting and touched the Holy Water that was in a side receptacle. There were candles placed between each window and about the altar. The singing was coming from behind an iron grille that separated the main sanctuary from the cloister. Lyle thought it sounded like Mozart's Mass in C major, *The Coronation*, and was happy to find that the Spanish enjoyed this music as much as the Americans liked it.

There were a few people kneeling in prayer and Lyle, along with the others, joined them in quiet meditation. *It is good to be at Mass again*, thought Marie as she began to pour her heart out to God for the safety of Ben. She wanted to pledge Christ something for Ben's safe return but she could not decide what to give. Then she decided to promise Him that she would always be true to the Church and that she would defend its precepts in the face of all adversity. The incense from the altar spiraled toward the gates of heaven along with the smoke from the candles and the singing of a dozen voices. Hearts were refreshed with God's peaceful blessings once again.

After Mass had ended and the procession had passed, they followed the Bishop to the entrance and waited for an appropriate moment to approach him.

"Are you Bishop Jon Damasus?" queried Lyle as he shook the hand of the priest.

"*Si*, I am he," replied the Bishop with a twinkle in his eye.

"My name is Lyle Longsworth. These are my close associates and friends," continued Lyle as he introduced them.

"We have come a long way searching for something important and would like for you to give us a moment of your time."

"*Si, mi amigo,* " Bishop Damasus looked about to see if there were other parishioners left to greet and then motioned for the four travelers to follow him. They left the sanctuary through a marbled arch and walked down a long, sheltered sidewalk that had pillars on one side. It ran along the edge of a courtyard that was crossed twelve times by cobblestone paths and filled with the fragrance from several gardens of white lilies. Even the mist from the fog didn't seem to dampen their beauty.

The Bishop led them through another door and down a corridor until they arrived at the end. Turning right, he opened a door that led to a spiraled staircase that curled upward.

"Please follow me and I will take you to my private study," he said as he started the climb.

They made four complete turns as they proceeded upward on a staircase that Lyle thought was crafted from white oak. There were three small windows that opened over the coastal shores and a hand-rail that seemed to be highly polished by the palms of many hands.

They arrived in a large room that overlooked the harbor where the walls were covered by shelves loaded with a variety of books ranging from philosophy to science. Bishop Damasus motioned for them to take chairs that were encircling a granite table located in the center of a multicolored rug.

"Now tell me about yourselves, and your request of me," stated the Bishop.

After seating themselves about the table, Lyle began by telling him of their interest in the Knights Templars and the possibility that there was a treasure to be found. Most of all, they were discovering the truth about the circumstances that surrounded the demise of the Order and noted that the real reasons for their subjugation were indeed the fault of King Philip. Lyle told of their journey across the Atlantic, the ill-fated flight, the kidnapping of Ben, and their trip into the Spanish territory. He told the Bishop that his friend from the United States, Father Marcos, had recommended that they come to him and request his assistance.

The Bishop looked at them through his wire-rimmed glasses while studying them closely. He was a stocky man in his late fifties with hair that was beginning to show gray along his temple hairline. He appeared to know what they were talking about but was hesitant about revealing his attitudes on the subject of the Knights Templars.

"You folks have been through a lot, that's plain to see. It is also apparent to me that you were led here by a power greater than mere human desire and therefore I am obliged to tell you everything that I know about the matter."

Lyle smiled and looked at Bill who was sitting on the edge of his chair. Marie was also listening with great interest and only Oliver seemed to be relaxed during this revelation.

"I do know of the events that transpired in France during the thirteenth century and of the demise of the Knights. I studied extensively on the matter during my years at the seminary in Rome. What you have discovered about the incident is all true. The Knights were accused wrongly and executed even in the absence of guilt."

"Why did all of this hostility toward the Catholic Church happen?" asked Bill. "I remember from history that France was devoutly Catholic during the 11th and 12th centuries. King Louis IX was a Christian king and led the country into prosperity. They were considered to be the strongest nation and were growing not only in wealth but intellectually as well."

"Yes, you are right about all of this," replied the Bishop as he rested his arms on the table. "Everyone was of one mind or religion and so they were basically without conflict on questions regarding virtue, God, creation of the world, and man's purpose, amongst other things. Then in the year 1200, the Paris University was established and strove to become the greatest educational institution in Europe. Its teachers were drawn from far and wide; among them were Thomas Aquinas, Duns Scotus and William of Ockham. William was known as the invincible physician because of his dynamic judgment, and for opening the philosophy of nominalism or reasonableness. By this he meant that man was able by his own intellect to figure out the science that was about him and provide logical explanations without the assistance of God or the Church. He started the movement toward intellectual freedom."

"I can see the trouble coming," interjected Lyle.

"Yes, there was a crisis building. Harsh words were exchanged between William and Pope John XXII. Then in 1294, Pope Boniface VIII became increasingly alarmed when he heard that the members of the University were calling themselves 'The Athens of Europe' and 'The Goddess of Wisdom.' They were even claiming to have authority on theology and that there now were 'two' beacons of light, the Church and the University."

"So this was the beginning of the division?" questioned Lyle.

"Yes, there were those who believed that the Church should no longer have authority and the situation began to worsen. Then in 1285, King Philip IV became ruler of France and started to unify the government against the Church, saying that he wanted to create a new country and establish a centralized government under his control. That was the beginning of the decline for the Catholic Church and the Knights Templars." The Bishop paused to take a drink of icewater that was brought to them by the housemaid.

"Trumped up charges were brought against the Knights, because they were one of the strongest military bodies in Europe and had an enormous amount of money. Philip probably figured that they might someday rise against him, in an attempt to defend the Church."

"This was certainly an interesting and yet a sad time in history," said Marie as she took a deep breath. "Why do you suppose that the Church didn't see it coming and do something?"

"I want you to come with me to the archives. There is some information there about Pope Clement that I think you will find fascinating," responded Bishop Damasus.

The Bishop stood and led them to the right wall. He pushed a button and two maple panels opened, revealing an elevator car within.

"Come, I'll take you in our elevator down to the archives; they contain most of the historical information in Spain. Not very many people know about this collection and I would prefer that you not reveal its location either." He led them into the car and pushed a button labeled LL2. The car started to move downward and the excited group waited in silence.

After a few minutes, the car came to a stop and the doors opened into one of the largest libraries that Lyle had ever seen. Rows of books reached from floor to ceiling and then extended from one end of the chamber to the other. Bishop Damasus went over to a computer that was sitting on a desk and switched it on. It appeared to Lyle that he was entering the description of some desired information and began scanning lists that were being shown. Several minutes passed as he searched the computer's database and then the marker came to rest on a particular name.

POPE CLEMENT V.

"If you will excuse me, I shall go and retrieve something that may be interesting," said the Bishop as he turned and disappeared down one of the aisles. Lyle occupied his time by studying the computer that the Bishop used and looking at some of the books that were on a shelf nearby.

"Here it is," the Bishop's voice came from the direction in which he had disappeared. He walked toward them displaying a leather folder that was wrapped around a sheaf of papers.

"Please, sit down at the table and I will read you what is inside. Then we can discuss the information and what you should do."

The five of them pulled up wooden chairs and seated themselves about the round oak table that was located near the computer setup. The Bishop turned on a large bone china lamp that was sitting in the middle of the table and proceeded to open the packet of papers with great care. They were obviously aged, by the looks of the discoloration.

"We've had the pages treated with special oils that soften and preserve old paper. This way, they will be saved indefinitely." He paused and reflected upon the material that had always interested him. "This is a letter that was written by Pope Clement in the late autumn of 1310 after being subdued by King Philip and being made to cooperate with his commands. It was brought to this land by one of the Pope's Cardinals."

11

Lyle stood at the window of his hotel room back in Santander and gazed at the sunset, which was casting beams of light through the remaining clouds. The air was fresh and clean from the day's rain and it now seemed appropriate for light to come bursting upon the earth.

His heart was sad as he remembered the letter from Pope Clement that Bishop Damasus had read. He agonized over the terrible events that had occurred and wished that things would have been different. Marie had been so touched by the words of this Pope that tears filled her eyes and streaked her face before the reading was over.

The sun was sending its last rays across the waters and Lyle pondered about the life that the Pope had lived.

The year was 1310 and evening was spreading its shadows of fading light across the city's structures. Pope Clement was standing on his balcony watching the ships as they sailed along the Rhone River into the sunset. It was a beautiful city that was chosen for him by King Philip, but he was quite saddened with the thought that he would never see Rome again. It was reported that the Italians would have him killed if he tried to enter the city, and he was advised by the College of Cardinals to stay near France. He had accepted the papal throne being moved to Avignon, which adjoined France's southern tip. This region at that time was a part of Sicily.

The air was heavy with humidity and the heat from the

late autumn day. Perspiration beaded the Pope's forehead and he struggled to loosen his garments. Why was he chosen to become head of the Catholic Church at such a time of turmoil? He was sickened with the thought that King Philip had arranged his election and that this king was manipulating decisions that were made for the Church.

"Your Holiness," came the voice of his assistant, Cardinal Rossi. "I've brought a refreshing drink and a selection of fruits for you. May I take it to the balcony and place it on your table?"

The Pope looked at him painedly and then motioned for him to go ahead. The Cardinal had been his only friend over the past several months and the Pope appreciated his loyalty in the present dangerous environment.

Cardinal Rossi, an Italian by birth, was dedicated to the Catholic Church and he agonized over the dilemma that had come upon its head. He placed the tray on the table and made a gesture for the Pontiff to be seated. He assisted in moving the chair as the tired man sank heavily upon the seat.

"It pains me deeply about the outcome of our Knights Templars," choked the Pope. He cleared his throat noisily and continued. "The Order has always been devoutly Catholic and devoted to me, their leader, and I've failed them." His voice cracked and he slumped forward, resting his head on his hands. His shoulders shook for several minutes. Raising his head slowly, he used his handkerchief to wipe away the tears that had filled his eyes, and then mopped the sweat from his forehead. "The King has forced me and my position to become prostitutes for his wishes. He wanted more money for his Flemish War and so decided that the best source was the suppression of the Templars in order that their possessions could be confiscated. I was powerless and I gave in, not knowing what else to do."

There was anguish in his voice and a look of devastation upon his countenance. His hands shook as he tried to pick the wine goblet up from the tray and then set it down quickly.

"You are a captive in your own land," replied the Cardinal. "The Church has been weakened by this assault and has left our organization greatly disturbed. The priests are devastated and are acting inappropriately. Everywhere, people of the Church seem to have lost or forsaken their faith and are becoming an abomination to God and man. They have been demoralized."

"Yes, that's exactly right," admitted the Pope as he stared into the setting sun. "It's like Christ's light to this world is growing dim and I'm the one to blame for all the tragedies that are occurring."

"This is indeed a dark period in the life of our Church, but I don't believe that you are to blame for the change in the attitudes of individuals and the beliefs that were being fostered by the professors at the Paris University. God is still in His universe and will someday straighten out this chaos."

"I feel that I must do something to make amends for the catastrophe that has occurred to the Templars," Pope Clement said with a quavering voice.

"I've heard that there were several Knights who fled Paris when the arrests were being made. Reports have it that they went to Spain, where attitudes and people are much more accepting of them. Why don't you write a letter, informing them of the political overtones in this matter and saying that you are helpless to assist them?"

The Pope's brow was downcast as he pondered this thought. Could there be a chance that they would read a message from him and understand the complexity of the problem? Would they forgive him for his inability to come to their aid? He could at least try. He turned to his friend and said, "Yes, would you take a letter for me and see to it personally that it gets to the Templars in Spain?"

"Let me get paper and an inked quill," answered the Cardinal as he walked across the room and gathered his materials. Returning, he seated himself near the Pope.

"Begin with these words," began Pope Clement.

My Dear Brethren of Our Lord's Knights Templars:

These words come difficult for me to say, but say I must. God knows how lost you must feel after the tragedy that has occurred in France. Let me try to explain what has transpired and then if you can find it in your hearts to forgive me, so be it. If not I will understand.

The King, Philip the Fair, has undertaken to establish a government that is to be devoid of any Church involvement. The Church is now only an instrument for him to unleash his own agenda. He is organizing all military factions to be under the control of his nephew and is angered that Master Molay will not consent to his wishes. Desiring to obtain more money for his ever-expanding products, the King decided to suppress your Order and appropriate your possessions. The trials that are being conducted against your brethren are meant to place shame upon the entire Order so that it may never rise again.

Now, I must tell you that King Philip has all but taken over the control of the Papal Throne. He manipulates the law so that it will benefit his desires. He has men appointed to Church positions in order that they may contaminate God's truth. Even how his priests sell pardons for sins, from adultery to murder. Money is buying positions for the religious, and dispensations from Church regulations. Bogus "priests" are given positions when they cannot even read, or deliberately garble the Latin Mass so that people won't know that they cannot speak the language. Our clergy and Cardinals are spending their time strutting about in furs and jewels, concerned about nothing more than entertaining guests of foreign lands. They compete with each other over the lavishness of their quarters. It's as if our Church is transferring its purpose from God's precepts to temporal prestige.

My hands are tied so that I cannot assist in coming to your defense. The King has perverted the use of the Church's Inquisition so that it now does the will of the government. My heart aches and I wish that I might die rather than see the tragedy that is coming upon our blessed Order. I advise you not to return to France, and to be aware of the hostilities that exist in England, Portugal, and Germany. These governments have taken King Phillip's advice and are arresting Knights there. May you find it in your hearts to forgive me for not coming to your rescue as I am indeed helpless and may God forgive me for all my weaknesses and my sins.

May the blessings of our Lord and Savior be with you always.

Yours in the body of Christ
Pope Clement V of Avignon, 1310

Cardinal Rossi laid down his quill and looked sympathetically at the Pontiff. How much sadness could one man bear? Was this a type of suffering that Christ had experienced while here on earth? He wished with all his heart that this period in time would pass and that somehow God would judge them in kindness.

"Please," choked the Pope in a broken voice that carried with it the pain of the ages, "see that this letter arrives at the quarters of our Templars in Spain." The Pope stood slowly, shoulders bent in sorrow and stumbled toward the edge of the balcony. His once magnificent frame was now separated from this present anguish. He struggled to gain another glimpse of the sun as it disappeared over the mountains and then sank into an irresolvable depression.

* * *

The night had turned unseasonably cold as a black BMW sedan arrived in Santander. The moon could be seen between the clouds rising over the distant Picos de Europa. Mons. Jacques Gerard was sitting stiffly in the back seat as he directed Bones, the driver, to their destination. He had made arrangements to stay at a hacienda that belonged to an associate of his on the outskirts of the city.

"There it is," Gerard said as he leaned forward and tapped Bones on the shoulder. "Pull into the driveway and stop the auto under the shelter near the house."

They came to a stop and Gerard instructed his men to take Ben into the downstairs apartment.

"Mind you that you don't hurt him anymore. I want him to be able to converse with us."

The men unloaded their luggage and Lewis took Ben by the arm and steered him toward the side door. They walked through a short hallway and then turned down a dimly lit staircase. Ben's arm was aching terribly in the grip of Gerard's man, Lewis, who refused to relax his hold, causing the pain to become even more stinging to the prisoner's flesh. And Ben's head also ached noticeably from the beating that was administered to him in Paris. He wondered if this was going to be the end or if they would continue attempting to force out of him the information that he had sworn to Marie and Father Hugues never to reveal. His hopes for escape were thin, but he resolved that if there was a chance to run, he'd do it. It was unfortunate about the plane crash and the death of Lyle. Here, there was nobody who knew where he might be, or how to rescue him. Ben allowed himself to be pushed into a dark room and heard the door being locked, and then the retreating footsteps of Lewis.

* * *

The phone rang by Oliver's bed and he jumped to his feet without a second wink.

"*Bonjour.*" He rubbed his eyes with the back of his left hand and glanced at his watch. It was 2:00 in the morning and someone must have something urgent to say, to awaken him at this time.

"*Senor*," replied the voice of a man. "I have some consequential information for you. Can you come down and talk with me?"

"Who are you?"

"Do you remember the fishermen you met on the beach the other day?"

"Yes, I remember talking with someone about the Knights Templars, why?"

"I am one of those men and I have an important message for you; can you come down and meet me in the lobby?" The man's voice was urgent and after a brief hesitation Oliver consented to see the man. Dressing, he jotted a quick note to Lyle and left it on the bed, just in case he didn't return.

The lobby of the hotel was empty, with the exception of the desk clerk and a few cleaning people. As Oliver approached the desk the clerk looked at him and averted his glance toward the front door. Oliver turned to follow the direction suggested and noted the fisherman still dressed in his work clothes just outside the double glass doors. After catching a nod from the clerk, Oliver turned and proceeded towards the entryway.

The man saw him coming and motioned for him to follow. Oliver began to wonder about this intervention but decided that it might be potentially significant and followed him out into the night. The air was cold and a northerly wind was beginning to build from the ocean. The only sounds that could be heard were the waves crashing on the beaches, and an occasional auto engine running nearby.

They walked for several blocks along a stone road that ran parallel with the ocean. The man hadn't bothered to speak yet and Oliver decided that he would in his own time.

The light from the street lamps flickered as the wind penetrated the cracked globes. They provided minimal light to see the path and the waving trees nearby as the two men hurried on.

The stranger stopped suddenly, his face turning toward a house on the corner. "A black auto arrived here about three hours ago," he whispered, just loud enough for Oliver to hear. "Four men got out and then they dragged another man out of the auto and marched him into the house. I live just across the street and happened to see the whole incident."

"What makes you think that this situation should attract my attention?" asked Oliver in puzzlement.

"I did disregard what occurred until I noticed two men leave the house about an hour later. Then I received a phone call from one of my friends who said that there were two men wandering about the square asking questions concerning visitors from Paris, especially one woman and three men with a black Rolls-Royce." The man stopped and looked intently at Oliver, then he continued, "These are not good men and you seem to be, that is why I wanted to warn you."

The wind was coming now with greater force. Oliver struggled to hold his coat about him.

"Thank you for apprising me of the situation. This may be trouble for us," he said as he glanced back down the street from which they had come. "I will get back now to the hotel and warn the others." He turned to thank and shake the hand of the fisherman, but he had vanished.

Startled, Oliver whirled about and searched the immediate area for signs of the man, but not a trace of him could be found. Oliver started back to the hotel at a quick pace.

"Lyle, Lyle," called Oliver softly but emphatically through the door. There was silence from the inside and

Oliver knocked again. "Lyle, Lyle."

Then a sleepy voice could be heard faintly from within. "I'm coming, just a minute."

Lyle opened the door and looked at Oliver through half-shut eyelids. "What is it, Oliver? Is something wrong? For a minute I thought I was dreaming again. Come on in."

Oliver gave an affirmative nod and followed Lyle into his room. It was now about 3:00 in the morning and the hotel was quiet.

"I've just had the most unusual encounter," said Oliver as he took off his coat. He told of his conversation with the fisherman he had met on the beach, and of the men who had just arrived from Paris.

"I had a feeling that they would show up," Lyle stated as he went to the window and looked out over the ocean. "What do you think we should do?"

"Let's wake up Bill and see what he thinks."

Lyle went to the telephone and dialed Bill's room. "Bill, sorry to awaken you at this hour but something has arisen that needs our immediate attention. Can you come over?"

Lyle received an affirmative answer and replaced the receiver. He went to the closet and took out his robe. "They must have Ben with them. I wonder if we should attempt a rescue?"

"Let's wait till we talk with Bill," suggested Oliver, as he seated himself on the sofa.

There was a knock at the door and Lyle called for Bill to enter.

"Say, what's going on?" he said as he saw Oliver fully clothed with a worried look on his face.

Lyle explained the situation and the likelihood that Ben was being held by Gerard's men.

"Lyle," began Bill after a moment's thoughtfulness, "They're baiting us. I think we should leave immediately for Burgos and the Monastery of Santo Domingo De Silos. Bishop Damasus recommended that we go there soon."

"But what of Ben?" asked Lyle.

"It is not yet the time for a rescue," stated Oliver from the corner.

"Yes, I think you're right," replied Bill as he went over to the sink and took a drink of cold water.

"Okay, if that is what you both think, then we probably should leave immediately," answered Lyle, who was now pacing about the floor.

"Let's pack our gear; I'll waken Marie and tell her of the change in plans and then we'll meet in the lobby in thirty minutes," said Bill as he started towards the door.

"No," interrupted Oliver. "Let's meet here in Lyle's room, and then go out the back way. That way no one will know we have left and therefore no one will be able to give any information to anyone who asks. I'll leave a note for the hotel in my room, in case the management comes looking for us before we return."

The others agreed and departed to prepare for the journey ahead.

* * *

Father Hugues awoke with sweat oozing from every pore of his body. The window shutters were flapping noisily against the sills and the wind was howling around the corners of the rectory. What was it he had just experienced? Why was his heart throbbing so strongly in his chest and neck?

He threw back the covers on his bed and sat on the edge for a moment. Yes, that was it. The dream of three men and a woman being pushed over the edge of a cliff. He could still remember seeing the terror in their eyes and hearing them scream desperately for help. But no one was about who could help them escape from their pursuers. Who was chasing them?

Father Hugues arose shakily and after slipping on his robe he went over to the windows and secured the latches. Yes, he remembered now! The French art thief, Jacques Gerard, was chasing the four who had left Paris only a few days ago and now this hardened criminal must be hot on their heels. What could he do to help them? He knew that this dream must be a warning about impending danger to these young folks.

He went into the library and located the atlas near the telephone table. Thumbing quickly through the pages, he found a map of Spain and located the city of Santander. He started to pace the floor. What could he do? He rubbed his eyes with his hands, trying to remove the sleep that still lingered. Abruptly he stopped pacing and stared at the map. He would follow the group to Spain and find the Bishop of Santa Maria. Perhaps together they could be of assistance. He felt guilty for having encouraged the four travelers to proceed with this adventure without having offered to go along.

Father Hugues jotted a quick note to his secretary and stuffed it into an envelope. He would be gone for several days and he would contact her when he could. In the meantime, she should notify Father Callone to take over the celebration of masses. Leaving the letter on the desk, he telephoned for a taxi to come immediately.

He waited in the anterior lobby with his suitcase for the headlights of the taxi to round the corner and prayed that he might not be too delayed to be of help. There must be something he could do to ensure the safety of these dear young people. Suddenly he realized why he felt so distraught. This must have been the same way that Pope Clement had felt when he knew that his Knights were going to be destroyed and could do nothing.

* * *

Dawn broke over Santander with the sky still full of clouds and a dark gray fog filtering across the land from the ocean waters. The unusual chill was noted by the townspeople and unwelcomed by Mon. Jacques Gerard as he strolled on the porch. His pupils were unusually dilated and his breath came in short and uneven gasps.

"Louis," he bellowed. "Where are you?"

"Coming, sir," came a voice from within. The screen door opened and Louis hurriedly came stumbling out. "What is it, sir?"

"Did you find out anything last night?"

"No sir, no one seemed to have seen them."

"Louis, I'm going to get rid of you. You're absolutely no good," Gerard growled angrily.

"Sir, I will keep looking. I'm sure we will turn something up this time," Louis was perspiring heavily and stammering again. "We were awfully tired last night. I'm sure we can find the information we need today." He reached into his pocket and pulled out a roll of bills.

Gerard nodded approvingly and his lips began to curl at the edges. His eyes cut into Louis like a sharp steel knife.

"See to it that we get the material we need today. And make it soon," he snapped as he turned and looked again toward the town square. He couldn't see further than a block because of the fog, but he knew in which direction the business district lay. He pulled his robe up tightly about his neck. *Damn this weather, damn these men, and damn the whole human race.*

* * *

The Rolls had reached a higher elevation as Oliver

pulled away from the fog that had rolled in the evening before. The sun was shining in beautiful streaks through the low clouds, and the fresh greenness of the grass and trees stood out in breathtaking loveliness. They were on a winding road that wove in and out of lush valleys. It traveled up and down hills that were filled with fields of spring grain and blooming fruit orchards. Small groups of cottages were intermittently clustered among groves of long-limbed ash. Light wisps of cooking smoke could be seen in the distance as the morning air shifted into the ascending direction, first east and then west.

"I hope our absence will not be detected soon," said Marie as she broke the silence that hung over them since their departure from Santander.

"I hope not, too," replied Lyle, who was studying the map. "We should be arriving in Burgos soon."

"This city was founded in about the 8th century. This was the city that El Cid, or Rodrigo Diaz de Vivar, was born in. He became a hero when he defended Valencia against the Moors." Marie paused. "There is a magnificent cathedral here which is a mausoleum to El Cid. It was built at the center of the city and all the roads lead away from here. During the busy time of the business day, the priests have to close the doors in order to prevent the people from using the church's passageways for their convenience."

The city was now well in view on the high plains. Lyle could see the steeples of the cathedral in the distance and hoped that someday he could visit the tombs of El Cid and his wife.

"Let's stop a moment for a little breakfast," said Bill, rubbing his stomach.

"Okay," replied Lyle and noticed Oliver pointing to a coffee shop that was just opening.

After a brief breakfast, during which they discussed their plans, they were on the road again.

"We should follow this road, N1E5, on down to Lerma. Then take a left toward the monastery,"' Lyle said as he plotted the way. "It looks to be about twenty miles past the village of Nebreda."

"Who is it that we should ask for when we arrive?" questioned Marie.

"Father Francisco is the one that Bishop Damasus recommended."

They arrived at the monastery about noon. The sight of the old Romanesque cloister was thrilling for all of them. Marie had said that this was one of the finest surviving architectural structures in all of Europe. As they entered the gates, Oliver parked in a area that was posted for visitors. They got out and entered the main door marked DIRECCION.

"*Bienvenida,* " a voice said behind them.

"*Hola, amigo,* " answered Lyle with a smile and extended his hand toward the monk. He was dressed in a floor-length brown robe with a white cord that was wrapped about his waist. His face was filled with a beautiful calm and his lips radiated a friendly smile that immediately put them all at ease. He couldn't have been over thirty, thought Lyle as he shook his hand and said, "*Nosotros visitamos Padre Francisco.*"

The young monk nodded and motioned for them to follow him. They walked down a long stone corridor that led to a room at the end. Through the door, the monk motioned for them to sit on the wooden chairs that were lined against the rosy stone wall.

It was cooler inside, away from the sunlight. The site of the monastery had been perfectly chosen in the rolling hills of the Castile, a welcome comfort for pilgrims as they journeyed toward Santiago de Compostela. Those pilgrim footsteps have been silenced now, as modern highways bypass this former haven of rest. Still, the monks continue their day's work and occasionally welcome a visitor who has heard about the place. These visitors come because of the angelic music that has satisfied many hungry souls and will fill them again with God's peace. The music of the Gregorian chant that was started over 1,500 years ago, is a unison of voices held by one note that has traveled through the corridors of the monastery. It eventually weaves its way into the hearts and souls of its listeners.

* * *

Father Hugues was in the air, aboard a 747, and on the way to Santander. The pilot had just reported a large fog cloud blanketing the whole northern coast, but stated that with the plane's instrumentation they could get through it safely. Father hoped that was true.

"Sir, I mean Father," exclaimed a young hostess as she blushed becomingly. "Could I get something for you to drink?"

"A cup of coffee would be fine," replied Father Hugues with a smile.

She returned directly with a cup of black coffee and a pastry. The aroma was wonderful and Father remembered that he hadn't had any breakfast yet.

"Thank you."

The ride was becoming more difficult as they neared the Spanish coastline. The seatbelt sign came on and the voice of the captain said, "We're going to have rough weather ahead. Please remain seated and have your seatbelts fastened."

The plane began to rise and fall suddenly. Some of the

passengers were becoming excited and some started calling for the stewardess. Father Hugues tried to remain calm. He knew that these men had flown through weather far worse than this and he himself had been through many flights that were quite hair-raising in comparison.

The plane started a dangerous downward projection. People gasped for air and clung at their seats in fright. Downward they plunged, seemingly headed straight for the ocean. The lights flickered and someone screamed. Down they continued until Father Hugues's ears felt ready to explode. He swallowed several times and clung to the armrest until his fingers started turning white.

Minutes continued to pass as the plane persisted in its downward course. Father Hugues was just beginning to wonder if this might be the time when he wasn't going to make it; then the plane began to level out and the jet engine slowed their descending whine. The change in motion sent many lunging forward, almost hitting their heads on the seats ahead. Then the wheels of the plane squealed on the asphalt runway and the aircraft began turning toward the terminal gate.

Father Hugues' legs were a bit shaky as he descended the plane's stairs onto the damp tarmac. He was glad that they had arrived safely and thanked God that he was once again able to breathe the fresh salty air. He gazed over the countryside and began plotting his next move in order to forget the dreadful flight.

* * *

Louis and Bones had scouted most of the city without a trace of the group from Paris. Everywhere they went they were met with negative responses. The men on the seashore knew nothing; the men in the square knew not a thing; the managers of hotels and restaurants could tell them nothing.

"Do you think that 'The Boss' was correct in assuming that these four people came to this city?" asked Bones, dropping into a chair near a street-side café.

"I don't know if he's right or not, I just know that I would never question him," replied Louis as he joined Bones and motioned for the waiter.

The day was still foggy and it was already about noon. It was not a day to be out scouting about the city. Their search seemed utterly futile and the answer to their questions hidden in the gray mist that deluged the city.

After eating ham sandwiches and consuming cups of black coffee they got up and started for the El Sandinero Casino. Perhaps someone there would have seen or heard something about the Americans and their associates.

The Casino was bustling with activity as people came and went from the word-famous gambling establishment. Tourists always found it an extremely attractive location to spend their money, and different nationalities had no trouble exchanging their cash into Spanish currency. The atmosphere was gay and lilting guitar music filled the air within.

"Let's ask the tour guide at the visitors' desk if he knows of anyone coming through this area," whispered Louis as he started toward a well-dressed Spaniard who was arranging a few pamphlets on his desk.

"*Senor*," addressed Louis as he held out his hand for a friendly shake. "We've lost some of the party we were traveling with and wondered if you might know of their whereabouts?"

"*Si*, what do they look like? Are they men or women?" His black eyes twinkled and a wisp of a smile lifted the corners of his mouth.

"There is one woman, Marie. There are two Americans,

Bill and Lyle. Then there is one French fellow by the name of Oliver who is acting as their driver." Louis looked at Bones to see if there was anything else that he should add to his statement. Bones nodded affirmatively.

The Spaniard frowned slowly and scratched his head. After a few moments he said, "There are many people who pass through here. Can you give me any other information?"

"They were driving a black Rolls-Royce."

"Now that you mention it, I did see one of those fancy autos leaving the city very early this morning when I was on my way in from the country. It was too dark to determine whether it was black or not, though."

"Which way was it headed?"

"It was going south towards Burgos on N623." He looked at them quizzically. "Can I ask for our manager to come and assist you?"

"No," replied Louis quickly. "You have been very helpful. I'm afraid our friends just decided to go on ahead, I guess. We'll call them this evening and see if they arrived safely."

"Very well," said the Spaniard as he again shook their hands and continued with his work.

Louis and Bones walked casually from the Casino and down the front stairs. After arriving on the street they turned and proceeded hastily toward the residence where Gerard was impatiently waiting. The heavy mist in the air was beginning to dampen the faces and moisten their coats. *This weather is becoming annoying,* thought Louis as he wiped his eyes and pulled the collar of his coat up about his neck. At least they would have good news for the boss. He'd be pleased. The moisture from the clouds was becoming heavier now and their feet were splashing in puddles that were forming in shallows of the cobblestone street. Thunder suddenly crashed above them and flashes of lightning began to pierce the semi-darkness. Winds were bringing in salty ocean dampness and a dark, ominous spell gripped the men as they started to run.

*   *   *

A large arched oak door opened and an elderly monk entered. He walked toward Lyle and the others with an outstretched hand and a broad smile on his thin face.

"*Hola, Bienvenida,*" he said as he warmly shook their hands. He stopped in front of Oliver and studied him for several seconds, then turned and started toward his desk.

"Do you like our monastery?"

"Yes, very much," answered Lyle as he came closer to the monk. "We are here on a special mission. Would you allow us to tell you a story and then perhaps you might find a way to assist us on our quest?"

The monk looked at Oliver again and then smiled at Lyle, "My name is Father Francisco. I am the one in charge of antiquities. Am I the person you wish to see?"

The room was suddenly silent and each looked at each other in amazement. Father Francisco smiled and motioned for them to be seated.

"I don't believe it," exclaimed Marie as she laughed. "How could you have known that you were just the one whom we desired to talk with?"

"I didn't know. That is just the way some things occur around here." He paused and pointed to the icon of Mary, the Mother of God of the Passion, that was hanging on the wall behind him. This 14th century icon depicted the infant Christ anxiously clasping His mother's comforting hand as they look toward two angels holding the passion cup. Her expression shows sorrowful but trusting resignation. Lyle nodded his understanding and said, "We've come in search of information concerning the Knights Templars after they fled from Paris in 1310. We have talked with Father Hugues in Paris concerning their problems with King Philip, and have learned that there were twelve who got away while most of the others were being arrested. We were wondering if they could have come down this far into Spain, after being near Castro Urdiales for a while?"

Lyle opened his briefcase and took out the manuscript that Ben had sent him. He showed Father Francisco the passage that said much gold and jewels were taken with them. He then turned on his computer and brought up the TABLE OF DISCOVERIES and went through all the entries relating major occurrences from the time he had left Duluth for New York City.

"I know it may look like we're just after the gold," stated Bill fervently, "but we're just as interested in knowing where these gallant men might have spent their last years and what they have done about the continuance of the Order."

"*Si,*" replied the Father, "I do understand. I have a feeling that you would not do anything to disturb the remains of these Knights or to defame their characters." He got up from his chair and walked to the window, slightly parting the draperies. There was a look of melancholy on his face as he stared out beyond the rolling hills. It was as if he were remembering some great sadness in history that filled his cup to the brim and the slightest disturbance would cause tears to spill if those thoughts were remembered aloud.

"Father," began Lyle quietly, afraid of speaking too loudly for fear of interrupting a precious thought.

The man turned slowly and Lyle looked in astonishment at his face. He had changed! The face was now wrinkled with age and the dark blue eyes were deeper into his head. His hair had turned to a snowy white and his hands were gnarled from years of labor.

"Don't be afraid," he whispered, "what you see is the real me. I am Master Molay. I was the one with whom King Philip was angered. It was my fault that the Order was destroyed. I would not go along with his plan to unite all the Holy Orders under the leadership of his nephew."

"But it wasn't your fault, Master Molay. It was the greed of King Philip that made him take your possessions. It was the love of power that made him give the order to execute your Knights and force Pope Clement to dissolve the Order. It wasn't your fault." Lyle's voiced was filled with passion as he electrified the air.

"Thank you for telling me this. It will help to set my heart at rest."

"I can't believe my eyes," gasped Bill as he and Marie stared. They were obviously shaken by the appearance of the Master Knight who had lived so long ago. Bill tried to rack his brain for something meaningful to ask this famous person.

"Tell me sir, where did the men go who escaped from Paris?"

The old man smiled gently and shook his head. "You are on a quest for the truth and you will find it when the road comes to an end." He turned and walked toward the door through which he had come. His kind eyes were filled with a deep but beautiful sadness.

"Wait," cried Marie as she went running after him. He put up his hand and stopped her short from touching his garments. "Please, stay and talk with us longer. I feel that I know you somehow."

"What is your name, my dear?"

"Marie de Molay," she answered and after a moment, a look of happiness slowly passed over her face.

"Yes," he said with great sensitivity, "you are a descendant of my family and I will continue to live on. Come, I will show you the way out." He opened the door and the others followed him into the corridor. They walked quietly past the granite arches of the cloister and heard in the distance the singing of the Benedictine monks. Their melodious voices echoed through the chambers and filled the listeners with a tranquil feeling of God's presence and His benediction. The sound seemed to be coming from the distant past; redeveloped and enjoyed again; and growing even more wonderful as it aged.

Master Molay paused at the entrance and looked at them. Then raising his hand in farewell he said, "You have found the truth, I can tell. May God be with you as you return home." He turned and disappeared through an archway.

"Holy Mother! Can you believe what we've just experienced?" said Bill as he headed toward the auto.

"I wouldn't have believed a word of this if I hadn't have seen it for myself," answered Marie.

"Now you can believe the things I've been telling you about along the way," Lyle said with confidence. "But I don't know what we're going to do now. It seems like we're at a dead end."

"Master Molay suggested that we head back," inserted Oliver as he opened the auto doors.

"Yes, I suppose we should," admitted Lyle sadly. "By the way, Oliver, why was Master Molay looking at you that way?"

"I don't know, maybe I looked familiar to him."

"He seemed to sense something about you, I think. Anyway, we should visit Bishop Damasus again and decide which way to venture now."

The Rolls was pulling away from the monastery as the

sky was beginning to fill with dark clouds from the north. *I hope we're not going to have trouble getting back,* thought Lyle as he settled back into the comfortable leather seat. What a magnificent supernatural manifestation they had just observed! Lyle hoped that Master Molay was at rest now and that his Knights would also find peace.

12

Father Hugues arrived at the Church of Santa Maria and proceeded directly to the office of Bishop Damasus. He was disappointed in the rainy weather and hoped it was causing Gerard a great deal of difficulty. The grounds of Santa Maria were engulfed with a heavy fog that caused the evergreens to give a ghostly appearance about the old Gothic church. The eerie calling of foghorns could be heard in the distance and an occasional cry of sea gulls added to the intensity of the dramatic helplessness of his friends.

He approached the rectory door and lifted the iron knocker that was under the small iron-framed glass window. The door opened immediately and a woman ushered him into the warm lobby.

"I'm Father Hugues, recently come from Paris and have an urgent need to talk with Bishop Damasus." He removed his raincoat and hat, placing them on the wall hangers near the door.

"He is in his office," replied the woman. "I shall go and tell him at once."

She turned and walked several paces down the blue-carpeted corridor, then knocked at the second door. Hearing a response, she opened the door and entered.

A moment later she reappeared and motioned the guest to come.

Father Hugues entered the office and smiled at the Bishop who was standing with obvious anticipation.

"Welcome, Father," stated the Bishop cordially as he

came around the desk and shook the outstretched hand heartily. "You're the priest who advised Lyle and Marie? I'm not surprised to see you, I must say, after the story I heard from your young associates."

"Thank you for seeing me," replied Father Hugues," and selected a tapestried armchair near the Bishop's desk. "I surmise that you have heard the story about the Knights Templars from our young enthusiasts."

"Yes, I've heard the whole story and am impressed at their spirit of adventure."

"I think that they're on the right track and have the best intentions, but I am extremely concerned about the international art thief, Gerard, who is also after the Templar treasure and has already kidnapped a university professor from his Paris home."

Father Hugues arose suddenly and started pacing the floor. "I had a terrifying dream last night about the four being in imminent danger. Is there anything else you can do which might assist them or keep their risks at a minimum?"

"I told them that the Templars were in this area after their escape from Paris and that their having gold was not known to anyone, or least nothing that has been recorded on paper." Bishop Damasus rubbed his chin thoughtfully, "I also showed them a letter that had been written by Pope Clement V; it was addressed to the exiled Templars and the words seemed to move the group very deeply. I don't suppose that we can notify the authorities to have these men apprehended?"

Father Hugues shook his head. "The information about the art thieves was given to me in confessional, but said that I could notify the concerned persons about their danger."

"Yes, I understand. I just wish that there were something we could do."

"Where are they now?" questioned Father Hugues as he seated himself again.

"It was reported in one of the journals that was left at the Castle of Santa Ana, a Templar stronghold, that the Knights from France had journeyed towards Burgos and the Benedictine monastery that lay beyond. We surmised that they probably went to spend time with the monks at the cloister of Monasterio de Santo Domingo de Silos for a while."

"So the group is planning on talking with the monks there about the Knights." Father Hugues nodded his affirmation and stood to stroll again about the richly decorated office. There were hallowed paintings of the Lord's Last Supper and one of Christ's Mother Mary who was receiving blessings from heaven before her Son's birth. There was one rather large painting that depicted the coming of Christ and His angels to this earth which held the attention of Father Hugues for several minutes.

"I suppose that all we can do now is pray for the safety of our young friends," said Father Hugues as he turned slowly away from the display of art works.

"Yes, let's go into the sanctuary and ask our Blessed Savior for intervention on their behalf," agreed the Bishop.

They left the office and entered the church by the side door. There were several local people from the nearby community praying at different locations near the sanctuary. The light from candles were lit for intercessions and prayers brightened the large space and brought warmth to the hearts of the supplicants. The two priests approached the niche that contained a white marble statue of Mary, the Madonna and Child. They knelt and each lit five white candles and then reverently bowed their heads in prayer.

As the smoky wisps from the candles mixed with the petitions of these men, the silence of the church became alive with musical whisperings of the wind about the pillars and corners of the stained glass windows. They prayed with closed eyes to avoid any distractions from their communion with God, and remained on their knees for a long time, enjoying oneness with their Divine Lord. They arose with a deep confidence that He would undoubtedly protect and strengthen Lyle, Bill, Ben, Oliver and Marie.

* * *

Ben Sully was lying on a small bed in the room where Gerard's men had placed him the night before and was listening to the thunder as it became louder outside. The small window near the top of the outside wall lighted with the flashes of lightning and he could hear the rain as it started to splash against the glass pane. His fears had lessened as time passed and he now wondered what was going to happen next. Then he heard a key turning in the door's lock.

"Well, it's now time to tell us about the contents of the manuscript that you took from Saint Martins," growled Gerard as he pushed open the door and approached Ben. His eyes were filled with hate and his face reddened with anger.

"I don't know what you are talking about," replied Ben as he sat up.

"You're lying and your friends are going to suffer for this," said Gerard as he pounded the wall with his fist.

Ben was surprised to hear the mention of his friends and wondered whom he might be talking about.

"We are close on the trail of your two friends from America and Marie, your assistant."

Ben silently gasped without giving any sign of recognition on his face. *What were Marie and Lyle doing?* He had decided against providing any information and he knew that he must appear ignorant concerning his friends and their activities.

"You tell us now and you'll be released unharmed. Otherwise, you will meet a fate much worse than you've ever imagined," snapped Gerard.

"I tell you that I don't know anything," repeated Ben as he slumped forward and became even more determined that they weren't going to obtain any information from him. He decided that he would play their bluff and pursed his lips as the furrows in his brow began to deepen. He hoped that the others would remain safe and thought of his friend, Lyle from the United States. Could it be that he and his friend, Bill, had survived the plane crash?

Louis came into the room and whispered something to Gerard. Gerard turned abruptly and followed him from the room. Ben was aware of muffled voices and tried to hear what they were discussing, but was unable to decipher the words that were exchanged between them.

Louis entered the room again and strode over to where Ben was sitting.

"You are coming with us now," he began. "We're going after your friends and when we finish with them, they will be unrecognizable." He grabbed Ben by the collar and brought him roughly to his feet. "You don't know who you're dealing with here. If I were you, I'd tell Gerard everything or you won't live to see Marie again."

He looked directly into Ben's eyes with an evil scowl on his face. His death-hold clench tightened on Ben's shirt and began to bite into the skin on Ben's neck.

"There's nothing to tell," insisted Ben as he began to gasp for air and his eyes watered.

"You bastard," snarled Louis savagely, striking Ben across the face with the back of his hand. Ben reached up with his arms to protect himself as he fell back across the bed. Louis bent over and grabbed him by the jacket again, pulling him forcefully to his feet.

"You've not seen the end of this."

Louis steered Ben toward the door with an iron grip on his arm. Up the staircase they went and exited the house by the side door. They rushed through the falling rain and blinding wind into the waiting auto. The other men arrived soon and then Gerard himself came wearing a black trench coat, the collar closed up tightly around his neck. A woolen hat was pulled low over his brow.

"Let's go," ordered Gerard to Bones who was behind the steering wheel, anxious to be on their way. The auto started and they turned out onto the street which was rapidly becoming covered with water. The auto accelerated forward quickly and they were soon speeding along the highway that would lead them to Burgos.

* * *

The rain was pouring as Oliver maneuvered the Rolls around some potholes that had developed in the blacktop. Their speed started to decrease because visibility was becoming more difficult and Oliver was afraid of damaging one of the car's axles. They rode in silence as they reflected upon the experience they had just witnessed at the monastery. Emotions were drained by the privilege that had been theirs.

"We're coming back into Burgos," said Oliver quietly, careful not to disrupt their thoughts too abruptly.

"Shall we stop for something to eat?" Lyle was wanting to make his friends comfortable and felt badly that their progress was so slow.

"Yes, let's do," agreed Marie, smiling cheerfully. *She is always happy,* thought Lyle as he began to search for a restaurant.

"Over there," exclaimed Bill pointing to an attractive canopied entrance and a large sign stating the establishment served local dishes.

Everyone agreed and Oliver located a parking place on the opposite side of the road. He told them to wait until he retrieved the umbrella from the trunk so he could properly assist them to the restaurant.

After arriving in the front entrance, the maitre d' showed them where to hang their coats and then led them into a portion of the establishment that was located on the highest of three levels. The balconies were separated by exquisite black ironwork and rich green ivy cascaded over the banister, falling in low, graceful arrangements into the next section. Marie relaxed in her chair and gazed about the candle-lit room. Somewhere, Spanish musicians were entertaining with lyrical melodies from their violins and guitars.

"You realize that we may run into Gerard and his men from Paris as we near Santander?" asked Bill as he studied the menu.

"Yes, you're right," agreed Lyle and he looked at Oliver who nodded his head. "Maybe it's time that we earnestly look for them and find a way to free Ben before they trap us."

"I think it is the right time," Oliver said in agreement.

The waiter arrived and each placed his order for dinner. Lyle suggested that they start their meal with a bottle of sherry from Jerez and the waiter brought four glasses.

"Well, my friends, *mi amigos*," toasted Lyle after filling the glasses. "Here's to *mañana*." He lifted his glass and the others laughed as they joined him.

"Master Molay said, 'you will find it when the road comes to an end.' What did he mean by that statement?" asked Marie as she studied them. Her face was beautiful, but Lyle thought he noticed signs of strain beginning to show around her tired eyes.

"I don't have the vaguest idea," replied Lyle. "Do you know what he might have meant, Bill?"

Bill's mind must have been thousands of miles away, for it took him several minutes and Lyle's prompting again to get an answer.

"No, I don't know either." He stopped for a minute and thought. "But there is certainly something curious about that statement."

Lyle looked across the table at Oliver and was about to ask him what he thought of the announcement that Master Molay had made before they left, but decided not to when he noted that Oliver was also buried in thought. He was gazing out the picture window, across the rolling hills at the clouds as they slowly moved toward them. He felt great sadness as he tried to remember the old days and found it somewhat difficult to arouse the same feelings that he had once experienced. Still he knew that these emotions would come if he tarried much longer in this dreamlike state. Lyle paid the waiter when they had finished and Oliver left a few minutes early to bring the Rolls around to the front of the restaurant. The time was almost 3:00 in the afternoon and the sky had become even darker with rain-filled clouds. Large, pelting drops spattered on the windshield as Oliver closed the doors and got back into the driver's seat. When the traffic was clear, he made a U-turn and started again down the road towards Santander.

"Thanks for that wonderful meal, Lyle," said Marie as she gave Lyle's arm a squeeze. Her smile was warming and took his attention away from the chilly, damp air that was starting to make him shiver.

"You are very welcome."

The wind was beginning to drive the blinding rain in pelting sheets against the auto. Great forces of nature were at play and their powers could be felt as the auto was buffeted to and fro.

"It's becoming extremely dangerous, isn't it Oliver?" asked Lyle as he leaned forward and peered through the front windshield. "Do you think we should go on?"

"I will be very careful," stated Oliver confidently. "I am going slowly now and I have adequate visibility of the road." Then he added, after a moment's thoughtfulness, "I will turn around though, if you think it is advisable. After all, it was my poor judgment that got us into a mess when we crossed the Pyrenees." He paused and looked into the rear-view mirror at Marie. "I'd prefer to keep on going so that we can find Ben."

Lyle and the others agreed.

"I still trust you, Oliver. I'd like to see Ben again too," said Marie, hoping to instill confidence in Oliver.

He was smiling now "I will be careful, I promise."

* * *

Bones pulled the auto into a gas station to refill the tank. Gerard had told the men that they could get out and stretch their legs, but that Ben would not be permitted to budge. They were in the northern part of Burgos and the weather had not been cooperating with their travel plans. Gerard was exceedingly upset that their progress was so slow and seemed on the verge of giving the driving over to Louis.

"Hey, Boss," said Bones, strolling around to the other side of the auto where Gerard was having a cigar. The rain was blowing against their faces as they tried to shield themselves from its pelting force. "What kind of auto did we think the Americans were driving?"

"You heard from the man at the Casino didn't you?"

"Yes, but I forgot." Bones turned away and went back around to the other side, strolling up to Louis. "What make of an auto are we looking for?"

Louis turned on Bones angrily. "You idiot! It's a black Rolls-Royce, stupid!"

"I just wondered," answered Bones defensively. "One that fits the description went by a few minutes ago."

"What are you saying?"

"You heard me, Louis. I said that a black Rolls-Royce just went by here."

Louis threw down his cigar and ran over to talk with Gerard. Within seconds, both men were back around the auto. Gerard pulled a revolver from his coat pocket.

"Why didn't you tell us this information before?" screamed Gerard so loudly that Ben could hear from inside the auto, despite the storm raging outside.

"I tried to tell you, but you wouldn't answer me," explained Bones lamely.

"You didn't say that you saw them. You said that you wanted to know what kind of auto they were driving!" Gerard waved the pistol in the face of Bones.

"I just wanted to make sure it was the correct auto before I alerted you." Bones stepped back in an attempt to distance himself from Gerard, who was seething with anger.

Other autos could be seen in the dim light passing north and south on N 623. Their headlights were on, their windshield wipers working vigorously.

"Which way did they go?" bellowed Gerard as he wiped the rain from his beady eyes.

"They were headed north," replied Bones, who by now was becoming frightened for his life.

"Well, let's go and Louis, you drive this time. Bones, you take care of our friend."

They were moving again, but this time headed back over the road they had just been on a little earlier. Louis was trying to be careful, but seemed unable to make time and still avoid the potholes. Gerard, his eyes forward, strained to get a glimpse of the Rolls, and also was still swearing profusely about the ignorance of Bones.

"Can't you go faster?" demanded Gerard as he pounded the dash with his fist.

"Not if we're to stay on the road," replied Louis respectfully. "I am going as fast as I can and still watch out for and avoid obstacles." He knew that it wasn't a good time to anger his boss more, but he also knew that Gerard trusted him.

The auto sped on through the ever-increasing darkness and pounding rain. Knuckles were whitened as the occupants gripped their seats for steadiness as they were thrown about. Perspiration began to gather on the upper lips of Gerard and Louis as they gritted their teeth in determination.

The rolling hills of the countryside soon turned into steeper grades and sharper turns. Vision was becoming even more difficult as the road began to disappear into the fog and Louis started slamming on the brakes more frequently.

The storm appeared to be moving slowly and deliberately along the route that joined Burgos with Santander. The branches of roadside trees were swaying vigorously, threatening to break if twisted any further. Rivulets were growing larger as smaller streams joined others until there was water coursing along beside them, strong enough to wash the road away. The shrill sound of the wind screamed about the hollows and blasted its way over the mountains. The northern part of Spain was experiencing one of the worst spring storms that had ever occurred in the area.

* * *

Oliver strained his eyes to see the road ahead as he

guided the Rolls through the rain water that was pouring everywhere. He slowed to a mere 20 kilometers per hour so they would not accidentally go off the road. The wind lashed the auto about and everyone could feel its wild surges. Marie clung to the overhead handgrip with one hand and the other grasped the seat ahead.

"This is one of the worst storms I think I've ever experienced," said Bill, straining his eyes to see the road ahead.

"It is the worst one for me," replied Oliver who thought he had seen everything.

The auto had now slowed to about 10 kilometers per hour and the sound of crashing thunder could be heard above the noise of the auto's motor. They began to notice that flashes of lightning brightened the horizon and provided spectacular views of the mountainous terrain.

"I wonder if we should pull off and wait for this to pass." Lyle seemed tense with anxiety and didn't want anything to happen to them.

"I'll just go slow," replied Oliver as he decelerated even further.

The landscape was now aglow with the mixture of blue, green, red, and yellow lightning flashes. Crashing and booming thunder shook the whole countryside and vibrated the auto. The atmosphere seemed to split with bolts of electrical charges and then rip the sky into pieces. The road was barely visible ahead in the light, winding downward around a steep hill and glistening brightly with running water.

"If I ever get home, I don't think I will ever go out in a rainstorm again," breathed Marie, quivering with the excitement. Everyone now had their eyes riveted on the road which curved in sharp turns around the sides of the wooded mountains like a snake making its way through the blackness to an unknown home.

Suddenly a crashing bolt of lightning shot from the clouds about 20 kilometers ahead of them, and hit the mountainside. Lyle could feel his skin tingle and a feeling of lightheadedness came over him. The auto's exterior seemed to glow with light. An explosion followed and the sky lit up, daytime-bright, as several trees burst into flame. Thunder cracked immediately overhead, making the whole area quake violently. Oliver brought the auto to an immediate halt and waited to see what was going to occur next.

"My God, I don't believe it," exclaimed Lyle as he peered out the windshield.

"That bolt of lightning is the biggest one I've ever seen," added Bill.

"Look there," shouted Marie, pointing to something ahead of them.

Down the road, just below where the lightning had ignited the side of the hill, a large section of earth was sliding across the roadway. As they watched, another huge piece of earth mixed with brush, and trees started to shift and slide from the hillside. A huge crevasse was being torn in the ground as stone boulders dug trenches with the downward movement. Muddy water spilled into the cracks and became torrents of rushing dirty streams that continued to undermine plant life that was still attached.

"Oliver," said Marie excitedly, "do you think we're too close?"

"I'll back up," he answered, immediately putting the auto in reverse and moved them back about two kilometers.

"Well, I guess that does it for this route to Santander," remarked Bill. "I'm certainly glad we were not any closer when that scorcher hit."

"You can say that again," added Lyle as he peered through the rainy windows into the darkness that was lit only by the continued flashes of lightning. The road was out ahead and debris continued to pour down from the hillside in a now decreasing amount. He could see where a large section of earth had become a crater and thanked God for saving them from this catastrophe. A shiny object caught his eye and he strained his eyes to catch sight of the device again. Another flash of electricity illuminated the area. Yes, there it was again. An object that seemed rather large and glistening with each lightning flash.

"Hey, you all," exclaimed Lyle, motioning toward the side of the hill that had just been washed away. "There's something up there. Wait—you'll see it with the next streak of lightning." Everyone gathered on the right side of the auto and strained their eyes to get a glimpse of the strange object that Lyle was describing to them. There, another bolt of bluish lightning blazed across the sky for several seconds and they all could see the shiny article through the downpour.

"I wonder what it is?" Bill said excitedly, sitting on the edge of his seat.

"Something has been uncovered by the avalanche," suggested Marie, her face full of renewed enthusiasm.

"It's obviously an item that's large in order to reflect that amount of light down this far," said Bill with growing exhilaration in his voice. "Shall I go up there and see what it is?"

"Oh, Bill, do you really think that is wise?" Marie had a worried look that did not quite conceal her desire to go with him.

"I suppose it wouldn't hurt to go," stated Oliver, "but I think I should go with you, just in case there may be trouble along the way. You do realize that there is a chance of getting struck by this lightning?" He looked at Bill with questioning eyes.

"Yes I do," replied Bill assuredly. "Lyle, you and

Marie watch our progress from here."

The two slipped on rubber boots and tightened their raincoats before stepping out into the storm. It wasn't long before they were sloshing through soggy grass with mud covering their legs. The rainy wind whipped about their faces and stung their cheeks. With one hand shielding his face and holding a flashlight, Bill used the other to grab onto small brush and trees in their ascent. A branch slapped him across the face and he grimaced. Then he felt his foot slip and down he went, sliding several inches before he could halt himself and return to where he had left Oliver. Just ahead, Oliver was trying to create a pathway by removing rock, branches and other debris from their trail. He wanted to make sure that the way back would be easily navigated if they had to retreat in a hurry.

Several minutes passed as they continued to ascend and steadily drew closer to the mysterious object. By this time, they were thoroughly soaked and covered with mud from their climb. With each flash of light they were able to obtain a better glimpse of the article and became more certain that this was something that demanded investigation.

Bill stood on the edge of the crevasse that was filling with rushing water. At the very beginning of the ditch to their right was a ledge protruding from below the roots of an enormous evergreen. Another flash of light enabled the two men to see what appeared to be a cave and inside was the object that reflected the light. As they stared at it, Bill was suddenly overcome by a powerful feeling that seemed to be beckoning them to come closer.

"Shall we chance a trip across?" asked Bill as he turned toward Oliver. He didn't see him and startled, began to search the area for some sign as to where he might have disappeared. About one-half kilometer away, Bill spotted Oliver as he stepped across the expanse on several large rocks. By the time Bill arrived at the point of Oliver's departure, Oliver had already reached the mouth of the cave.

"Come on over," he called above the rumblings of the thunder. Bill took a deep breath and stepped out upon the rocks. Five large stones and five big steps; he arrived alongside Oliver safely.

The cave had an odor of aged materials. Their lights showed a large, damp cavity that obviously hadn't been exposed to daylight for several centuries. They stepped carefully toward the object which was now taking on the shape of an old shield. As they arrived closer, Bill shone his flashlight directly at it. There, despite the dirt and grime, was a shield with the insignia of a red cross.

"Look Oliver, it's a Templar shield!" exclaimed Bill as his heart pounded. "The storm has uncovered this cave and exposed what has been hidden for hundreds of years."

"Yes, I think you're right," answered Oliver, touching the shield reverently

Bill arose to his feet and started searching further into the cave. Oliver could see the darting of his flashlight about the damp walls and hear his footsteps becoming more distant. He lingered at the shield, touching it again with a fondness that brought a smile across his lips.

* * *

"What do you suppose has happened to them?" asked Marie as her eyes searched the side of the hill. The last sighting of the two men had been 15 minutes ago and they could no longer see the beam from their flashlights.

"I'm sure they're okay," assured Lyle. He also was a little uneasy, but did not want to alarm Marie. "Bill is experience with such adventures and I'm sure he will be okay with this one."

The wind continued to blow with unrelenting force about the auto as if trying to wear down the occupants' faith. Lightning played about the rolling clouds with a variety of colors and display of electrical arrangements. The thunder caused the ground to quake and a slight tremble passed through Marie's hand as she reached for Lyle in the darkness.

* * *

The blackness was exaggerated by the rumbling thunder and the closeness of the cave. Bill turned off his flashlight momentarily to see if other impressions could be felt. His intuition was sharper when he didn't depend on his eyes and ears or the sense of touch. He lingered several moments quietly, waiting to pick up a signal or a feeling. Suddenly, he turned and started to walk toward the right wall, nearer to the entrance. He jumped when his shoe came into contact with a hard object and he turned on his light again.

"Oliver!" blurted Bill enthusiastically as he knelt beside several chests that were partially covered with what looked like numerous shoddy rags. "Come quickly. I found something that is unbelievable." His hands shook as he uncovered the closest chest and discovered that it was without weather damage and seemed new as it must have been over 600 years ago.

"I knew it!" exclaimed Oliver, sinking to his knees beside Bill. His large hands reached up, touching the chest with respectful regard.

"This must be the Templar gold that we've been searching for," said Bill as he began to shakily unlatch the clasp that held the lid shut.

"Yes, I am sure it is," agreed Oliver as he helped raise the lid and moved the light about the contents. There were thousands of gold coins, still shiny as the day they were minted. The discovery caused the two to become weak and they sank backward for several moments, awaiting the return of their strength. The lightning from the storm continued as the men opened each of the five chests and examined the contents. They seemed to be caught in a time that stood still as they became even more dazzled by the significance of the discovery.

* * *

"Go faster, I tell you," ordered Gerard, prodding the arm of Louis with his pistol. He was becoming even more impatient as he considered that they were so close to their quarry.

"I am going as fast as is safely possible," explained Louis again, stepping on the accelerator. They were now dangerously approaching the edge of the road with each hazardous turn, and clinging to the side of the auto as it swung about.

Ben could hear the tires squealing as they accelerated and braked on the wet road. He knew that they could suddenly go over the edge and thought about his life, and of the friendships that he had experienced over the years. It was a good life, despite the difficulties encountered, and only regretted that he did have the time to know Marie better. He admired her inner beauty and thoroughly enjoyed her company. Now that things seemed so desolate for him, he regretted not having become more serious about her and for having neglected asking her to marry him.

The thunder shook the auto and jarred Ben from his thoughts. Was there a possibility that his captors would overtake his friends? What would Gerard do to them? Ben vowed that if it were at all possible he would throw a wrench into their schemes and began to pull at the ropes that tied his hands together, forgetting the bruises that encircled his arms.

"I know we should be coming upon them at any moment," said Bones. "They weren't that far ahead of us when we turned around."

"Maybe they took another road?" suggested Louis.

"Why would they think of that? They don't know we're following them," snapped Gerard, whose patience had run out.

The auto continued swerving dangerously back and forth as it followed the mountainous curves downward into a gorge. Rain pelted the metal so hard that it sounded like bullets hitting them from above. Every time a flash of lightning streaked, it seemed to come closer and the men would suddenly jump in terror. The darkness of the storm seemed to grow more oppressive as it continued to build above them and follow them into the valley's blackness.

13

"There's the light," Marie suddenly exclaimed, grabbing Lyle by the arm.

Sure enough, a small wavering light was making its way down the side of the hill in approximately the same location that Bill and Oliver had last been seen on their way up.

"I'm glad to know that everything is okay," stated Lyle as he watched with anticipation at the approaching light. "I wonder what they found? I don't see the shining object anymore."

"They probably have it with them."

The small light from the men's battered flash appeared to be moving much slower than Lyle thought it should. Logically, the return trip downhill should go faster than the one ascending the mountainside. The rain was still persistent in its downpour as if someone were siphoning the ocean with the intent of drowning them. Lyle shuddered as he thought of the group being so far away from safety and watched intensely as the men came slowly closer.

"I'm going out to meet them," announced Lyle, fastening his coat. "I just can't sit here and wait any longer." He opened the auto door and stepped out into the downpour. Pushing his hat snugly down with one hand, he clutched at his upper lapels and started running across the road and up the side of the hill toward his friends. What had they discovered? He sloshed through the puddles of water and soon had mud covering the lower portion of his slacks. The wind howled in an eerie way about his ears and the reflection of the lightning played about the slopes that lay ahead.

"Hey Bill—Oliver!" called Lyle through cupped hands. He waited for a few seconds and, hearing no answer, he called again. "Bill. . . Oliver!" Still no answer; no human voice could be heard in the stormy night. Where had they gone? The spot of brightness that he saw a short time ago was now missing. Lyle began to wonder if they had been hallucinating when they saw the light approaching them a few moments ago. He slowly walked on a few steps, his eyes searching each clump of brush and every gathering of rock.

Then he noticed the light again, coming around a large boulder, heading toward the point where he was standing. Lyle waited for several moments and then called. This time there was a response. "Hey, Lyle! You'll never guess what we found." Bill's voice sounded good to Lyle's ears and he smiled to himself in relief.

"What did you find?" Lyle was getting closer to them and he could make out their figures in the fog as his eyes adjusted to the darkness.

"The Templar gold!" Bill exclaimed. "Five chests of gold coins! We've got one with us and will need to go back for the others."

Lyle was dumbfounded as he arrived at their location. Bill and Oliver set the trunk down and opened the lid for Lyle. There were several minutes of silence when only the distant thunder could be heard. Lyle was certain that the sound of his throbbing heart would also be noticed as he stared speechlessly, first at the others, then at the gold. He motioned with his flashlight for them to follow and led the way down the rocky footpath to the auto below.

"My God," gasped Marie, emerging from the auto and

running toward them. Oliver opened the auto's trunk and with the assistance from the others, lifted the chest inside. Bill again opened the lid for Marie to see the treasure and stood back screaming in glee. "My god, I don't believe it. I DON'T BELIEVE IT!" She held her face in both hands and tears of happiness could be seen sparkling in her eyes. "This is unbelievable!"

"Yes, this is really a miracle," said Lyle, putting his arm about her waist. "This must have been what Master Molay meant when he said, 'You'll find it when the road comes to an end.'"

"And indeed, the road did come to an end," replied Bill as he closed the chest. "Here is the shiny object that we saw from below." He produced the Templar shield from the ground beside him. "It was the reflection of the lightning off the shield that enabled us to locate the cave." He polished the edging with his coat sleeve. "We've got four more chests to retrieve and then we must find a way to get out of here." Both Marie and Lyle examined the old shield closely.

"This is certainly a find," Lyle said as he caressed the cross that was centered on the iron armor. "I'll go with you to get the remaining chests."

"No," came the kindly voice of Oliver. "You and Marie study the road map and see if there's another route to Santander. Bill and I will retrieve the chests."

They all agreed and Lyle opened the auto's door for Marie to climb in out of the weather. He looked back over his shoulder as the men again started up the mountain. This time their steps seemed a little brisker and the rain a little less intense. The rolling thunder was growing more distant as the tempest moved away into the neighboring mountaintops. The flashes of lightning could only now be noticed if one deliberately looked for them, and then they were only a glow on the horizon.

While Marie and Lyle studied the map for another route, Bill and Oliver brought the other chests of gold down to the auto. After everything was secured in the trunk, Oliver put the Rolls in reverse and backed up until he was able to locate a turnaround area. Then headed in the direction from which they had come. Soon they spotted the sign that indicated the alternate route they were looking for and were again headed for Santander.

"Can you believe there's another auto out in this weather," Oliver stated as he glanced in the rear-view mirror. The others turned to look at the advancing auto. The headlights were on a blinding high beam and the auto seemed to be gaining on them rapidly.

"I can't believe they're traveling at that speed on these roads," blurted Bill. "They must be crazy!" The auto was now very close to their rear and appeared to pause for an instant, seemingly to study them without trying to pass.

Oliver kept the Rolls at a steady speed, not wanting to take any chances with going over the side or losing any of their treasure to unknown strangers. The roads were still curving about the mountainsides and the slightest wrong movement could send them careening over the side into the steep, rocky gorge. He didn't like this new situation. If he stopped the auto, the strangers might try to intercept them. If he went faster or permitted them to pass, someone could go over the ledge. A frown came over his brow as he tried to figure who it might be that was harassing them. Could it be the rebel force that lived in the area? No, the locals had said that the Basque Separatists didn't bother visitors. They were usually known to go after government officials. Could it be the men from Paris?

The strange auto was still hugging their bumper as they sped around the still drenched and winding roads. Marie was hanging onto Lyle's arm with one hand and clinging to the door's armrest with the other. "Who can they be?" she asked just as the advancing auto sped up and struck Oliver's Rolls. The blow caused them to lunge forward and Oliver swiftly checked the wheel so that they did not start sliding sideways.

"What the hell!" exclaimed Bill. "We've got to do something soon. Oliver, can you outrun them?"

"Not on this wet road, I'm afraid and then there's the extra weight in the back that would cause a problem on the curves."

"Ten to one it's those criminals from Paris," said Lyle as he tried to rack his brain for a solution.

"I bet it is," agreed Oliver. "I began to get that feeling a few minutes ago."

The auto jerked again as they were rear-ended. Then they heard a sound that everyone had feared. The sound of a machine gun.

Oliver was silent as he quickly pulled the Rolls over to the side of the road by the mountain and came to a stop. "Well, that's enough of this! I've had it with those guys. Stay inside and don't unlock the doors for any reason." He quickly got out of the auto and disappeared into the night.

"What can he do?" Lyle was dumbfounded by Oliver's action and wondered what he could do to stop these men from harming them.

There was another blast from the machine gun and this time bullets hit the rear windshield.

"It didn't break!" exclaimed Bill as he examined the window. "It must be bullet-proof."

The other auto was backing away to prepare for another assault. Suddenly they could faintly see something moving around the intruder's auto and watched intently to see if the men were getting ready to come after them on foot.

"Damn," Bill said to himself "I knew we should have

brought a gun with us. I never like to go on dangerous missions without a weapon in my luggage." He began to feel under the driver's seat in case Oliver had a weapon stashed away, but could find nothing.

Suddenly, a large white horse streaked by the Rolls, straight toward the villains. Lyle couldn't believe his eyes and grabbed Marie by the arm. "My God, it's a Knight!" His eyes were wide in disbelief.

The Knight was in full mail armor and wearing a white cloak with a red cross on it. The Knight surged forward toward the pursuers, and flashed his large sword back and forth in warning. The darkness lifted in the light that radiated from this Knight and the rain temporarily ceased while this battle was drawn. The great horse reared up and pawed the air with his mighty forelegs. The whinny that came from his throat was more like a scream that sent shivers through all who heard. His eyes were filled with fire as the whites about the pupil glistened brightly. *This animal seems to know what is going to happen*, thought Lyle, gazing at the awesome creature.

Circling the enemies' auto a couple of times, the Knight was careful not to come into the open line of fire from their guns. He charged; the horse hit the vehicle's side with his hoofs and caused the auto to move sideways several feet. Guns could now be heard as the men tried to shoot blindly at the Knight. The Knight moved skillfully out of their aim and charged in again. The swift, mighty sword swung down again and again, slicing large gaping holes through the metal.

"Damn those men, what do they think they're doing, pretending to have a Knight fighting for them," growled Gerard. "Get out, Bones and shoot him!" Bones jumped quickly from the vehicle and swung about, trying to locate the horse and rider. He aimed his AK machine gun at the unseen Knight and fired a round of ammunition into the darkness.

Abruptly, behind him appeared the Knight. With one swift and mighty swing from his sword, he lifted the head of Bones from his body and the corpse crumbled to the ground. The Knight's horse rose again and sounded his bellow so that all could hear of their triumph. His white ears were laid back against his head and his nostrils flared. The great mouth was opened wide and a large plume of steam shot from his throat.

"Did you see that?" exclaimed Lyle. "I can't believe that this is really happening. Where is Oliver? He shouldn't be missing this!"

"A Knight of the Temple has reappeared and is defending us! That's just what they did during the Middle Ages, defend the pilgrims." Bill stared in wonderment at the spectacle that was unfolding before them. A miracle was occurring before their eyes. They had been saved again!

The Knight was again charging the intruders' auto, intending to totally destroy what remained of the enemy. Then he stopped abruptly, and looked intently inside. Raising his sword high, he seemed to pause again as if waiting for something to happen.

Inside Gerard's auto, Ben Sully noticed the hesitation of the Knight and was convinced that it was a signal for him to make his move. He threw his body forcefully at the side door. By this time he had been able to unfasten the ropes that held his hands together and could now help himself in this one chance for freedom. The door burst open under Ben's force and he rolled out upon the road.

Before Gerard or Louis could apprehend Ben, the Knight rode forward and with a powerful arm reached down for him, pulling him up and over the horse's withers. Quickly, the horse wheeled about and started in a gallop towards the Rolls.

"It's Ben!" shouted Marie, moving to unlock the door. As she opened it, the Knight halted his horse, letting Ben slip down its side to the ground and into the waiting arms of Marie.

"Ben, Ben," cried Marie, showering him with kisses. Her arms clung tightly about his neck and he laughed joyfully as he returned her hugs.

The Knight was rapidly approaching Gerard again. Bullets spraying from Louis' gun were being deflected by the shield on the Knight's left arm, and his white cape waved gracefully in the breeze as he slowed his approach to a deliberate walk. The time for the execution was at hand and still there was no sign of surrender from the enemy. The Knight paused and his horse snorted loudly.

The clouds were beginning to break overhead and strands of moonlight started to shine through upon the scene that was being played out on Spain's lonely mountain road. A Knight of the church had been summoned again to defend the helpless and protect its possessions.

The Knight raised his sword again, traced the sign of the cross in the air with it and signaled with his leg for his horse to attack. They lunged forward, the two moving as one mighty force in the darkness. The impact of their strength began to move the auto closer to the edge of the road. Another surge from the might of these heavenly beings and the vehicle started to teeter on the rocky brink. The Knight made a vigorous thrust forward with his blade. At the same time, a bolt of lightning exploded from a dark cloud overhead, striking the vehicle and throwing it over the ledge into the blackness of the rocky gorge below.

Lyle and Bill jumped from the Rolls and ran over to see what had happened to the remains of Gerard's auto.

"I don't think that we'll ever be bothered by them again," said Bill as he scanned what was left of the burning auto, two hundred feet below. No sign of life was noted after several minutes and they decided against going down to search for bodies.

"That was a miracle, you know. Ben was in the right place at the right time." Lyle gave a sigh of relief as he turned toward the Rolls and looked about for the Knight. The area was silent again and there was no trace of the mighty warrior anywhere.

"He's gone," Lyle's voice showed his disappointment. He wanted so much to talk with one of the Knights and to learn from them about their Order. But alas, these were not usual times and one only takes what one is given from miracles such as this.

Arriving back at the Rolls, Lyle was surprised to find Oliver sitting behind the wheel.

"You just missed the greatest excitement of your life," he said, slapping Oliver on the shoulder. Oliver looked at them from the window and smiled. "I can imagine it was remarkable. God has a way of making things right, either now or later."

Once again the group was on the road, headed for the northern coast. The remainder of the trip was spent reminiscing about the startling occurrence they had witnessed in the hills and updating Ben on what had transpired since his kidnaping. He in return told them about his ordeal with Gerard and that he was, for the most part, unafraid. Lyle wondered about that, but didn't say anything because of the look in Marie's adoring eyes. She was in love with Ben and it sent a surprisingly sharp pang of loss through his heart.

Alas, this was meant to be and Lyle was happy that Ben had been returned to them.

The remainder of the time was spent silently contemplating all that had happened on the trip, wondering what might transpire next that could possibly surpass what they had already seen.

It was late when they arrived in Santander and they quietly entered their hotel by the side door.

"Let's all meet in Lyle's room in an hour and order dinner sent up," suggested Bill. The others agreed and later concluded an exciting day over fresh club sandwiches. As they toasted to their success with a glass of Spanish port, the moon was just rising over the Picos mountains. The sky had once again become a sea of tiny lighted islands that shone brightly against a backdrop of black velvet. The air was fresh and clean as it gently blew from the northerly oceans. The four, safe again, did not notice a small white dove that had settled itself on the balcony railing. She watched them for several minutes, blinking and nodding before her wings lifted her once again into the night sky.

The following day, the group met at the hotel restaurant close to 10:00 in the morning. It was good that they could catch up on their rest after the strenuous activity they had been through lately.

"Well, I think we should head over to see Bishop Damasus today and fill him in on recent developments. Can't you just see the look on his face when we tell him about the monastery and the gold, let alone the Knight's fight with Gerard?" Lyle was so excited that he spilled his coffee into his lap. Jumping up, he quickly wiped his trousers with the napkin and laughed. "Isn't this crazy? I'm acting like a kid." The others agreed and laughed with him.

"Do you think it's right to keep the gold?" asked Bill. *He's serious!* thought Lyle.

Marie and Ben looked at Bill in questioning incredulity. "You are thinking of giving it back to the Templars?"

"Hey," Bill raised his hands. "I'd like to have this gold just as much as the next guy, but after everything we've seen and learned, I would feel funny about keeping it." He gave a helpless little shrug and sipped on his orange juice.

There was silence for several minutes and then Lyle broke the spell. "I think you're right, Bill. The gold should be returned to the Church and they will do with it as seems right."

"I agree," said Oliver.

"I agree," stated Marie.

"I agree," replied Ben. "Just let me feel one of those gold coins before these riches leave me and make me forever destitute!" He flung his arms the air, pretending helplessness. They all laughed and began to eat the breakfast that the waiter had just brought.

Early afternoon, Oliver and the others were once again headed for Santa Maria. Lyle had telephoned ahead to notify them of their coming and discovered that Father Hugues had arrived from Paris. He smiled with gratitude when he learned of their special prayers, deciding that those special petitions were undoubtedly the power that brought the Knight to their aid.

Arriving at the church, the four got out of the auto and headed for the rectory. Before they arrived near the entrance, the door opened and both priests came towards them with open arms.

"My children," murmured Bishop Damasus as he gave each a welcoming embrace. "God is good." His rosy cheeked face was beaming and his eyes twinkled with kindness towards them.

"I don't believe, no, I shouldn't say that," began Father Hugues as he put his arm about Ben. "I am so glad to see you safe again. What you must have gone through during those dreadful hours with those men."

"It wasn't so bad," stated Ben as he strolled with the priests about the grounds. "I knew that you were doing everything in your power for me and that somehow things would work out."

Lyle started walking towards the Rolls. "Father Hugues, Bishop Damusus, would you like to see the treasure?" They agreed unanimously and followed him. Lyle opened the trunk and then the chests, and stood aside as the priests came forward.

"It isn't true," exclaimed Father Hugues as he stared in awe at this vast amount of gold.

"I can't believe it," whispered the Bishop as he steadied himself on the auto. "One in ten million persons comes upon a discovery like this."

"Yes," began Lyle as he adjusted his jacket. "And we have all discussed the situation, that is, the Templar Gold and its origin, and have decided that its rightful owner is the Church."

The priests stood in silence and stared first at Lyle and then the rest. They all nodded their agreement with this statement.

"You are most generous," replied the Bishop. "I am certain that the Roman Catholic Church will accept it and thank you for this return of the Templars' treasure." He paused, rubbing his cheek and then began again. "Because I am a Bishop in the Catholic Church and administer according to her percepts, I do now state that each of you will receive a portion of this treasure as a reward." He turned and went into the rectory and returned with five leather briefcases. Placing them on the ground, he opened each and then began to fill them with gold coins from the chests. "Please, help if you can. Fill up each with as much as possible." Lyle, Bill, Marie and Oliver quickly began to scoop up handfuls of gold and fill the cases with as much as they could hold and still be able to latch the case.

"Thank you," Lyle choked as he tried to find words that would begin to show his appreciation. "I wish though, that we could do something for the Knights Templars. Something to show our love and our great esteem for their past and current activities."

"Yes, that sounds like a good idea," agreed Bill and the others as they struggled to close the lid on their briefcases.

"What do you have in mind?" The Bishop secured the chest lids.

"What about having a Mass for them?"

Bishop Damasus thought about this suggestion as he adjusted the chain about his neck. The gold cross he was wearing resembled the cross that was on the Templar shield. "That sounds like a good idea. Let's hold one this evening, say about 7:00. It will be a Requiem Mass."

"It will be the last Mass of the Knights Templars." Lyle suddenly felt exhilarated and warm. He didn't know why except that this had been a long and extremely emotional experience for him. He now knew for certain that there were good spirits around and wondered idly if they would know that there was going to be a special service for them this evening.

"We'll meet here then at 7:00. I will have a few flowers brought from the garden shop and some artifacts from their era near the altar." The Bishop paused and looked at the chests of gold and then at the men.

"Oh, yes," began Bill. "We'll carry them into your office."

"It would be better if you would take them to my private study."

The gold was laboriously transferred to the Bishop's secret hiding place. Marie looked about his study once again, remembering the first time they had been there and the letter that the Bishop had read from Pope Clement V. *What an enormous amount of history there is in the Church,* she thought as she walked over to the leaded glass window and gazed toward the old Templar castle. The sun was beginning to set in the westerly sky and evening shadows were starting to grow longer among the evergreens. Rich colors sprang forth from the gardens as the brightness of the day gave way to the dim evening's splendor. The tops of the trees seemed to stretch higher and higher as they tried to cling to the sun's last rays. As her thoughts moved across the landscape, her heart was full of love and she was happy for Ben's safe return; for Master Molay's recognition of her; and for the dedication of the Knights Templars. Marie felt complete in who she was and where she was going. There was a past, a present and a future waiting for all of them. God was the originator and planner of everything that was or ever would be. She was peaceful as she returned to the study and discovered that the men had finished storing the gold in a secure place.

"Let's go down to the dining area," said the Bishop. "I've asked my housekeeper to prepare a few hors d'oeuvres for us before the evening mass." He turned and headed for the door. The others followed him downstairs into the dining room where the glowing candles were giving the atmosphere a pleasant warmth.

After the light snack, there was pleasant conversation over coffee and port near the warm crackling fireplace. The

Bishop arose and stated, "I must go over to the church, pray the Divine Office and then prepare the altar for Mass. Father Hugues, would you like to assist me?"

Father Hugues nodded his agreement and the two left the room. Lyle and the others continued to relax in the comfort of the living room, discussing future plans.

The clock on the mantel struck the half hour and Lyle lifted himself from the leather armchair. "I think I will go over to the church and pray this last thirty minutes before Mass."

"Let's all go," stated Ben as he knocked his pipe out and stood with Marie.

"I'm going to stay behind for a while," said Oliver, looking at Lyle with a strange sadness in his eyes. "I've got a few things I need to do before I go."

As they neared the sanctuary, the sound of men's voices could be heard through the trees. The beautiful Gregorian chant was being practiced by the monks for the celebration. Lyle hoped that it would be a significant Mass for those involved, one that would never be forgotten. He knew that if he prayed devoutly for God's presence and blessings, it would happen.

The sanctuary was illuminated by the light of many candles. Long stemmed red roses had been placed in vases around the altar and to the right was a table where the Templar Knights' shield, sword and mantle were displayed. Prayer came easily to the four as they knelt in silent meditation. Many were the thoughts as they lifted their hearts in prayerful contemplation. Time slipped by as each communicated with the Holy Spirit and gave love to the Most High.

Singing began at the entrance of the church. Lyle looked around as a procession of monks slowly started in pairs up the center aisle. Their heads were bowed beneath black hooded robes and their arms folded in the sleeves of the robe.

"Requiem aeternam dona eis domine. Et lux perpetua luceat eis. Te decet humnus Deus in Sion, et tibi reddetur votum in Jerusalem. Exaudi orationem meam, ad te omnis curo veniet."

(Rest eternal, Give to them, Oh Lord. And light perpetual shine upon them. Sing a hymn to God in Zion. Hear our prayer.)

The words of the Latin chant were beautiful. Lyle absorbed them into his heart and felt his soul elevated.

The monks slowly divided near the altar and completed a circle around to the back, through the iron grilled doors. They seated themselves upon seats that once were reserved for the knights that belonged to the region.

The Bishop and Father Hugues had entered and seated themselves to the left of the altar. Bishop Damasus now rose and pronounced a blessing upon the congregation as they stood in reverence. Villagers were also present for the Mass, since it was held at the usual evening time.

"Kyrie eleison. Kyrie eleison. Kyrie eleison. Christe eleison. Christe eleison. Christe eleison."

The sweet melody of the Mass chant floated heavenward as it mixed with the prayers of the people. Marie felt herself lifted higher than ever as she let herself soak in the spiritual significance of the service.

After the reading of the Gospel by Father Hugues, the Bishop stood and approached the Templar shield.

"This evening's Mass is in dedication and remembrance to the brave Knights of the Temple who lived from the 10th to the 13th centuries." His hand rested on the shield for a moment. "They were a dedicated order of men who strove to uphold the Church's precepts and protect wayfarers as they traveled on their pilgrimages to different Holy Shrines throughout Europe. They lived a chaste life; denying the flesh; upholding the faith; and adhering to the disciplined life of a monk. These were some of the reasons that the Knights succeeded so well in their endeavors. These men should be and will be counted among the blessed."

The sanctuary was so silent that you could hear a pin drop. The Bishop prepared the bread and wine while the monks began to chant the Offertory. Father Hugues rose and brought over the lighted incense. The Bishop took it after being blessed and then turned toward the items that once were articles of defense for the Templars, blessing them with the incense.

The low voices singing the chant could be heard in the background.

"Domine Jesu Christe, Rex gloriae, libera animas omnium fidelium defunctorum depoenis inferni et de profundo lacu libera eas de ore leonis."

(Lord Jesus Christ, King of Glory. Free the souls of all the faithful departed from hell and in our deep sorrow rescue us from the lion's mouth.)

The Bishop brought out a piece of paper and began with these words.

"Let us pray. May the soul of Grand Master Jacques de Molay and Hugh des Paynes be at peace in paradise." He again made the sign of the cross with the incense.

"May the soul of Godfrey St. Omer and Arnaut de Bouchart be at peace in paradise." Again he made the sign of the cross and the smoke from the incense rose heavenward.

"May the soul of Gerard de Caux and Hugues de Pairud be at peace in paradise.

"May the soul of Visitor of France and Geoffroi de Charney be at peace in paradise.

"May the soul of Oliver Templar and Raymond de la Costa be at peace in paradise."

Lyle caught his breath with the mentioning of the name Oliver and looked quickly about to see if he could locate their gallant driver. He was not to be found.

"May the soul of Preceptor of Normandy and Guigo Adhemar be at peace in paradise.

"May the soul of Piene de Modies and Jean de Chatuauvillians be at peace in paradise."

The air was filled with the sweet fragrance of perfumed incense as it created a cloud of translucent whiteness about the altar. Ben leaned forward in his seat as he soaked in the meaningful display of honor for the Knights.

"May the soul of Roger de Flor and Everard de Barres be at peace in paradise.

"May the soul of Thomas Berard and Brother Guillaume de Sonnae be at peace in paradise."

The Bishop continued reciting the names of Knights that had been recorded in history while the monks quietly continued chanting.

"Ne absorbeat eas turtarus, ne cadant in obscurum."
(And let us not be forgotten forever.)

When the Bishop completed the reading of names he proceeded to bless the bread and wine. Lyle looked over at Marie who had tears streaming down her cheeks. She tried to wipe them dry without anyone noticing. Ben took her hand in his own and gave it a tender squeeze as they knelt. Raising his hands heavenward, the Bishop consecrated the sacraments while the monks chanted.

"Sanctus, Sanctus, Sanctus Dominus Deus Sabaoth. Pleni sunt caeli it terra gloria tua. Hosanna in excelsis. Benedictus qui venit in nomine Domini."

Bishop Damasus came forward with the bread and Father Hugues came with the wine. As they stood on the top stair before coming down to the ground level, the Bishop once again raised his hands. "This is the Lamb of God who takes away the sins of the world. Happy are they who are called to His Supper."

Suddenly, Lyle heard movement in the back of the church and turned his head to see what it might be. His heart leaped into his throat and his hands started to tremble. There, entering through the arched doorway were the Knights of the Temple. They were marching two abreast, clothed in the chain mail armor with the white cape and red cross that was their costume. On their left arm was the shield of the Order and their right hand rested on the handle of their sword.

Lyle blindly reached behind him as he tried to grab Marie and get her attention. Then he heard her gasp. The others also were obviously watching by now. Lyle looked toward Bishop Damasus and could see shocked surprise lighting his face. Father Hugues' face was turning white as he stared in disbelief at what was happening.

The Knights came quietly on, turning their heads neither to the right or left. The footsteps were in time with the chant as it led their way to communion.

"Lux aeterna luceat eis, Domine. Cum sanctus tuis in aeter-

num. Requiem aeternam dona eis. Domine et et lux perpetua luceat eis."

The magnificence of their stature was marvelous to behold. The determination on those faces seemed to tell of actions and beliefs that had grown deep into their characters. As they passed the location where the four were sitting, Lyle suddenly recognized some of the faces.

He remembered the two Americans who had assisted them during the snowstorm near the top of the Pyrenees, Thomas Berard and Robert Craon. They were here with the other Knights now being reconciled with the Church and given a special blessing from the Bishop.

There was Robert Raymond, the bellman who had helped them in the New York hotel. His face looked the same beneath the now bushy beard. Then there was the cabby who had taken them over to Ben's house in Paris. Lyle smiled as he passed and made a gesture of recognition, but the Knight proceeded on without a sideward glance.

"Lyle, look," whispered Bill. Lyle turned and focused his attention in the direction that Bill was pointing. There, standing on the right side of the Bishop was the smiling figure of Master Jacques de Molay. It was the same figure that they had seen and visited with at the Santo Domingo monastery.

Lyle looked again and took a deep breath. There, standing on the left side of Father Hugues, was the figure of a Pope. *Who could that be?* though Lyle.

"That's Pope Clement," whispered Ben. "Who else is so closely connected with this occasion?"

The Pope had a look of love and benevolence on his face as the Knights came towards him. He briefly rested his hand upon their heads before they reverently received communion from the Bishop and Father Hugues. The Knights then moved to each side of the sanctuary where they waited for the others to finish. *They have forgiven him*, thought Lyle.

Lyle looked up again into the faces of the Knights as they slowly passed by him. He gulped as his breath quickened; there was Oliver! There was the friend who had saved them from the ocean, rescued them from Gerard, and had escorted them over so many miles through France and Spain. It must be Oliver the Templar. Lyle motioned for the others to look.

"Requiem aeternam dona eis Domine et lux perpetua luceat eis."

The haunting music brought chills to Lyle as he wished that his friend would look at him for one last time. *Dear friend*, he thought, *please don't pass me by. Please don't forget me.*

Suddenly, Oliver stopped and looked down at Lyle. A smile came across his face as he saw the four travelers. He reached out with his hand and slowly touched each as they in turn touched him back.

"Good-bye, my friends," he said softly. "Thank you for everything that you've done for me and for our Order. God be with you always and peace be with you until that day when we shall be reunited in Paradise." A trace of a tear could be seen in the corner of his eye as he struggled to be on his way. The heartache of leaving friends was painful to him.

"Good-bye, Oliver," replied Lyle as he swallowed a growing lump in his throat. "Until we meet again, my friend." They watched as he turned and proceeded to the front. He knelt first in front of his Pope and then in front of Master Molay. Lyle and the others then rose to receive communion. As they followed the Knights to the Lord's table, Lyle was filled with joy over the privilege of having known one of them and for being allowed to celebrate this Mass with them.

The evening's Mass was completed before either Lyle or Marie could believe it was really happening. The air was electrified with intense emotion that left all of them weak.

The Bishop lifted his arms in benediction. "May the Peace of the Lord be with you always."

The congregation completed the sign of the cross and said "Amen."

The monks began to chant the recessional as they led the way from the church.

"In Paradisum deducant te Angeli. In mo adventu suscipiant te Martyres. Et perducant te in civitatem sanctam Jerusalem. Chorus Angeturum te suscipiat, et cum Lazaro quondam paupere aeternam . habeas requiem."

Tears filled Lyle's eyes as he joined the monks in the song.

"Go forth to Paradise. Let Angels take thee by the hand. And at the gate of Heaven, may the Martyrs greet thee at thy coming. May they lead thee in the city of Jerusalem, the Holy place of God. May the choirs of Angels sing in joy to welcome thee and with Lazarus who once was so poor. May thou find eternal peace at last."

The last of the Knights disappeared into the night, taking with them Master Molay and Pope Clement who left walking side by side.

Minutes passed by before anyone could either say or do anything. The grandeur of the occasion was almost too much to fully assimilate.

The Bishop and Father Hugues were waiting in the foyer for them. The other townspeople were starting to leave, most of them quietly thoughtful and in amazed silence.

Lyle arose and waited for the others to follow him. After bowing toward the altar, they solemnly filed out of the sanctuary as the church bells began tolling their mournful cadence.

"Do you believe what we just witnessed?" asked Bill as he shook the Bishop's hand. "Never will I forget this day."

"One does not always experience such a display of God's power. This is certainly an experience that shall always affect my life," responded the Bishop as he wiped the perspiration from his forehead and upper lip with his handkerchief.

Lyle, Bill, Ben and Marie gave their farewells to the priests late that evening and headed towards Santander. Lyle and Bill would be flying home to the United States the following day. The evening was filled with continual reminiscing about their adventure. Humorous events were relived and solemn experiences remembered with humility. Each promised to keep in touch with the other as they separated to rest for the night.

Spain and France were indeed ancient lands of enchantment that held many secrets of days past. Around every corner; in the darkness of the windswept hills; by the lapping ocean waters; beneath the smile of every stranger there lives the possibility that each instance contains undisclosed and limitless possibilities.

As the night closed in upon the sleeping figures of Lyle and his friends, the mystical dove passed by his window again. Not stopping, but only to turn her head slightly and wing her way toward home.

The next morning, Lyle and Bill said good-bye to their friends and took a taxi to the airport. There was a short delay in the departure, but soon the plane was rising into the blue westerly sky.

Bill thought about what he would tell his wife and whether she or anyone would believe the story. What could he ever do that would surpass such an experience? He vowed that he would stay closer to home and be a more devoted husband. Nothing he could do now would ever surpass the excitement that this trip had given him.

Lyle looked down upon the beautiful coastal waters and watched as the city slowly became smaller. He then rested back in his seat as he thought again of their adventure and wondered how Madeline would react to their experiences. The Knights were some of the most daring, courageous, and dedicated men that had ever served the Church. Lyle pondered about the possibility of there being such men like this again in the present civilization.

The Church needed men that would be brave and who would work with passionate dedication. He closed his eyes as the plane rose higher in the sky and the small white dove that was following turned, winging her way to the south.

THE END

ACTUAL CHRONOLOGICAL HISTORY

1119   Hugh des Payens and Geoffrey de St. Omer were the first two men to take vows for the Temple of Solomon; the name was later to be changed to the Knights of the Temple.

1128   Bernard of Clairvaux, a priest and founder of the Cistercian order was commissioned by the Council of Troyes, under Pope Honorius, to draw up a rule for the Knights Templars.

1200   France was becoming a leader among the civilized nations, noted for its Christian devotion, its learning centers, and chivalry among the people that was greatly influenced by the French knights.
The University of Paris was established. It drew all the great thinkers of the time such as Thomas Aquinas, William of Ockham, and Duns Scotus to teach there during the twelfth century.

1226   King Louis IX was called the "Most Christian King." He led his country in rightness and the people lived in prosperity. He led two crusades and was later canonized a saint.

1285   King Philip IV was made ruler of France. His elusive management style and compassionless impertinence was soon obvious. He was a man of unlimited ambitions and went to great lengths to obtain what he wanted. It wasn't long before he exiled the Jews and Lombards in order to confiscate their wealth. Then he instituted taxes upon the wealth of the Church and its clergy.

1294 Pope Boniface VIII and the Vatican became alarmed at the claims of the professors from the University of Paris. They were calling themselves the "Athens of Europe" and "The Goddess of Wisdom" and even had the authority of theology, saying only after being reprimanded by Rome that they were equal with Rome in being a beacon of Light.

1303 Pope Boniface VIII drew up a decree excommunicating King Philip but before he could issue it, the papal palace at Anagni was attacked by William de Nogaret, one of Philip's aides, and 2000 mercenaries. The pontiff was freed but died a few days later.

1303 Pope Benedict excommunicated Norgaret and those who participated in the assault on Pope Boniface VIII. He was poisoned one month later.

1309 King Philip manipulated with money and negotiations the next papal election of a Frenchman named Clement V and moved the papal seat to Avignon. King Philip placed him under his laws and began to use the pope's influence to his advantage. Pope Clement V was forced to absolve the King and all those who participated in the attack upon Pope Boniface VIII. He also permitted the demise of the Templars.

1310 The Knights Templars were arrested and false charges were brought against them. King Philip had all properties confiscated and began proceedings against them for offensives toward the Church. Their belongings, lands and monies were taken by the King. Later, token amounts were given to the Knights Hospitalers, the Pope and friends of the King. The trials were lengthy and began to portend a favorable outcome for the Knights, so King Philip pre-empted the conclusion and had fifty-eight Knights burned at the stake. Many more died under the strain and some committed suicide. The remaining gave torture-inspired confessions and were later freed to live out their days under certain restrictions. Although never condemned or found guilty of any charge, the Order was officially suppressed.

1314 Master Jacques de Molay, the leader of the Order, and his associate Geoffroi de Charney were burned at the stake after two years in prison. Before Master Molay died, he called upon King Philip and Pope Clement to appear with him before the tribunal of God. Pope Clement V and King Philip IV did in fact die the same year.

1315 The dark horse of the apocalypse descended upon France and over the whole of Europe. Famine spread across the land. Everywhere doom hovered and peasants looked about for someone to blame. A bizarre movement called the Pastoureaux enveloped the people and they began to revolt against those who seemed to be oppressing them. Blood was spilt from landowners to government officials and members of the Church.

1345 The Black Death spread across all of Europe and millions of people perished. Not even the most intelligent doctors from the universities were able to squelch this disease.

Footnote: And so, the Age of Christianity had changed in the world. There was now a civil power that would rule the people, and the Church would act as God's representative, providing guidance where needed, reprimands when deemed necessary, and promising salvation to the faithful who desired life in the hereafter.